Clues to Interpreting Charts

Clues to Interpreting Charts

GAYATRI DEVI VASUDEV

MOTILAL BANARSIDASS
INTERNATIONAL
DELHI

Reprint Edition : Delhi, 2025
First Edition : 2003

© GAYATRI DEVI VASUDEV

ISBN : 978-81-19394-19-7 (Paper)
ISBN : 978-81-19394-27-2 (Cloth)

Also available at
MOTILAL BANARSIDASS INTERNATIONAL
H.O. : 41 U.A. Bungalow Road, (Back Lane)Jawahar Nagar, Delhi - 110 007
4261 (basement) Lane #3,Ansari Road, Darya Ganj, New Delhi - 110 002
Shop No. 6, Luz Ginza Complex, 241 Luz Corner, Mylapore, Chennai - 600 004
12/1A, 2nd Floor, Bankim Chatterjee Street, Kolkata - 700 073
Stockist : Motilal Books, Ashok Rajpath, Near Kali Mandir, Patna - 800 004

No part of this book may be reproduced in any form or by any electronic
or mechanical means including information storage and retrieval systems
without permission in writing from the publishers, excepts by a reviewer
who may quote brief passages in a review.

Printed in India
MOTILAL BANARSIDASS INTERNATIONAL

Preface

Jyotisha or astrology is India's great gift to the world, next only to Vedanta. The knowledge of astrology has been an integral and inalienable part of Indian cultural, political and social life down the ages. There are several standard classical works on the subject which deal with every single aspect of life.

In the present century, credit must go to my great grandfather Prof. Suryanarain Rao for bringing *jyotisha* before the English-knowing public in the form of a quarterly journal *The Astrological Magazine* he started in 1896 and through a number of books he authored on the subject. Unfortunately, *The Astrological Magazine* wound up for a variety of reasons in 1914.

The Astrological Magazine was restarted in July 1936 initially as a quarterly by my father Dr. B.V. Raman. Since then it has growth into a prestigious forum for high-level discussion, month after month, on every conceivable aspect of astrology under his dedicated and selfless labour.

My father Dr. Raman took it as his life's crusade to bring astrology into the comity of sciences and towards this end, worked tirelessly. His innumerable books on *jyotisha* have dealt with all aspects of the science right from the basics to the more complicated techniques of interpretation. And honestly speaking, there is no area of astrology which he has not brought before the astrology-conscious readership.

I have endeavoured to apply the standard principles of astrology from different angles to chart interpretation and the pages that follow carry my own insights into the subject and the treatment of countless cases that have come to me for astrological interpretation. It is a book on practical astrology. I have also tried to look at contemporary issues in social life from the astrological angle. Some of these were not known during the 50s, 60s or even the 70s.

In relation to *dhana yogas*, every book has a list of yogas. But what has not been discussed so far is how to locate these yogas and interpret them in a chart to be in a position to make a decision, such as giving up one's job and going in for self-employment or even business or sticking to the job itself when the *dhana yogas* though literally present, may not effectively work. Periods when losses occur, if known much before hand, can diffuse the impact of the blow. These and several such questions relating to finances are astrologically assessed here.

For example, under education, I have tried to figure out what planetary factors point to a child's ability to cope with the tougher central syllabus or what factors restrict his potential to just manage with the state syllabus at the school level. Such insights into a child's intellectual potential can help a parent understand the child better and plan his or her educational career. Even twenty years ago such issues were non-existent. Likewise, matters related to birth of children, adoption and test-tube babies are new concepts. Adoption, though present from ancient times, was a very limited option and was seldom exercised. Today, more and more couples are going in for adoption in the case of inability to have their own children. A decision to adopt a child becomes easier to make if one is aware of the indications for the absence of one's own progeny. This is again an issue very relevant to my generation. Likewise, AIDS is the 'gift' that the civilization of warped, perverse reckless lifestyle has given mankind in the last three decades of the century. I have attempted to analyse AIDS astrologically, basing my conclusions on adaptation of traditional principles to undersand this frightful curse of Nature.

Housing posed no problem three decades ago. Today, owning one's house seems to be a herculean task. A chart, studied from this angle, can lighten one's worries on this count.

Preface

Likewise, the subjects of foreign travel, surgery, heart ailments, mental sickness, marriage and its attendant problems of exploitation, suffering, divorce, death of spouse as relevant to our times have also caught my attention in this volume.

The treatment of these topics in this volume is by no means exhaustive; nevetheless, an attempt has been made to understand certain contemporary issues and all-time matters in the light of astrology.

Most of the papers included in this volume have appeared in the pages of *The Astrological Magazine* with which I have been associated for over 28 years.

I believe this volume will, like a tiny drop in the ocean, contribute to the momentum of the crusade for astrology initiated by my father Dr. B.V. Raman.

Gayatri Devi Vasudev

Contents

Preface   v

1. The First Steps to Understand Charts   1

2. Importance of Muhurtha   11

3. Financial Prospects   21
    (a) Indu Lagna   23
    (b) What Makes One Rich by Birth?   33
    (c) How to Gauge Financial Setbacks?   40
    (d) Choosing Between Business and Service   48
    (e) Timing Financial Success and Failure   57

4. Owning Your Own House   69

5. Progeny   81
    (a) Principles of Family Planning   83
    (b) Your Own Child or Adoption   90
    (c) When Jupiter Ceases to Help   94
    (d) Children — Bane or Blessing?   100
    (e) Are Test-tube Babies Safe?   112

6. Education   123
    (a) Deciding Children's Education   125
    (b) Judging Educational Progress and Performance   132

7. Health and Diseases   139
    (a) Diagnosis of Disease and Surgery   141
    (b) Asthma and Consumption   152

	(c) Detecting Heart Problems	165
	(d) The Scourge of AIDS	171
	(e) What Causes Mental Sickness?	177
8.	**Marriage**	**183**
	(a) Marriage Timing	185
	(b) Happy and Unhappy Marriages	192
	(c) Blighting Factors in Marriages	196
	(d) The Tragedy of Divorce	204
	(e) Is Matching of Charts Necessary?	212
9.	**Locating Foreign Travel**	**225**
10.	**Careers**	**235**
	(a) Mars and Working Women	237
	(b) Medical Profession	245
	(c) Lawyers and Judges	255
	(d) Art and Artists	263

Chapter One

The First Steps to Understand Charts

There are many areas in classical astrology that have received only scant treatment at the hands of the ancient Rishis and even the later writers and commentators. The Vargas or the sub-divisional charts are mentioned everywhere but nowhere are we told how to make use of them.

What the different divisional charts stand for has been given in most textbooks.

I shall only list the Shodasavargas and their significations here:

Rasi — the physical appearance, health and entire life.
Hora — wealth, securities, assets.
Drekanna — happiness through brothers.
Chaturtamsa — fortune.
Saptamsa — sons, grandsons, children.
Navamsa — wife.
Dasamsa — matters of great importance, career, honour, awards, fame.
Dwadasamsa — parents.
Shodasamsa — benefits and adversities through vehicles.
Vimsamsa — spiritual life, Ishta Devata, Sadhana.
Chaturvimsamsa — learning, education.
Bhamsa — strength and weakness.
Trimsamsa — evil effects.
Khavedamsa — auspicious and inauspicious effects.
Shashtiamsa - totality of results.

Of all the Shodasavargas, Trimsamsa is commonly referred to glean all about the chastity or otherwise of a female by almost all writers.

Fundamental principles of horoscopic delineation can be applied to the divisional charts to obtain fairly good results. Natural benefics, generally, tone up a Bhava and their influence on the Ascendant or concerened Bhava in a divisional chart will have a benefic effect. But it must always be remembered that a divisional chart is but an off-shoot of the Rasi chart and must perforce be read against its background.

To start with, the Rasi chart must warrant an event or signification in the first place. For instance, the Chaturvimsamsa (1/24th) chart gives clues as to one's Vidya or education. In Chart 1, the native had a distinguished educational career throughout Mercury Dasa. Her education had mainly to do with science and mathematics at this point of time. Mercury as the 5th lord is exalted, even if in the 8th. Further, there is a particular Yoga which says Mercury in the 8th gives fame, success and distinction. This is from the Rasi chart.

Chart 1: Born 24-10-1949 at 3-33 p.m. (IST) at 13 N, 77 E 35.

Rahu			
Ascdt.	Chart 1 Rasi		
Jupt.			Mars Sat.
	Moon Venus	Sun	Merc. Ketu

			Ascdt. Mars
Venus Rahu	Navamsa		Merc.
Jupt.			Ketu
Sun	Moon Sat.		

Sat. Sun		Ascdt.	Moon
Venus Rahu	Chaturvim-samsa		
Mars			Ketu
Merc.			Jupt.

In the Chaturvimsamsa chart, the Ascendant is aspected by a benefic Jupiter. Mercury occupies the 8th house in a sign ruled by Jupiter. He is, again, the 2nd and 5th lord related to acquisition of Vidya or learning. Education progressed very well in his Dasa continuing into Ketu Dasa. In Rasi, Ketu joins Mercury. In the divisional chart, Ketu occupies Leo whose lord Sun aspects the 5th house or house of education. Jupiter-

The First Steps to Understand Charts

Saturn influencing the Sun, whose results Ketu must reflect, took the native over to legal studies. But this was only until the end of Mars Bhukti. Mars as Bhukti lord is in Shashtashtaka (6-8) to Dasa lord Ketu. The native finished her course with distinction but the mutually adverse positions of the directional lords brought her formal education to an end. Another factor of importance is the play of transiting planets in the Varga charts. Transit Saturn was on the Chaturvimsamsa Lagna afflicting the relevant signification (education) and in the 12th from the Varga Moon gripping him in his seven-and-a-half year cycle. Naturally, the native's scholastic pursuits came to a grinding halt for reasons beyond her.

The Navamsa is the only popularly used Varga chart. It gives important clues relating to marriage and married partner. The 7th Navamsa from Lagna gives a general description of the husband or wife. The description is both of the mental and physical characteristics. It also gives clues to the time of marriage, of stress in married life as well as of divorce, death or separation from married partner.

Chart 2: Born 1-5-1932 at 8-03 p.m. (IST) at 13 N 04, 80 E 17.

Moon Merc Rahu	Sun Mars		Venus
			Jupt.
	Chart 2 Rasi		
Sat.			
	Ascdt.		Ketu

Ascdt. Merc.			
	Mars Sat.		
			Rahu
Jupt. Ketu	Navamsa		Moon
	Venus		Sun

In Chart 2, mark the mutually adverse positions of Mars and Venus in the Navamsa chart. These two planets are the Lagna and 7th lords in Rasi. It was in Venus Dasa, Mars Bhukti that the native lost her husband. Transit Saturn was in the Navamsa 7th house over the Navamsa Moon. The Navamsa having to do with marriage and the Moon with the mind, the native suffered a severe emotional blow in the loss of her husband by this Saturnine transit in the appropriate Varga chart.

Going back to the Rasi of Chart 2, the transits and directional influences operating at the time of the tragedy give little indication of its occurrence. But a deeper scrutiny reveals the Dasa is of the occupant of the eighth house (Mangalyastana) while Bhukti is of the lord of the sign occupied by Venus in Navamsa. The Navamsa chart gives a clearer picture of the bereavement suffered by the native than the Rasi chart.

Chart 3: Born 7-10-1954 at 10-00 p.m. (IST) at 12 N 18, 76 E 42.

		Ascdt.	Ketu		Sat. Merc. Ketu			
	Chart 3 Rasi		Jupt.			Navamsa		Sun Moon Venus
Moon								Ascdt. Jupt.
Mars Rahu	Venus	Merc. Sat.	Sun		Mars			Rahu

In yet another case (Chart 3) of a young girl rendered a widow months after her marriage, the Rasi chart is sufficiently transparent on the point.

Mars and Rahu in the 8th are a clear indication of the loss of husband. Most certainly, if their periods are on. The girl's husband died in a drowning accident in Rahu Dasa, Mars Bhukti. This is too simple for an explanation. In the Navamsa chart, Rahu afflicts Mangalyastana. Rahu and Mars afflict the 8th house. Come to the transits now. Transit Saturn was in the 8th from Janma Rasi. This indicates a period of frustration and sorrow. But what kind of frustration ? Turn to the Navamsa chart. Transit Saturn in Leo afflicts the Navamsa Lagna and is the 2nd from the Navamsa Moon. So the frustration has to do with marriage. The Rasi and Navamsa charts, read together, point to a marital tragedy in plain black and white.

The transits of Saturn are of great help in forestalling tragedy and disappointment with reference to the Varga charts. The transits of Jupiter are equally helpful in fixing good events — marriage, success, distinction, acquisition of property and all other bright sectors of life.

From the Drekanna chart, we may study the birth and death of brothers. Apart from the Dasa-Bhukti Vichara, the transit of Jupiter and Saturn can be effectively employed for anticipating such events.

Chart 4: Born 29-9-1946 at 11-58 a.m. (IST) at 13 N, 77 E 35.

		Rahu	
	Chart 4 Rasi		Sat.
Ascdt.	Ketu	Venus Moon Mars Jupt.	Sun Marc.

		Merc.	Moon Venus
	Drekanna		Mars
			Ketu
			Jupt.
Sun Rahu			
Ascdt.	Sat.		

In the Rasi in Chart 4, the 11th house and the 3rd house ruling elder and younger co-borns respectively are influenced by benefic planets. In the Drekanna chart, the Ascendant is aspected by benefic Venus and the Moon while receiving no malefic aspects. But the Drekanna Ascendant comes under a Papakartari Yoga between Sun-Rahu on one side and Saturn on the other. When transit Jupiter was in Gemini influencing the Drekanna Ascendant and Drekanna Moon, a brother was born to the native. The Drekanna Moon was under the influence of benign Jupiter. Again, when transit Saturn was in Capricorn in the 8th from the Drekanna Moon causing *Ashtama Sani* to it, an elder brother died.

The Saptamsa (1/7th) chart is a good tool in finding out the possibility or otherwise of progeny. I have found it gives far better results in female charts than in male charts.

Chart 5: Born 25-12-1935 at 9-45 p.m. (IST) at 13 N, 77 E 35.

			Ketu
Sat.	**Chart 5**		
Mars	**Rasi**		Ascdt.
Rahu Merc. Sun Moon	Jupt.	Venus	

	Venus Merc.	Rahu Sat.	
Sun Moon	**Saptamsa**		
			Ascdt.
Mars	Ketu		Jupt.

In Chart 5, the 5th house in the Rasi chart is badly afflicted. New Moon with Mercury and eclipsed Lagna lord in the 5th have rendered it an empty sector. The 5th lord is in the 12th therefrom.

Considered from the Moon, the 5th lord Mars, though exalted, is caught between malefics in signs on either side of him. Karaka Jupiter is in the 8th from the 5th. Venus aspects the 5th but his Dasa was over before marriage.

In the relevant Saptamsa chart, the Ascendant Leo is aspected by Lagna lord Sun and New Moon. The Moon is also the 12th lord and his association with the Lagna and Lagna lord cannot improve matters. The native has been married for over thirty years now and has so far not conceived even once. She is now past the child-bearing period.

The Dwadasamsa has mainly to do with Pitru (father) according to Parasara, although many later writers attribute both parents to the Varga.

The 9th house in the Dwadasamsa in Chart 6 is occupied by Karaka Sun aspected by malefic Saturn. It has no benefic aspects. The Dwadasamsa Lagna is afflicted by the Nodes. No benefics aspect it. The 9th lord Moon is in the 6th with 8th

Chart 6: Born 14-7-1913 at 12-35 a.m. (CST) at 41 N 16, 95 W 58.

Rahu	Ascdt. Mars	Venus Sat.	
	Chart 6 Rasi		Sun Merc.
Jupt. (R)	Moon		Ketu

Mars	Moon Merc.	Rahu	
	Dwadasamsa		Sun
Sat.			Jupt.
	Ascdt. Ketu	Venus	

lord Mercury, subject to a Papakartari Yoga but aspected by benefic Jupiter. In Rahu Bhukti of Saturn Dasa, the mother of the native divorced his father. Note the strength of the 9th lord in the Rasi chart even if he is retrograde. The native found a father in the man his mother married shortly after. The afflictions to the Dwadasamsa Ascendant and ninth house denied the native the benefit of his natural father while the eccentric (retrograde) strength of the 9th lord Jupiter in the Rasi gave him at least a step-father.

Momentous events, honourable and otherwise, can be gauged from the Dasamsa chart. Although according to classical works, this Varga denotes distinction and attainment in life, afflictions can cause reverses and loss of reputation.

Chart 7: Born 9-1-1913 at 9-30 p.m. (PST) at 33 N 53, 117 W 49.

	Rahu	Sat.	
Venus	Chart 7 Rasi		
Moon			Ascdt.
Mars Sun Jupt. Merc.			Ketu

	Jupt.	Ascdt. Sat. (R)	Rahu	Venus Moon
	Merc. Mars	Dasamsa		
		Ketu		Sun

The Dasamsa chart in Chart 8 has Neecha Saturn (R) in the Ascendant. No benefics aspect it. The Dasamsa lord Mars is in a Badhaka house with sixth lord Mercury. The Rasi chart has a worse picture to present. Saturn, the dreaded Raja Yogabhangakaraka, stands in the 10th house signifying a fall. The chart is of an erstwhile U.S. President who had to resign the chair following a nation rocking scandal. The Dasamsa chart only reiterates sinister forebodings found in the Rasi chart. At the time of the resignation, transit Saturn was over the Dasamsa Moon. Expectedly, this transit proved disastrous to the native's prestigious career and personal reputation.

In the same chart, three years before when Jupiter was crossing Sagittarius over the radical planetarium, the native won the presidential elections. In the Dasamsa chart, this Jupiterean transit over Sagittarius influences the Dasamsa Ascendant and the Dasamsa 10th lord signifying success and distinction. This occurred in Mercury Dasa, Venus Bhukti. According to general rules of astrology, both planets hold potential for great benefits. That these benefits have to do with career is borne out by transiting Jupiter's influence on the Dasamsa chart. That the same success held seeds of destruction can be gathered from the presence of transit Saturn in Taurus about to enfold the Dasamsa Moon but kept in check by transit Jupiter's influence over this Varga chart.

Using Varga charts for making predictions is no easy job. Clues offered in the classical works are few and for in between. But genuine efforts and diligent study can reward us with some insights (09-81).

Chapter Two

Importance of Muhurtha

Time is the essence of astrology. The time of birth of a child, of a sapling or an animal carries with it the history of its product. Now, let us look at it the other way round. Mark out a point of time as astrologically propitious. Plan the birth of a child or the planting of a seed or even the beginning of a venture. Should it give good results in the form of a child that will live long and well or a tree that will prove highly productive or a venture that leaves behind only a trail of success ? If the answer is yes, then we are right and probably, fairly acquainted with Muhurtha, a branch of astrology that has been successfully applied to all kinds of human endeavour from the Vedic times. Muhurtha is the yardstick which gauges the quality of time.

In the Mahabharata, we read of Parasara and Matsyagandhi uniting to bring forth Veda Vyasa. We are told Parasara is carried away by the rustic beauty of Matsyagandhi. Well, that is how the poet puts it and we must give him a wide margin for it. The poet is far too imaginative to see the truth in its objective blandness. He must paint it in the riotous colours of poetic imagery. But to a mind trained to make a proper and objective assessment of a situation, there is more to this episode than being a mere romantic interlude in the mighty epic of battles and kingdoms.

Let us stop to ponder what kind of a man Parasara was. He was a *tapasvi* who had burnt away the dross of his gross nature in the dual fires of austerity and discrimination. He had reached a stage where Nature and her offspring were nought but the One Indwelling Spirit. Duality had ceased to exist for him. In his infinite compassion, he identified himself with the suffering humanity lost in the maze of Avidya — he was a seer — the past, the present and future lay unwrapped before him. No wonder he gave the world the science of astrology which, in later days, Varahamihira calls a boat to cross the ocean of life. Would such a man fall prey to carnal urge depicted in the fisherman's story?

Parasara waiting on the banks of the river to cross it looked up at the sky to note an amazing configuration of planets was about to take place. He saw that in a short while from then, the sign rising on the eastern horizon was so powerful and so full of auspicious signs that it could only forebode good to the world. He speculated a birth taking place now, or even an *Adhana*, could be of a *Mahapurusha* who could work towards ameliorating the human agony born of the dualities. Appropriately enough, he saw the young maiden approach him to ferry him across the river. This is how and why Matsyagandhi brought forth Veda Vyasa who not only wrote the epic Mahabharata much before the events in it took place and the devotional treatise Srimad Bhagavatam but also codified and classified the Vedas. What greater evidence does one need to appreciate the astrological importance of a moment? This is then the science of Muhurtha which enables one to judge the worthiness or otherwise of time.

The basic tool for determining a suitable Muhurtha is the Panchanga. This is an ephemeris that carries the astronomical computations of planetary positions.

What are the *pancha angas* or the five limbs of time?

They are Vara (weekday), Tithi (lunar day), Nakshatra (asterism), Yoga and Karana. The definitions of these terms are simple and can be found in any text-book on the subject. Each of these elements must be carefully chosen before venturing on any project — secular, spiritual, political or social.

Of the seven days in a week, Tuesday and Saturday are invariably avoided. Tuesday comes under Mars, the planet of strife, discontent, accident and turmoil. Saturday is ruled by Saturn who stands for decay, delay, obstacles, frustration, loss and death.

Tithi is the lunar day. The full-moon and new-moon days, the 4th, the 8th and 14th lunar days in the dark and bright halves of the lunar month are not recommended for any Muhurtha.

Importance of Muhurtha

Nakshatra is the arc of 13° 20 and for purposes of Muhurtha, the Moon's exact location is vitally important.

Krittika and Bharani, Pubba, Poorvashada, Moola, Makha, Aslesha, Jyeshta, Aridra and Poorvabhadra are constellations that are avoided for all constructive works.

In drawing up a propitious chart for any venture, it is important to ensure the strength of the Ascendant and the Moon, the latter both by himself and also in relation to his natal position in the chart of the native for whom a Muhurtha is sought.

All constructive works must have a vacant 8th house. Not even a benefic should occupy it. The tragic Challenger space-shuttle take-off (Chart 1) in 1986 at Cape Carneval had the dreadful Mars in the 8th house in Scorpio.

Chart 1: 28-1-1986 at 11-30 a.m. at Cape Carneval.

	Ascdt. Rahu					Merc. Sun	
Jupt.	**Chart 1**				**Navamsa**		Rahu
Venus Sun Merc.	**Rasi**		Moon	Ketu			Mars
	Mars Sat.	Ketu			Sat.	Jupt.	Moon Venus

Pubba is the constellation in which the Moon was placed when the Challenger took off (Chart 1.) Pubba is one of the more destructive constellations. It is pre-eminently suitable for "nefarious schemes, poisoning, deceit, imprisonment, setting fire and other evil deeds". Sadly enough, the shuttle exploded into a gigantic fire-ball moments after blast-off. All seven crew members were killed and the 1·2 billion dollar spacecraft completely destroyed. The weekday was Tuesday, totally unsuitable.

The Tithi was Shashti or the 6th lunar day of the dark half. This Tithi is not so bad as Charturthi (the 4th lunar day),

Navami (the 9th lunar day), Chaturdasi (the 14th lunar day), Pournami (Full Moon) or Prathama (first lunar day) of the bright half and Trayodasi (13th lunar day), Chaturdasi (14th lunar day) and Amavasya (New Moon) of the dark half. Nevertheless, it is not recommended for Muhurtha.

Aries rising is not welcome either. Signs of Mars and Saturn are invariably unfortunate.

But the most outstanding flaw here is the presence of two malefics, Mars and Saturn, in the eighth house. Mars is in a Sarpa Drekanna (serpent decanate) and Saturn is in a Pasa Drekanna (noose decanate) strongly indicating violent termination of the project.

Let us take our minds back to the Apollo Explosion of 1967. It occurred on 27th January. It was a ground explosion which killed three astronauts. Unfortunately, the time of the explosion is not available to us but the close coincidence in the dates is remarkable. Even more frighteningly coincidental is the position of the Moon that day nineteen years ago. It was also in Leo in Pubba 18° 54'. The Moon was at 18° 29' at the Challenger take-off. In both cases, we have the Moon occupying the fiery sign Leo and the Sun occupying Capricorn in the proximity of the 16th degree. That also means the same Tithi or lunar day was operating on 27th January 1967. It was also Krishna Shashti. One more coincidence is the presence of Rahu and Ketu in Aries and Libra respectively at the time of the two space accidents.

This brings us to another vitally important precaution in fixing up a Muhurtha. Affliction to the rising sign (Ascendant) and the 7th house (*Udayasta shuddiheeno*) must be avoided. A railway accident is a case in point.

In August 1986, two trains set-off within an hour of each other from Garwa Road Station in Bihar.

A goods train with 44 empty wagons started at 2-05 a.m. (IST) on 6-8-1986 from Garwa Station, 24 N 10, 83 E 52 (Chart 2).

Somewhere in transit, six of the rear bogies got decoupled. About 9 km. from Tolara, it was detained because of this. But at 3-05 a.m. on the same day, through sheer negligence, the

Importance of Muhurtha

Chart 2: Goods Train Left Garwa Station on 6-8-1986 at 2-05 a.m. (IST).

	Rahu		Ascdt.
Jupt. (R)	**Chart 2 Rasi**		Sun Moon Merc. (R)
Mars (R)	Sat. (R)	Ketu	Venus

	Rahu		Jupt. (R)
Venus	**Navamsa**		Rahu
	Sun Moon		Merc. (R)
	Ascdt.	Ketu Sat. (R)	Mars (R)

Amritsar Tata Express was released on the same line under the assumption it was clear. Racing at a speed of nearly 80 km. per hour, the Express within minutes of its leaving the station crashed into the breakaway wagons. The Express engine and its wagon fell into the stream below killing nearly 71 people and injuring many, not to speak of the heavy monetary loss involved in the accident. A study of these two charts reveals many principles emphasized in Muhurtha.

Chart 3: Amritsar Tata Express left Garwa Station on 6-8-1986 at 3-05 a.m. (IST).

	Rahu Ascdt.		Jupt. (R)
Venus	**Chart 3 Navamsa**		
Sun Moon			Merc. (R)
		Ketu Sat. (R)	Mars (R)

The two charts have Mars in the 7th, a terrible place for a malefic to occupy. In both, the Moon is weak in Paksha Bala having just come out of Amavasya. The 8th lord Saturn in the two charts occupies a Pasa Drekanna.

The lunar day was the first day of the bright fortnight or Sukla Prathama (1). The Nakshatra was Aslesha, the 9th from Aswini. The Zodiacal sign was Gemini, 3rd from Aries. The weekday was the sixth day, a Friday. Working out the Panchaka for this data, we get $1 + 9 + 3 + 6 = 19$ which leaves Mrityu Panchaka. Ironically, this is a classic example for the need for Panchaka Suddhi or a safe Panchaka.

The 7th house is an important place because any planet there has a complete and sweeping influence on the Lagna. Every planet has a full aspect of the 7th sign from is own position. That is why although malefics are to be avoided in any Kendra (quadrant), they are positively barred from occupying the seventh house since their influence on the Lagna will be total here.

In the Navamsa charts of both, a Martian sign rises. It is very important to avoid a malefic Navamsa in any Muhurtha. Chart 2 has a relatively less afflicted Navamsa Lagna. In Chart 3, Aries as Navamsa Lagna is afflicted by all the malefics — Mars, Saturn, Rahu and Ketu. The gravity of the accident is intensified by the retrograde position of Mars in the 7th in Rasi.

There are certain broad guidelines given to us by Narada. These are known as the 21 great evils or Mahadoshas and must be avoided in any election chart. Their description is given in Dr. B.V. Raman's book **Muhurtha** or **Electional Astrology**.

Our sages took stock of the difficulties attendant on locating a good Muhurtha and came up with a practical piece of advice. They said, choose a time that has a predominance of good points over the bad ones. The bad ones cannot be eliminated *in toto*. Therefore, let the plus points be more in number. As a general rule, avoid the heavy afflictions listed as Mahadoshas, they said.

Of the Tithi, Vara, Nakshatra, Yoga and Karana, the Nakshatra is most important. Between the Lagna and the Nakshatra, the former merits greater attention. The Lagna

Importance of Muhurtha

must invariably be strong. Render Jupiter strong for marriage, Venus for travel, Mercury for learning, Mars for all kinds of competition, the Sun for meeting officials and those in positions of authority and influence. Irrespective of the nature of the undertaking, make the Moon powerful.

What safeguards should a Muhurtha have ? Jupiter or Venus in Lagna is an overall shield against most adverse factors in the Muhurtha. Their aspect on the Lagna is also good. So also the disposition of Jupiter, Venus or Mercury in quadrants which can neutralise some of the other malevolent factors.

The Moon in the 11th for night Muhurthas and the Sun in the 11th for daytime ones is also good.

Then the Hora factor can also the considered.

Each hour of the day is called a Hora. Each day, from sunrise to sunrise, has 24 Horas of equal duration. Each Hora is governed by each of the planets in cyclic order in a particular way. Sunday begins with the Hora of the Sun at sunrise. Then follow the Horas of Venus, Mercury, Moon, Saturn, Jupiter, Mars in that order and the cycle keeps on repeating until on Monday morning at sunrise, the Hora of the Moon will run to be followed by the Horas of Saturn, Jupiter, Mars, Venus and Mercury. This is a very simple process and anyone can plan his venture to begin in a proper Hora easily.

How are the Horas interpreted ? **Kalaprakasika** says : The Sun indicates danger to life, Venus favors marriage, Mercury is good for delivery. The Moon rules general welfare. Saturn signifies fetters. Jupiter bestows monetary benefits and Mars rules war.

By timing a project to start in an appropriate Hora, success can be expected. For instance, we know the Moon takes care of general welfare. So any project can be begun in the Moon's Hora. Let us suppose the Moon is in Scorpio and with Saturn. Here, not only is the Moon weak but also suffers from the proximity of a malefic. So although the Moon Hora would have been advisable, in this particular instance, it has to be rejected. The Horas of Venus and Jupiter can be chosen.

As natural benefics, regardless of the nature of endeavour, these two planets can be depended upon.

As another illustration, let us take the case of a woman undergoing labour pains. The Tithi is Amavasya and Nakshatra also is unfavourable. In such a case, we cannot wait for a favourable Tithi or Nakshatra. The woman can be taken to the nursing home in a Lagna occupied or aspected by Jupiter or Venus or in a Hora of one of these planets or of Mercury. Likewise, depending upon each case in the worst of Panchanga-conditions, a relatively safe period can be found.

By choosing a proper Muhurtha, we can ensure the quality of time and screen off adverse influences. Would this have been possible if fate or destiny had been all powerful ? The very fact that there is such a subject as Muhurtha allowing scope for free-will quashes all charges of fatalism against astrology. In such circumstances, how can anyone in his senses charge astrology with determinism ? (03-87)

Chapter Three

Financial Prospects

(A) INDU LAGNA

The Purusharthas or four pillars of life according to Sanatana Dharma are Dharma, Artha, Kama and Moksha. Each is as important as the other for the fulfilment of life's objectives. That is from the standpoint of Dharma. Too much of anyone of these can tilt the balance and invite misery. However, from a spiritual standpoint, Moksha is more important than the other three. But the sages of India, in their vast wisdom, emphasised all the four pursuits equally. For an average man, average in terms of intelligence, abilities, potential as well as spiritual evolution, money becomes overwhelmingly important. And common-sense as well as life teaches us again and again money is dangerous. That is why the compassionate *Rishis*, aware of the limitations of the mind and flesh as well as the dangers of desire springing from them, laid equal emphasis on Dharma and Moksha along with the material Artha and Kama so that the average man while enjoying the pleasures of the world would be held back from going to extremes by the checks of Dharma and Moksha.

The wisdom of the ancient Rishis found expression in the different Vidyas they bequeathed to posterity. The Vidyas or disciplines derive their merit not for reasons of antiquity but for their role in making life more meaningful in today's confused societal life. Astrology is one such legacy we have inherited from the Rishis. It is called Jyotisha Sastra and sheds light on all aspects of human life. It is a language in itself and reveals human life in astronomical terms. It is also synonymous with the Purusharthas for it brings in not only Dharma, Artha, Kama and Moksha in its sweeping embrace but also shows where each stops in each individual life and how hankering for what is not within one's reach can only bring in frustration.

The role of each Purushartha is identified in an individual chart by planetary groupings against the background of the twelve signs of the Zodiac. Certain planetary combinations in the chart emphasise the ethical and spiritual structure of a native, certain others highlight the fiscal features in his life and how far he may aspire for it. Yet, others concentrate on material enjoyment and lacunae in its acquisition, if any, and on all other aspects of life.

A sizeable section of astrological lore is related to dhana or wealth, one of the more important of the Purusharthas of life today. Of the twelve Bhavas or divisions of the Zodiac, the second house (Vitham or wealth), the fourth (maheepayaankshiti mandiraani or royal vehicles, lands and houses or influence), the ninth (bhagya or fortune) and the eleventh (akiladhanachayapnoti or accumulation of incoming wealth) have to do with Artha or material prosperity. That is although Artha was originally envisioned as having equal status with the other three objectives, today, in actual practice it gets four Bhavas out of a total of twelve Bhavas or thirty-three and one-third per cent of the total share of importance allotted to life's various activities. This in itself shows how far-sighted and pragmatic the ancient Rishis were in judging and assessing human nature on which the whole edifice of astrological combinations is built.

Economical considerations outweigh all others. So much so, parents are, many times, more concerned with the financial future of the proposed groom than if he will be faithful to their daughter. But luckily, no competent and conscientious astrologer will comply with such specific requirements while comparing charts for matrimony.

Apart from an academic review of the relative merits of the Purusharthas, the importance of money cannot be underrated. Astrological literature carries countless combinations for judging financial prospects.

A simple method of determining the fiscal strength of a chart is to judge the strength of Kalas or special forces (if you can call them that) ascribed by definition to 2 key planets in a chart. The key planets are the 9th lords from Lagna

(Ascendant) and Chandra Lagna (Moon-sign). The Kalas for these lords are added and their sum divided by 12. The quotient is set aside. The remainder counted from Chandra Lagna (Moon-sign) gives a sign which is known as Indu Lagna. Two or three simple rules are all that are needed to know if one will have very great wealth or moderate finances.

The Kalas ascribed to the planets are:

Sun	—	30 Kalas
Moon	—	16 Kalas
Mars	—	6 Kalas
Mercury	—	8 Kalas
Jupiter	—	10 Kalas
Venus	—	12 Kalas
Saturn	—	1 Kala

1. If this Indu Lagna is aspected by benefics, Jupiter, Venus and Mercury — very wealthy.
2. If Jupiter, Venus or Mercury aspect Indu Lagna and no malefics taint this benefic by aspect or conjunction — moderately wealthy.
3. Only malefics are in Indu Lagna — moderately wealthy.
4. A powerful malefic in or aspecting Indu Lagna — very rich.
5. A malefic and a benefic aspect the Indu Lagna or are in it — moderately wealthy.

Some illustrations will explain the rules better.

	Moon Rahu	Lagna	Sat.
Sun Merc. Jupt.	Chart 1 Rasi		
			Ascdt.
Venus		Mars Ketu	

The 9th lord from Lagna (Chart 1) is Saturn who gets 1 Kala. The 9th lord from the Moon is Jupiter and he gets 10 Kalas. The sum of their Kalas is 11. Since this is not divisible by 12, we take 11 itself and counting this from the Moon-sign, we get Indu Lagna as Aquarius.

Three planets, the Sun, Mercury and Jupiter, occupy the sign Aquarius which is the Indu Lagna. The Sun is a cruel planet and slightly afflicts Jupiter and Mercury, both benefics. Therefore, the native was wealthy, especially in Jupiter Dasa. If the Sun had not been there, and he causes combustion to the two planets, perhaps the native would have enjoyed limitless riches which was not the case.

In the next example (Chart 2), the lord of the 9th from Lagna is Mars who gets 6 Kalas. The 9th lord from the Moon is Saturn who gets 1 Kala.

Lagna	Sat. Merc.	Moon Sun	Venus Rahu
			Mars
	Chart 2 Rasi		
Ketu	Jupt.		

Their sum 6 + 1 = 7 being less than 12, we can count from the Moon-sign itself seven to get Indu Lagna. This falls in Scorpio, occupied by benefic Jupiter and aspected by the Moon and the Sun. The native was a very wealthy man.

In yet another case (Chart 3), the 9th lord from Lagna and the Moon being Jupiter and Mercury respectively, the sum of their Kalas works out to 10 + 8 = 18 which divided by 12, leaves a remainder of 6. Counting 6 from the Moon-sign, we get Pisces as Indu Lagna. Ketu, a malefic, occupies it. Jupiter and Mars aspect it. Ketu gives the results of his sign-dispositor who being Jupiter is exalted. The native possessed fabulous riches.

Financial Prospects

	Sat. Merc. Sun	
Ketu		
	Chart 3 Rasi	Lagna Venus Jupt.
		Mars
	Moon	Rahu

In the next example (Chart 4), the 9th lord from the Lagna is Venus who gets 12 Kalas. The 9th lord from the Moon is Mercury who gets 8 Kalas. Their total works out to 20 and we get a remainder of 8 on dividing it by 12. The 8th from the Moon is Taurus occupied by malefic Saturn. The native is one of the richest film-world celebrities.

		Sat.	
Lagna Ketu	**Chart 4 Rasi**		Jupt.
			Rahu
Ketu		Moon	Mars Merc. Venus Sun

However, this simple numerical method may not give very clear indications and it is far more advisable to take recourse to an analysis of the planetary positions to assess the financial strength of a chart.

Certain simple but very effective Dhana Yogas arise when :

(1) The Lagna and the 9th house are connected in any manner. The Lagna lord must be powerful and the 9th lord should be in his own or exaltation sign identical with a quadrant

or trine. This Yoga is known as Lakshmi Yoga. Variations of it include the mutual association of the Lagna lord and the 9th lord, the 9th lord in a trine or quadrant or exalted while Lagna lord is also well-disposed and a slightly different version occurring when the 9th lord and Lagna lord being in own or exaltation signs are in quadrants or trines. That means, if the Lagna lord and 9th lord are related but with reference to Dustanas, the 6th, 8th or 12th houses, the Yoga may be said to be proportionately diffused.

(2) The Lagna lord in the 2nd, the 2nd lord in the 11th and 11th lord in the 2nd is a very effective Dhana Yoga.

(3) The Lagna lord, being strong, should occupy a Kendra in conjunction with Jupiter and the 2nd lord should join Vaiseshikamsa.

(4) The lord of the sign in which the Lagna lord is placed in Navamsa should be strong and join a quadrant or a trine from the 2nd lord or should occupy his own or exaltation sign.

(5) The 2nd lord should occupy a quadrant or trine from the 1st lord or the 2nd lord, being a benefic should be either in deep exaltation or in conjunction with an exalted planet.

(6) The Lagna and 2nd lords should have exchanged signs.

Equally interesting are Yogas for losing wealth and money.

Moon			Mars	Rahu		Mars	
Ketu	Chart 5 Rasi		Sun Merc. (R) Rahu	Sun Venus	Navamsa		Moon
Mandi	Lagna	Jupt.	Venus	Mandi Jupt.		Lagna Merc.	Sat. Ketu

Financial Prospects

The outstanding feature of this example (Chart 5) is an Adhi Yoga involving only benefic signs. The 9th lord is in the 5th and is the center of this Yoga.

From Chandra Lagna, the picture is clearer. The Moon-sign lord Jupiter aspects the 2nd and 9th lord generating a Lakshmi Yoga.

The Kalas for the Moon and Mars being 16 and 6 respectively, Indu Lagna works out to Sagittarius. It is aspected by Mars and its own ruler Jupiter is in the 11th from it.

The most important event that occurred was the death of the father in 1923 coinciding with the closing of Mercury Dasa. Mercury is in the 9th with the Sun, Rahu and Saturn. Mercury is a Maraka from the 9th lord Moon. So also Saturn. This event was significant as giving the native substantial properties. Mercury is the 11th lord placed in the 9th with 4th lord Saturn indicating huge inheritance.

			Mandi
Merc. Rahu	Chart 6 Rasi		Moon Jupt.
Sun			Ketu
Lagna Mars Venus		Sat.	

	Mandi		Sun Venus Sat.
Moon	Navamsa		Mars Ketu
Rahu			
	Merc.	Jupt.	Lagna

In Chart 6, Indu Lagna is Libra occupied by exalted Saturn.

The Lagna is a powerful sign and its lord Jupiter is exalted in the 8th with the 8th lord Moon. Mars as 5th lord joins 11th lord Venus and the two are aspected by exalted 2nd lord Saturn. Further, the 9th lord Sun is in the 2nd house aspecting Lagna lord Jupiter. Thus, we find the Lagna, the 2nd, the 9th and the 11th houses inter-related.

The Lagna is extremely powerful. The native began life as a clerk and rose to be a great industrialist. Viewing from the Moon-sign, we find the 2nd lord is in the 7th while the 9th lord is exalted in Lagna aspecting the 2nd lord. Further, the 2nd and Lagna lords being exalted also are under a Nakshatra Parivartana. The Lakshmi Yoga involves an exalted Lagna lord and manifests in full strength.

It was in the Dasa of Venus that the native's ascent began. Venus is the 11th lord and is followed by the 9th lord Sun's Dasa. The Sun is very well-placed being aspected by the Lagna lord exalted Jupiter and this led the native to becoming one of the most successful industrialists in the country.

Contrasting sharply with this chart is Chart 7 of a man who lived and died in penury.

	Rahu Sat.		
	Chart 7 Rasi		
Lagna			
		Sun Jupt. Merc. Ketu Mars Venus	Moon

Indu Lagna is Aries badly afflicted.

The Lagna lord is debilitated in the 4th with Rahu. The 9th lord Mercury is in the 10th with 11th lord Mars and draws Saturn into their orb of influence but being combust in the 8th lord debilitated Sun, whatever good this Yoga can convey gets automatically nullified. Saturn's Papadhi Yoga with reference to the weak waning Moon may also be noted as having given the native utter poverty and suffering. Two powerful Kendras are afflicted by powerful natural malefics — Rahu-Saturn (debilitated) in the 4th and Ketu afflicted debilitated Sun in the 10th house which suck the vitality of the chart and make the native lacking in motivation and endeavour.

The native of Chart 8 was born in very humble straits. His father was only a poor school teacher. The native was so badly off he could hardly manage two square meals a day. This state

Financial Prospects

		Rahu	
Lagna	Chart 8 Rasi		
Moon			Mars Sat.
	Sun Jupt. Venus Ketu	Merc.	

	Mars Sat.		
Moon Merc.	Navamsa		
Rahu			
			Sun Mars Jupt. Moon

of affairs continued well into the fag end of Rahu Dasa. In Mars Bhukti of Rahu Dasa, fortune smiled on him. The native began a share business and soon he was one of the leading lights in the Stock Exchange. The Lagna lord aspects Lagna but he is in a cuspal degree. The 2nd lord Jupiter is in the 10th with 9th lord Venus. Jupiter is also the 11th lord. But Jupiter is combust to the exact degree with the 7th lord Sun. The Moon suffers from Papadhi Yoga. In early 1988, in Saturn Bhukti, the native suddenly went bankrupt losing crores of rupees in different investments he had made. Jupiter, though 11th lord, is combust and the Bhukti lord Saturn is weak.

The Dhana Yoga caused by the relationship between the 2nd, the 9th and 11th lords is quite obvious. But what has failed to sustain this Yoga is a weak Lagna lord and a not so strong Moon-sign.

The Lagna is Aquarius aspected by its ruler Saturn. But Saturn in a cuspal degree is rendered very weak. The Moon is in the 12th and as 6th lord, this is not too bad, but his sign-dispositor Saturn in a Dustana occupies a cuspal degree. So also as 2nd lord with reference to the Moon-sign. The strength of the Ascendant and the Moon-sign can never be underestimated in assessing Dhana Yogas.

Chart 9 is of a mining magnate whose beginnings were very humble. In 1949, the native began manganese ore production and diversified it to iron ore also, later on becoming one of the leading mining men in the state.

		Jupt.	
	Chart 9 Rasi		Sat.
Moon			Lagna Mars
Rahu Venus	Sun Merc.		

Moon			
	Navamsa		Rahu
Sat. Ketu			Sun
		Merc.	Lagna Venus

The Lagna is Leo with its ruler Sun in the 4th in a quadrant with a Vargottama 2nd and 11th lord Mercury. The 9th lord Jupiter is in the 10th, also Vargottama, and aspecting and in turn aspected by 11th lord Mercury. The very powerful connection between the 2nd, the 9th and the 11th lords has generated an extremely powerful Dhana Yoga. The Lagna lord Sun has exchanged signs with Yogakaraka Mars in a Kendra and this is an additional source of strength to the existing Dhana Yoga.

Saturn Dasa was also good but many ventures failed sinking the native in huge debts. But because of the inherent strength of the Lagna lord, Mercury Dasa can be a financially very comfortable period.

Irrespective of the Dhana Yogas, 2 basic factors have been noticed in almost all cases of financial success. One, the Ascendant lord is invariably powerful, and occupies either a Kendra or a Kona or a sign of strength. Alternately, the Moon should be strong either sign-wise or house-wise or through Pakshabala.

The second factor is a powerful 9th house. The 9th is the house of good fortune and if the Lagna is strong enough, the 9th house factors get intertwined with qualities of industry, caution, acumen in helping one to make the most of available opportunities.

For instance, in Chart 8, the 9th house is rendered extremely powerful by its ruler being in the 10th. But the Ascendant is weak. While the 9th lord took the native to dizzy

Financial Prospects

heights of success, the weak Ascendant lord was unable to help him retain it for long and when trouble struck, dropped him like a live coal. Otherwise, no matter what the problems, the native survives through thick and thin. Chart 9 has his share of problems and they are such as to be mind-boggling (litigation, liabilities) but the sheer strength of the Lagna lord ensures the going is good and invests the native with resources to fight these problems. *(05-89)*

(B) WHAT MAKES ONE RICH BY BIRTH?

Yogas for financial prosperity may already be in operation at birth which means one is born with silver spoon in one's mouth. The primary astrological requisites for affluence and wealth at birth are not only a strong Lagna and Dhana Yogas but also the balance of Dasa of the right planet at birth.

Chart 10: Born 9-6-1966 at 3-25 p.m. (IST) Hyderabad with a balance of 0 years, 9 months and 22 days of Mars Dasa at birth.

Sat.	Venus	Sun Mars Rahu	Merc. Jupt.
Moon	\multicolumn{2}{c}{**Chart 10** **Rasi**}	
	Ketu	Ascdt.	

		Mars Sat.	
	Jupt.		Ketu
	Ascdt. Rahu Merc.	**Navamsa**	Sun
		Moon	Venus Sat.

The horoscope (Chart 10) of the grandson of the Nizam of Hyderabad illustrates this point very clearly. The Ascendant is Libra aspected by its own lord Venus who is extra-strong being in his own Nakshatra Bharani. The 2nd lord Mars is Vargottama in the 8th (the house of inheritance) joining the 11th lord Sun (Labhadhipati or the ruler of gains). Both planets come under a powerful Subhakartari Yoga caused by Venus on one side and Mercury and Jupiter on the other. The native inherited fabulous, legendary riches collected over generations by the Nizam's ancestors.

The Dasa at birth was of Mars, ruler of the 2nd primarily (since we are concerned with the Dhana Yogas) joining the 11th lord Sun in the 8th house. Mars is additionally strong being Vargottama. Rahu along with these two planets being in exaltation only reinforces the Yogas for riches.

Chart 11: Born on 20-9-134 at 2-10 p.m. (CET) at Naples with a balance of 3 years, 9 months and 2days of Mars Dasa at birth.

			Ketu Mars
Moon Sat. (R) Rahu	Chart 11 Rasi		Venus
Ascdt.		Jupt.	Sun Merc.

			Rahu Merc.
Venus	Navamsa		Ascdt.
Sat. (R) Mars			
	Jupt. Ketu		Moon Venus

In the next case (Chart 11) which also has a balance of Dasa of Mars at birth, the natal circumstances were radically different. A product of poverty, the father deserted the family which was constantly in hunger. The native had to pass through an impoverished childhood. Thin and scraggly, the native, her mother and sister often had to spend the night in dry water pipes by the roadside to protect themselves from the rains.

Mars here also is in the 8th house as in Chart 10. The Ascendant lord is well-placed in the 11th house but in the constellation of the 5th and 12th lord Mars and Mars, in turn, is in the 8th, one of the worst Dustanas in debility and eclipsed by Ketu. Mars is aspected by the 8th lord Moon which gives restrictive circumstances at birth while the 2nd lord Saturn's Vargottama (by virtue of his occupation of the same sign in Rasi and Navamsa) position in the 2nd is a latent Dhana Yoga.

Financial Prospects

The Dasa of the debilitated planet at birth gave a life of privation, of hunger and suffering. Rahu in the 2nd is also not favourable for finances which is rendered worse by his joining 8th lord Moon and occupying the 8th lord's constellation. The Lagna lord Jupiter in the 11th is good for material circumstances but since he occupies the constellation of Mars who is heavily afflicted and whose Dasa was current at birth, the native's birth and early life were in penury.

Mars gets his debilitation cancelled by not only his occupation of a Kendra from the Moon but because Saturn, in whose sign he gets exalted, is also in a lunar Kendra generating thereby a strong Neechabhanga Raja Yoga.

The 2nd lord Saturn is Vargottama and more importantly in the constellation of the 9th lord Sun which is a good Yoga for monetary prospetity. The 9th lord in the 10th is in a powerful Kendra with the 10th lord and sign-dispositor Mercury and both are hemmed between powerful benefics Jupiter and Venus. The Lagna lord Jupiter in the 11th is basically a Yoga for great wealth, poor circumstances at birth notwithstanding. Venus, the 11th lord, is in the 9th and is highly favorable for riches. Naturally, the native did not remain in poverty for long. By the end of Rahu Dasa (which was no better than Mars') she got her first big break in films and thereafter there was no turning back. Her success as an international star has been phenomenal and her income fabulous.

In another horoscope (Chart 12) we will now review, the native was born in good circumstances. Her parents were orthodox and cultured and she grew up in conservative comfort.

The Ascendant is Cancer. Its ruler Moon is not only in the best trine but also full and strong, rendered extra-powerful by his sign dispositor Jupiter being in a Kendra (quadrant) from him. The Dasa balance at birth was of Jupiter for about 5 months followed by Saturn's. These planetary dispositions gave her a conservative upbringing and what may be described as an upper middle class moral and monetary background.

Chart 12: Born 16-10-1948 at 12-30 p.m. at 10 N 30, 76 E18 with a balance of 0 year 4 months 24 days of Jupiter Dasa.

Moon	Rahu		
	Chart 12 Rasi		Ascdt.
			Sat. Venus
Jupt.	Mars	Ketu Merc.	Sun

	Jupt.		Sat.
	Navamsa		Rahu Moon
		Ketu	Ascdt. Mars
	Merc.		Sun Venus

The Ascendant is extremely powerful and the Dasa at birth was of Jupiter who, though in the 6th house is, otherwise strong, in a powerful Moolatrikona sign. Saturn whose Dasa followed soon after birth is the 7th and 8th lord in the 2nd house with 11th lord Venus. This is no Dhana Yoga; in fact it curbs access to financial luck and all that the native enjoyed during Saturn's period was a moderately good parental upbringing due to the strength of the Lagna lord. Come Mercury Dasa and the windfalls began which continued unchecked, year after year, taking the native to the topmost rung in the success ladder.

The foundation of the chart is strongly laid by the disposition of the Moon, not only as Ascendant lord but by virtue of his position as Janma Rasi as well.

The Moon is in the 9th, full, and this is made possible by the aspect of the 2nd lord Sun who is himself Vargottama and aspects the 9th house. In addition, Venus and Mercury occupying the 6th and 8th houses from the Moon generate a powerful Adhi Yoga. Mercury, as 3rd and 12th lord, is not a strong benefic. Further, he is afflicted by 7th and 8th lord Saturn. But he occupies the constellation of Rahu who is in the 10th. However, it is the tremendous strength of the pivotal point of the Adhi Yoga, the Ascendant lord Moon, Full in the best trine, the 9th, that has ensured the Yoga flows without

Financial Prospects

hitch. The Lakshmi and Adhi Yogas are the two Yogas that have worked in the chart, thanks to the strength of the Ascendant.

In the chart (Chart 13) of a Hollywood star whose success saga was intricately intertwined with personal tragedy, the balance of Dasa at birth was, again, of Mars, Yogakaraka for the Ascendant, in which she was born. Cancer rising aspected by the Moon made her a sensuously beautiful woman.

Chart 13: 1-6-1925 at 9-30 p.m. (PST) at 34 N 02, 118 W15.

	Venus	Sun Merc.	Rahu
Mars Jupt.		Chart 13 Rasi	Ascdt.
Moon			
Ketu	Sat. (R)		

		Rahu Merc.	Venus Mars
		Navamsa	Sat. (R)
Ascdt.			
	Ketu Jupt.		Sun Moon

Mars, ruler of the Dasa in operation at birth, is a strong functional benefic, being the ruler of the 5th and 9th, respectively, but is relegated to the 8th with 9th lord Jupiter. Mars occupies the constellation of Jupiter, who as the 9th lord is a benefic, but unfortunately rendered helpless to do good in the 8th house. Jupiter is further weakened by the fact, he is in Dhanista ruled by the powerless Yogakaraka. The Lagna is aspected by its ruler Moon, also from Dhanishta, a hopeless position that eventually destroyed the native's personal life as well as fortune. The circumstances at birth of the native were by no standards enviable either.

The Ascendant lord in the 7th helped her gain fame and success but the poor position of the Bhagyadhipati (9th lord) and Yogakaraka and the absence of any worthwhile Dhana Yogas never let her finances really grow. Note the 2nd lord Sun, though in the 11th is with 3rd and 12th lord Mercury, aspected by 7th and 8th lord Saturn and weak Mars. The 9th lord Jupiter is in the 12th from the 9th and the 11th lord Venus in the 12th from the 11th. With Jupiter Dasa, her income began to swell but she was constantly cheated and swindled out of her money by her marital partners, one after the other. Finally, she died tragically due to an over-dose of sleeping tablets.

The Ascendant is strong. The 10th house is not bad but the Dhana Yogas are conspicuous by their absence. Although the native had all the trappings of success and fame theoretically, she was never able to enjoy what they might have otherwise fetched her if the chart had a sound financial base.

Contrasting this chart with the previous, both Cancer-borns with strong Lagnas, the Dhana Yogas made all the difference though both ruled the roost as the reigning stars during their heydays.

Going back to the theme of riches, no better illustration can be found than that of Queen Elizabeth, the II of England.

The Ascendant Capricorn in Chart 14 is aspected by the powerful 7th lord Moon. The Lagna lord Saturn aspects the Lagna from the 11th house. The Ascendant lord is also the 2nd lord and his position in the 11th is a Dhana Yoga. In addition, the occupant of the Ascendant Mars is the 11th lord and has exchanged signs with the Ascendant lord Saturn favoring the Queen with the riches she commands.

Chart 14: Born 21-4-1926 at 1-40 p.m. (GMT) at 51 N 31, 0 W 06 with a balance of 11 years, 9 months and 23 days of Mercury Dasa.

Venus Merc.	Sun		Rahu
Jupt.			Moon
Ascdt. Mars	Chart 14 Rasi		
Ketu	Sat.		

			Rahu Sun
	Navamsa		Sat.
Ascdt. Moon Venus			
Ketu		Jupt. Merc.	Mars

Financial Prospects

The birth occurred in Mercury Dasa and Mercury in the 3rd is in Neecha (debilitation) but with Yogakaraka exalted Venus whose functions he imbibes. Further, Mercury is in Uttarabhadra, ruled by a very strongly placed Saturn. Jupiter in the 2nd is not welcome but he is redeemed by occupation of Dhanishta, ruled by exalted 11th lord Mars. Mars, in turn, is very powerful being in his own Nakshatra and otherwise well-placed.

Chart 15: Born 30-10-1950 at 12-08 p.m. (IST) at 16 N 44, 75 E 07.

Chart 15 Rasi				Navamsa			
Rahu			Moon		Sun Sat. Ketu		
Jupt.							
Ascdt.				Ascdt. Venus Merc.			Rahu
Mars		Venus Merc. Sun	Ketu Sat.		Jupt.	Moon	

Chart 15 is a study in contrast. It is of a native who was born in very ordinary circumstances. He lost heavily all his earnings of 2 or 3 years at the end of Jupiter Dasa, Jupiter being similarly placed in the Queen's chart.

The Ascendant is the same sign as the Queen's and its ruler Saturn is in the 9th with Ketu. The 2nd lord in the 9th is welcome. The Dasa, again, was of Mars (at birth), ruler of the 4th and 11th, but placed in the 12th. The Moon in the 6th is not particularly strong. The losses in Jupiter Dasa are largely attributable to his position in the 2nd in Dhanishta. As 12th lord, his position in the 2nd is baneful for financial matters. What is worse is his occupation of Dhanishta, as in the Queen's chart, but with the difference, its ruler Mars as 11th lord (ruling *labha* or gains) is devitalised of all energy to promote monetary luck by his position in the 12th house. The point is inspite of similar placements, the strength of the Lagna, the Moon and the Dhana Yogas make all the difference in promoting financial luck or marring it.

Reverting to Chart 13 and reckoning from the Moon-sign (Chandra Lagna), a whole bunch of similarities show up between it and Chart 15.

Capricorn is the Moon-sign and its ruler Saturn is in the 11th in Parivartana with 11th lord Mars. This ought to have given sound finances but mark 11th lord Mars is with 12th lord Jupiter and in Nakshatra Parivartana with him. This gave a good income but the money trickled through her fingers leaving nothing behind. Also, Saturn as 2nd lord is aspected powerfully by 8th lord Sun. In Chart 15, the 2nd lord Saturn in the 9th is no doubt good but is held back from forming a Dhana Yoga because he occupies the 8th lord Sun's constellation (*89/90*)

(C) HOW TO GAUGE FINANCIAL SETBACKS?

Determining Indu Lagna is a simple test for assessing the financial base of a chart. It does not say all about where the native stands financially, but it does offer some idea of his finances. It is simple enough but even here, there can be some confusion unless we are clear on certain points.

What would happen if there is no remainder or if the remainder is zero ? For example, if Lagna is Virgo occupied by the Moon, the 9th house would be Taurus and the Kala for Venus being 12, we get the sum of the Kalas of the 9th lord from Lagna and Chandra Lagna as 12 + 12 = 24. Dividing this by 12, the remainder is 0 or you can even say 12. The 12th sign from the Moon, namely, Leo, becomes Indu Lagna.

Further, the more powerful a planet in Indu Lagna or influencing it by aspect, the more wealthy will it make the native. Now, what is powerful? Is it Digbala or some other kind of strength ? There are different kinds of strength — sign-wise, house-wise, Yoga-wise, Nakshatra-wise, due to exaltation, Vargottama or other Shadvarga-Balas. It can be any one or more of these. What is important is the planet should

Financial Prospects

be strong in any one or more ways to enhance the Dhana Yoga strength. For instance, for Aquarius Ascendant, if the Moon is in Scorpio, Indu Lagna will fall in Aquarius. If Saturn (as a malefic), is in Leo, sign-wise he is in an inimical place but he has Digbala. Substitute the Moon-sign by Cancer. Indu Lagna for 9th lords Venus and Jupiter (12 + 10 = 22) divided by 12 = 1 plus remainder 10 will be the 10th sign from Cancer, that is, Aries. Saturn whether in Aries (if he has effective cancellation of debility) or Libra can still be deemed to be powerful. So, irrespective of the nature of strength, the Dhana Yoga gets support.

Next, what happens in the case of untenanted and unaspected Indu Lagna ? In such a case, the test of Indu Lagna may not be helpful and it goes without saying the chart has to be analysed exclusively on the merits of planetary juxtapositions and Yogas.

Another doubt that could arise is when the Moon is in Indu Lagna. How is it to be judged ? The Moon is not absolutely benefic or malefic. It also becomes functionally good or bad, depending upon its distance from the Sun, in other words Paksha Bala. Waxing Moon is benefic. Waning Moon is malefic and the same rules can be applied in judging the Moon in Indu Lagna. An illustration (Chart 16) will show us how.

The Ascendant being Virgo and the Moon in Taurus, the sum of the Kalas of Venus and Saturn being 12 plus 1 or 13,

		Moon	Jupt.
	Chart 16 **Rasi**		Ketu
Rahu			
	Merc.	Sun Sat.	Lagna Mars Venus

			Venus
Lagna Mars Rahu	**Navamsa**		
Sun			Merc. Ketu
Sat.	Jupt.		Moon

the remainder works out to 1 which makes the Moon-sign itself the Indu Lagna.

Taurus is Indu Lagna with exalted Full Moon there and aspected by benefic Mercury. Mercury is benefic, the Moon is full and benefic and also additionally strong being in exaltation. Further, for the Ascendant in question, the Moon's lordship is an asset as far as finance is considered. Therefore, financially good. How good are the Dhana Yogas and how far will they go as shown by Indu Lagna?

To begin with, the native was a jobless engineer. A rich matrimonial alliance came his way and he married in September 1988. Now, he has a comfortable job in his in-law's business, a car and even a house, not to mention a beautiful wife !

The Ascendant Virgo has 9th lord Venus, in debility, but with cancellation of debility. That is a good Yoga for financial fortune. The 2nd lord is in the Lagna, Lagna lord in the 3rd is aspecting the 9th and, in turn, is being aspected by 11th lord Moon. The Lagna and its ruler are powerfully influenced by strong Dhana-related planets, Venus and the Moon, as 9th-cum-2nd and 11th lords respectively. Mars in Lagna as 8th lord and his Dasa at birth gave humble early beginnings. Jupiter Dasa, Moon Bhukti brought him fortune with a bang. Jupiter as 7th lord in the 10th aspecting the 4th established links between marriage-career and house while it was the Bhukti of the Moon that set the mechanism of the Dhana Yoga moving. Here, Indu Lagna is clear in its implications and the rest of the chart only confirms it. Looking at Indu Lagna even more closely, we find the aspect on it by Mercury (whether from Lagna, Chandra Lagna or Indu Lagna) is highly favorable and unsullied. Indu Lagna falls in the 9th house (ruling *bhagya* or good fortune) and that in itself is a sufficiently strong factor to indicate the comfortable finances of the native. But the Dasa of Saturn was quite different. As 6th lord, Saturn is exalted in the 2nd. But he is combust in the 12th lord debilitated Sun. As Saturn Dasa began, the native lost all his riches with a divorce from his rich wife.

Financial Prospects

Jupt. Merc.	Ketu Venus Sat. Mars	Ascdt.	
Sun	\multicolumn{2}{c}{Chart 17}	
Moon	\multicolumn{2}{c}{Rasi}	
		Rahu	Indu Lagna

	Ketu	Sun Venus	Sat.
	\multicolumn{2}{c}{}	Ascdt. Moon
Jupt.	\multicolumn{2}{c}{Navamsa}	
		Mars Rahu	Merc.

The Indu Lagna is Virgo in Chart 17. It is aspected by powerful benefics, Mercury and Jupiter. Two benefics influencing Indu Lagna should give good wealth but do the planetary positions endorse this ? The Ascendant lord Venus is in the 12th with 12th lord Mars and Yogakaraka Saturn. This disposition of Lagna lord Venus has its own significance and can indicate earnings through certain sources. The Lagna lord Venus joining Saturn (Yogakaraka and 9th lord) is a favourable disposition. The 2nd lord Mercury joins the 11th lord Jupiter in the 11th house which is supportive of good finances. The disposition of Indu Lagna and its indications are endorsed by the disposition of the Lagna lord Venus, the 2nd lord Mercury, the 9th lord Saturn and the 11th lord Jupiter.

But how do we judge a case when the Indu Lagna clues are in distinct contradiction of the indications of the planetary positions in the chart ?

Jupt.	Moon		Sun Rahu
	\multicolumn{2}{c}{}	Merc. Venus Mars Ascdt.
	\multicolumn{2}{c}{Chart 18 Rasi}	
Ketu	Sat. (R)		

Ascdt.	Moon	Ketu	
Venus	\multicolumn{2}{c}{}	
	\multicolumn{2}{c}{Navamsa}	Merc.
Mars	Rahu	Jupt. Sat.	

The 9th lord from the Ascendant is Jupiter, so also from the Chandra Lagna (Moon-sign) in Chart 18. The Indu Lagna works out to Scorpio which has a most powerful malefic retrograde Saturn in it. Going back to the results attributed to different planets in Indu Lagna, we find "one powerful malefic in or aspecting Indu Lagna" is said to confer "fabulous wealth". Saturn as the 7th and 8th lord is an undoubtedly strong malefic and his retrogression further adds to his maleficence. Nor is he a benefic from the Moon-sign. Has that made our native roll in riches ? Jupiter also aspects Indu Lagna and where both a malefic and benefic influence it, moderate wealth is the result. Which of these results — fabulous wealth or moderate wealth — apply to this chart ? The native hailed from a very ordinary family (lower middle class but highly cultured background) with no pretensions whatever to wealth. The native in his youth entered a monastic order to become a monk. Though now a senior member of the order, author of deeply inspiring spiritual books and a great devotee and renunciate, by no stretch of imagination can we describe him as either moderately wealthy or fabulously rich. The Ascendant lord Moon is in the 10th in exchange of signs with 10th lord Mars and the life of the native has, indeed, been one of much achievement in spiritual life. The 2nd house Leo is aspected by retrograde malefic Saturn, 7th and 8th lord, and this is a dampening influence on the monetary potential of the chart. The 2nd lord Sun is no less uncomfortable being in the 12th eclipsed by Rahu.

Mars, Venus and Mercury are in Lagna and have contributed to the spiritual stature of the native in the process becoming quite forgetful of the financial part of life. Mars is a Yogakaraka but in the 12th lord Mercury's Nakshatra. So also the 11th lord (Labhadhipati) Venus. Mercury, the 3rd and 12th lord, is quite helpless in Pushya ruled by the restrictive 8th lord Saturn. The 9th house is well-placed being occupied by the 9th lord Jupiter, who is, again, in a Saturnine constellation. While this has ensured that the native's material needs, rather basic needs are taken care of, it has done nothing to promote his monetary prosperity (not that it matters to him, anyway).

Financial Prospects

So, an important deduction that is highlighted by this example is Indu Lagna has very little say in influencing the general pattern of the chart, if there are no combinations for financial success worth the name.

Indu Lagna occupied by a powerful malefic (but a functional benefic) does, indeed, confer great wealth. Chart 4 is a good example where Saturn is in Indu Lagna, Taurus. From Lagna, he is Lagna lord and from the Moon-sign, an excellent Yogakaraka and therefore, as a functional benefic, strong factor supporting the financial base of the chart. Planets, functionally benefic being either natural malefics or benefics, are helpful in Indu Lagna. Chart 2 has Scorpio as Indu Lagna, occupied by functional benefic Jupiter and aspected by functional benefic Moon. Natural malefics as malefic lords are of no help at all.

In Chart 19, the Lagna being Libra and the Chandra Lagna, Taurus, the respective 9th lords being Mercury and Saturn, the sum of their Kalas works out to 8 + 1 = 9. This leaves Capricorn as Indu Lagna, occupied by Saturn, a natural malefic but a functional benefic and going by the general rules is supposed to confer 'fabulous wealth'. This is true of the native as an analysis of the chart as a whole will also reveal.

Jupt. Venus Ketu	Sun Mars Merc.	Moon	
Sat.	Chart 19 Rasi		
		Ascdt.	Rahu

Moon			Sat.
Rahu	Navamsa		
		Jupt.	Ketu
		Venus Merc.	Ascdt.	Mars Sat.

The Ascendant Libra is Vargottama and its lord Venus is exalted in the 6th with 6th lord Jupiter. The 6th is not a Dustana here, but an Upachaya. Venus is in the constellation of Yogakaraka Saturn. The Lagna is aspected by exalted 11th lord Sun, 2nd lord Mars as well as 9th lord Mercury. Mercury is also the 12th lord, one may be tempted to point out. Yes, but being in a well-placed Lagna lord Venus' constellation, the 9th lordship dominates. Indu Lagna indications receive support from the whole chart. Saturn, a benefic, both from Lagna and Chandra Lagna has given only favorable results relating to Indu Lagna.

While on the subject of judging financial prospects, trying to find out when finances will bloom and when they will take a dip is also an interesting part of the study.

Reverting to Chart 17, 1964 to 1974 were average years in terms of financial success. 1974 to 1977 were prosperous. 1977 to 1979 moderate and 1980 to 1982 were marked by huge losses and total misfortune leading to bankruptcy and loss of all capital and savings.

The native was in service between 1964 and 1977. This period begins with the last Bhukti of Rahu Dasa and moves into Jupiter Dasa. Jupiter is the 8th and 11th lord with the 2nd and 5th lord Mercury. As 11th lord, he is good for finances and he is also the 8th lord. From Chandra Lagna too, as 3rd and 12th lord, he is good in the 3rd in his own sign but a none-too-strong money-generating planet. During Jupiter Dasa, there was gradual financial progress that comes naturally in anybody's life who works at his job consistently. This period came under the Bhuktis of Jupiter, Saturn, Mercury, Ketu and a small part of Venus Bhukti. The first thrust to betterment came in Venus Bhukti. Venus is the Lagna lord and his joining the 9th lord Saturn gave a catalytic push to the finances of the native which was carried to the Sun through the Moon Bhukti. Then came Mars Bhukti and Mars is the 12th lord when again the graph dipped. Rahu Bhukti put the chart under Dasa Chidra which unfortunately coincided with *Ashtama Sani* or the transit of Saturn through the 8th house from the natal Moon. The end of Jupiter Dasa (mark Jupiter's malefic 8th house lordship from Lagna and the 3rd and 12th lordship from Chandra Lagna) as in Chart 15 snatched away all that the native had collected over the entire span of Jupiter Dasa. Luckily, the chart is inherently strong, thanks to

Lakshmi Yoga which, even if in the 12th, involving as it does the conjunction of the Lagna and 12th lord, Venus and Saturn, throws a protective shield on the native. The native was lucky in that the Dasa of Saturn, a constituent of the Lakshmi Yoga, helped him to rebuild his financial life. As the Dasa progressed, the native was able to bring in some improvement but the fact Saturn occupies the 12th did not help him consolidate his financial base.

Any link between the Ascendant, its lord and the 9th lord is an indication that no matter what the financial disaster, the native, provided the right Dasa operates, will be pulled out to safe heights again.

As we have seen in all these cases, the Nakshtras hav a tremendous influence in charting the financial story of a native. The Yogakaraka well-placed becomes ineffective if in the Nakshatras of malefics or ill-placed planets.

The Sun as a Dhana Yoga causing planet is favorable for promoting financial prosperity. But if he is the 8th lord, as happens in the case of Capricorn Ascendant, his association with the 2nd, 9th or 11th lords, leads to their combustion and therefore, catastrophic results in money-matters. This is an especially important factor to keep in mind when deciding on making investments in business or the share market. As the Lagna lord, as in the case of Leo-borns, the Sun's proximity with money-related planetary lords is actually a good thing to happen. His joining the 2nd, 9th or 11th lords indicates monetary luck. For example, for a Leo-born farmer, the Sun in the 5th with the 2nd and 11th lord Mercury, 9th lord Mars and 5th lord Jupiter, the combustion did not really work and left the native a man of great riches at the end of his career.

As the 2nd lord for Cancer-borns, the Sun becomes one of the constituents of the Dhana Yoga forming combinations and his association, mind you, only in money-matters, loses the sting of combustion. As the 7th lord for Aquarius, the 4th lord for Taurus and the 10th lord for Scorpio, the Sun is not so bad but to some extent takes away from the total strength of the Dhana Yogas if he joins any of the planets causing them. As the 6th lord for Pisces, he is a shade better than as the

8th lord for Capricorn. For Virgo, being the 12th lord, he stands somewhere in between, not a harsh malefic but no benefic either. As the 5th lord for Aries and as the 9th lord for Sagittarius, he is positively helpful. As 11th lord for Libra, he is highly helpful if he is involved with the 2nd and 9th lords. The Sun's proximity to Mercury is not baneful to the Dhana Yoga where Mercury is one of the signatories. For Virgo, Pisces and Capricorn particularly, and for Taurus, Gemini, Scorpio and Aquarius, the best position for the Sun (I regret only in respect of money-matters) would be to stay aloof all by himself in the sign of his occupation. For Virgo, the Sun is not an out-and-out malefic, inspite of his 12th lordship, for he becomes pliable and can even indicate financial success through the positive significations of his lordship. (04-90.)

(D) CHOOSING BETWEEN BUSINESS AND SERVICE

Judging financial Yogas is not only a delightful exercise for all students of astrology but even more a dependable guide to making major decisions in life, such as giving up service for self-employment or for venturing into business or diversifying one's business activities. It is also the best guide when conditions at work irk one and one begins to think in terms of launching on one's own. In such cases, the financial Yogas, rather their absence, will help one bear the difficulties in the work-spot with patient endurance in the understanding that business is just not one's fate.

Indu Lagna			Ketu			Ketu Jupt.	Mars
Sat. (R)		**Chart 20 Rasi**		Merc. Sat.		**Navamsa**	Ascdt.
			Ascdt Sun Venus(R)				Sun
Rahu		Mars Jupt.	Merc. Moon		Venus Rahu		Moon

Financial Prospects

The native of Chart 20, after adequately qualifying himself academically, took up a job and had reached a fairly good position as a senior executive in a reputed commercial organisation by the time Saturn Dasa started.

Here, we see the Ascendant Leo is occupied by its ruler Sun in Vargottama. While the Sun is strong as Lagna lord by virtue of his own sign in Rasi as also in Navamsa, his occupation of Lagna itself is not so desirable as his aspect on Lagna would have been. We will look only at factors having to do with finances. The Lagna is only moderately strong, therefore. The 2nd lord Mercury is in his sign of exaltation, but the 2nd house is occupied by 12th lord Moon. The Moon, being Vargottama, is a plus point, no doubt. The 9th house Aries is aspected by 9th lord Mars, 5th and 8th lord Jupiter and 6th and 7th lord Saturn. The 11th lord Mercury is also the ruler of the 2nd house but then he joins the 12th lord Moon. From Chandra Lagna (Moon-sign too, the 2nd, the 9th and the 11th houses are not connected in any way. The 2nd lord Venus is in the 12th with 12th lord Sun aspected by Saturn, the 5th and 6th lord. The 9th lord is also Venus, again in the 12th. The 11th lord Moon is well-placed in Lagna. The 2nd house is occupied by 7th lord Jupiter and 8th lord Mars, neither being qualified particularly to promote finances. This kind of a horoscope, if the Dasa is not helpful, is best suited for a salaried job and apart from some ups and downs, can expect only moderate finances, enough to lead a life of comfort and self-respect. But unfortunately for the native, the lure of lucre proved too strong, so strong that when he met with problems in his job in 1978-'79, he quit it and decided to launch out on his own. Until then, he was quite well off. But once he gave up his job and opted for his own business, it was the beginning of the end of his financial luck. He did consultancy for a while, traded in metals for a couple of years with no luck and a stint in lorry transport business that left him with huge losses. All this was mainly because of an ill-timed decision.

The native's problems began with stress in his work-spot in 1978 when transit Saturn was in Leo just beginning to afflict the natal Moon. The Dasa of Saturn had already begun. Saturn is a powerful malefic, retrograde and afflicting both the Lagna lord Sun and 10th lord Venus. Saturn has no connection with any factor that has to do with finances in a positive sense. Both from the Lagna and Chandra Lagna, he is a malefic but since he is in Vargottama, he retains some dignity and suggests that if the situation is handled with caution, tact and prudent restraint, he will at least help to keep the show going. On the other hand, his maleficence can indicate no windfall, spectacular monetary luck or even moderately good dividends. But as we have seen, the native decided to make it big on his own and with no Dhana Yoga worth the name to support him invited upon himself financial debacle after financial debacle. Saturn Dasa is least suited for monetary gain and definitely cautions against any kind of investment. Luckily, the next Dasa is of Mercury, a favourable planet for money, both from the Lagna and the Chandra Lagna. But only in relative terms of modest and improved income. The Moon as the 12th lord from the Lagna in the 2nd does not help to stabilize the monetary foundation of the chart and the best course open to the native in these planetary circumstances is to stay content with a salaried job, which, of course, will not be difficult to land once the Dasa of Mercury starts. Saturn Dasa too can give employment but not on very attractive terms.

Reverting to Chart 15, this native too suffered a total loss of all capital but with a change in Dasa, he opted, under astrological guidance, to run a business on very, very modest lines. The Dasa here is of Saturn, again, the Lagna and the 2nd lord in the 9th and bound to be fortunate. But Saturn's power to do good is to some extent hampered by his occupation of Uttaraphalguni, ruled by the 8th lord Sun. Therefore, keeping these astrological constraints in the chart as also the 8th house transit of Saturn (*Ashtama Sani*) from the natal Moon that was due to start soon, in mind, the native was extremely cautious and kept his investments on a low key. This way losses are minimised and profits are only marginal but luckily financial catastrophes are avoided. As Saturn Dasa progresses, business picked gradually and since the 9th lord's Dasa will

Financial Prospects

begin thereafter, reasonably good gains can be anticipated. But until then, caution, contentment and restraint must mark all monetary decisions.

Dhana Yogas or combinations for finances are always welcome for they indicate the financial potential of the chart is far above average. Does it then imply that charts that have no specific Dhana Yogas must suffer abject poverty ? Not at all ! Charts that are lacking in money-causing Yogas can still give their natives comfortable circumstances in life, but such natives cannot aspire for big gains through business, shares and investments. They fare well in service or professional careers that do not require big capital. Dhana Yogas are an index of success in business and big windfalls, the degree depending upon the intensity of the Yogas.

Chart 21 is a powerful chart but it is slightly baffling. The planetary positions and the financial results run along parallel lines with no meeting point in sight.

Rahu				Ketu Jupt. (R)	Merc.		
	Chart 21 Rasi		Jupt. (R)		Navamsa		
Moon Mars Sat. Venus			Indu Lagna	Ascdt. Sat. Mars			
Sun Merc.			Lagna Ketu		Sun		Venus Moon Rahu

The Ascendant lord Mercury is in the 4th, a Kendra. The 2nd and 9th lord Venus joins the 11th lord Moon. Malefic Mars (ruler of the 3rd and the 8th) and Saturn (ruler of the 5th and the 6th) also join them and all the 4 planets are aspected by an exalted retrograde Jupiter. Saturn and Mars, the latter exalted and the former in his own sign are Vargottama. Mars apart, the Moon (11th lord), Venus (2nd and 9th lord) and Saturn (5th lord primarily, being in the 5th) together should have generated powerful Dhana Yogas. But they have not !

The native's financial status has been, more or less, static since 1964 and just moderate. Nothing to describe as Dhana Yoga ! What has happened to the Dhana Yogas we have just spotted ?

A closer look will reveal that Saturn is combust, so also Mars and the two become powerful malefics *vis-a-vis* Dhana Yogas. The combustion is a baneful influence on the money producing Yogas, especially that the Sun is the 12th lord ruling *losses* which is very relevant to the assessment of the Dhana Yogas.

However, reference to the Dasas will give better clues.

Jupiter Dasa was highly favourable, that is, upto about 1967 or so when Rahu Bhukti began. Saturn Dasa was none too gratifying although regular income of a modest amount was available. Saturn is combust in the 12th lord and in very close conjunction with the 8th lord Mars. Moreover, both planets are in Uttarashada, ruled again by the 12th lord Sun.

Venus and the Moon combining and aspected by Jupiter (exalted) are not, of course, ineffective and can give a financial windfall when right Dasas operate.

Mercury Dasa has begun and Mercury is in the 4th aspecting the 10th house as 10th lord. That he is with the 12th lord Sun cannot be ignored but the distance between the two is quite big, and unlike Saturn, combustion does not harm Mercury as much. And Mercury is beyond the orb of combustion ! So Mercury Dasa favours a shift in the nature of work from service to self-employment or business and favourable returns from it. However, the best part of the Dhana Yoga is, more or less, useless because it may surface only after Venus Dasa begins which is after 2012 when the native may no longer be interested.

Dasas and Dhana Yogas are like the two wheels of a cart. If one of them is flawed or not in operation during the productive years of life, the benefit of the Dhana Yoga simply evaporates.

There is nothing like the synchronisation of Dhana Yogas and Dasas to bring about financial luck. This simple fact is glaringly evident in the charts of all tycoons. Personalities

Financial Prospects

of the show world are some of the best examples to illustrate this equation.

Chart 22 is of one of the most successful stars of the singing world of this century. He was barely in his teens when financial luck descended on him like an avalanche. His albums have brought him and his sponsors millions of dollars. Funny, but it was Saturn Dasa, in strong contrast to Chart 21, that did magic to the young singer's earnings.

	Ketu	Mars Lagna	Mandi
Moon	\multicolumn{2}{c}{Chart 22 Rasi}	Venus
			Sun Merc. (R)
	Sat.	Jupt. Rahu	

	Sat.	Ketu	Moon Merc. Mandi
Venus	\multicolumn{2}{c}{Navamsa}	Lagna
	Jupt.		Rahu

The Ascendant is Taurus aspected by Yogakaraka Saturn who, in turn, is strengthened by the aspect of his sign-dispositer Mars. The Ascendant lord Venus is in the 3rd in an Upachaya, a house of elevation, with his sign-dispositer waxing strong in the 10th house.

Mercury, the 2nd lord, is in the 4th with the 4th lord Sun. The 9th lord Saturn is in the 7th with Digbala and aspects Mercury, the 2nd lord. The 11th lord Jupiter aspects the 2nd house. These planetary positions have given rise to a connexion between the 2nd, the 9th and the 11th houses but what puts life and vitality into this chain is the fact Saturn Dasa began early in life to act as a catalysing agent. Saturn is a strong benefic, primarily as the ruler of the 9th and 10th houses and, therefore, a Yogakaraka. But that apart, Saturn occupies Jyeshta ruled by the 2nd and 5th lord Mercury. This dual lordship of Mercury, indeed, qualifies him to boost monetary luck but this property of Mercury is further abetted by the Adhi Yoga generated in the 10th house due to the Moon being there with Venus in the 6th and Mercury in the 7th from him. The Moon is full and in a powerful Kendra with its sign-dispositer in the 10th from it. Further, Indu Lagna too falls in Aquarius, the centre of the Adhi Yoga, both of which have jointly contributed to an annual income running into millions.

In Charts 20, 21 and 22, financial luck has been of three distinct types and yet all three have had Saturn Dasa deciding the fate of their fortunes. The only difference is that Saturn's lordship has had a big say in boosting or retarding monetary success apart from the inherent strength of the Dhana Yogas themselves.

Adhi Yoga found in Chart 22 is one of the most commonly occurring features in the charts of those who have had sensational financial success.

Adhi Yoga as defined in classical works is not limited or confined to financial success only.

According to Varahamihira's **Brihat Jataka**, (XIII-2),

सौम्यै: स्मराრिनिधनेष्वधियोग इन्दो
स्तसिंमश्चभूपसचिवक्षितिपालजन्म।

meaning, when the benefic Mercury, Jupiter, and Venus are in the 6th, 7th and 8th houses from the Moon, the Yoga is known as Adhi Yoga. Further,

संपन्नसौख्यविभवाहतशत्रवश्च
दीर्घायुषो विगतरोगभयाश्च जाताः ।।२।।

meaning, they will get intimate friends, great pleasures and wealth, will have their enemies crushed, will live long free from disease and fear.

Soumyaih means the benefics (natural) Mercury, Jupiter and Venus. The waxing Moon usually classed with benefics is not implied for the simple reason, the remaining *saumyaih* have to be reckoned with reference to him. Clauses to this Yoga would automatically suggest that the benefics must be strong.

Financial Prospects

In other words, the intensity of the Yoga gets qualified by the strength of the planets (*saumyaih*).

According to **Mandavya** and **Saravali**, Adhi Yoga is classed under Raja Yoga in the sense of royal power or political power, and they further require the planets Mercury, Venus and Jupiter should not be combust and should not be with malefics.

In astrology, a rigid literal interpretation can lead us nowhere. A liberal interpretation within the framework of the basis tenets of the science will give better insight into the results of the Yoga.

Adhi Yoga can be of 7 different kinds as obtained from a combination and permutation of the planets and the houses involved. The following varieties emerge :

1. Mercury, Venus, Jupiter are in the 6th, 7th and 8th houses from the Moon.
2. The three benefics are all in the 6th house.
3. The three benefics are all in the 7th house.
4. The three benefics are all in the 8th house.
5. The benefics are distributed in the 6th and 7th houses.
6. The benefics are distributed in the 7th and 8th houses.
7. The benefics are distributed in the 8th and 6th houses.

More sub-varieties are possible if each of the 3 benefic planets changes order in the 3 houses and some more are produced by the different Nakshatras the planets occupy in each of the houses.

While malefics with the benefics are said to spoil the Yoga by some authorities of old, others hold that the malefics give the Yoga but, in the process, make the native tyrannical. We are not concerned with this part of the interpretation. All that we will look into is whether the Yoga can be said to be a Dhana Yoga of consequence.

In most of the cases where Adhi Yoga results occur, it is rare that all the 3 benefics Mercury, Venus and Jupiter are involved.

		Jupt.	
Sun Indu Lagna Merc. Venus	**Chart 23** **Rasi**		Ketu
Rahu			Ascdt.
	Mars	Sat.	Moon

Sat. (R)	Merc. (R)	Moon	
Venus	**Navamsa**		Ascdt. Ketu
Sun Rahu			Jupt.
	Mars		

In this case of a multi-millionaire's daughter, the Moon is in Virgo and Mercury and Venus are in the 6th from him. Jupiter is too far away to contribute to the Yoga. All other factors that promote finances are present but what sets apart the native is the degree of the riches she will inherit from her millionaire father.

The Ascendant is aspected by its ruler Sun and joined by 2nd and 11th lord Mercury. Venus also joins them. The 9th lord Mars occupies his own sign Scorpio and is aspected by 5th lord Jupiter. Mars, in turn, aspects the 2nd and 11th lord Mercury and also the Sun. Indu Lagna (6 for Mars and 12 for Venus being the rulers of the 9th from Lagna and the Moon respectively) is in Aquarius occupied by powerful benefics Mercury and Vargottama Venus and aspected by Vargottama Mars. That she was born with a silver spoon in her mouth is apparent from the Dasas in operation since birth being of the Moon, Vargottama Mars and Vargottama Rahu. Neither business nor employment but riches by birth is attributable to the strength of the Lagna lord joining the 2nd and 11th lord Mercury and the aspect on them by Vargottama Mars. (*11-89/05-90*)

(E) TIMING FINANCIAL SUCCESS AND FAILURE

Riches and poverty are diametrically opposite states and carry with them diametrically opposite conditions. Riches automatically bestow on one many blessings — social status, objects of luxury and acquisitions of all kinds, opportunities and prestige. Poverty, on the other hand, is a curse that brings with it hunger, privation, humiliation and many times even loss of independence. This is a very generalized view of the two states and exceptions cannot be ruled out. But we are here concerned not with the exceptions.

Riches bestow power. Perhaps that is why ever since the beginning of civilization, man has always striven to earn and accumulate money. In fact, wealth can get one just about every-thing under the Sun except, perhaps, mental peace and good health.

In ancient India, the importance of wealth was never underrated inspite of her great philosophy of renunciation and spiritual pursuit. The Vedic seers clearly defined the 4 objectives of human existence as Dharma, Artha, Kama and Moksha. Artha was held to be capable of even procuring Dharma. Valmiki in the **Srimad Ramayana**, *Yuddhakanda* (73-37) says:

यस्यार्था धर्मकामार्थास्तस्य सर्वं प्रदक्षिणम्।
अधनेनार्थकामेन: नार्थ: शक्यो विचिन्वता।।

meaning, a wealthy man seeking after Dharma and prosperity will succeed at all cost but a poor person hunting after prosperity will find it difficult to attain.

Money was recognised as omnipotent.

हर्ष: कामश्च दर्पश्च धर्म: क्रोध: रामो दम:।
अर्थादेतानि सर्वाणि प्रवर्तन्ते (नराधिप)

meaning, wealth is the root cause of every kind of joy and desire, vice and virtue, anger and self restraint.

Poverty, on the other hand, was held to give rise to suffering. And the efforts of a poor man were said to be of no consequence.

अर्थेन हि वियुक्तस्य पुरुषस्याल्पेजसः।
व्यच्छिद्यन्ते क्रियास्सर्वाः ग्रीष्मो कुसरितो यथा।।

(73-33)

meaning, all actions done by a penniless man of no high order dwindle to nothingness even as the flow of rivulets during summer.

Money being so important, classical works on astrology are replete with combinations both for riches and poverty.

For example, according to **Sarwartha Chintamani** of Venkatesha Daivajna, if the Lagna lord joins the 2nd lord in a Kendra or in deep exaltation in Navamsa and is with benefics or receives benefic aspects; or, if the 2nd lord joins the 10th lord aspected by the lord of the Navamsa occupied by the Lagna lord in a Kendra aspected by benefics; or, if a benefic is exalted, in a friend's house, or in Vaseshikamsa and occupies the 1st, the 2nd or the 11th and is aspected by the lord of Navamsa occupied by the lord of the 2nd house; or, if the Lagna lord is in the 2nd and the 2nd lord is in the 11th or the Lagna; or, if the 2nd lord is powerful, joins an exalted planet or is himself exalted; or, if the Lagna lord joins the 2nd or the 11th lord and if the sign-dispositer of the Lagna lord is powerfully placed, one becomes rich.

There are also Yogas called Daridra Yogas in contrast to Dhana Yogas that lead to penury. These Yogas are said to mar horoscopes and are classified as Raja Yoga Bhanga, Rekha, Preshya and even Kemadruma Yogas. Such Yogas can snatch

Financial Prospects

away the fortune one may have obtained by birth. In other cases, they may never let a native succeed financially. The results of such Yogas are simply results that go with extreme penury — no wealth, being hostile and wrathful in nature, constant mental distress, being disagreeable, reviling God and others and always subject to jibes and taunts. These results are inexorably interwined with poverty and the frustration it brings with it.

The Sun in Aries Rasi and Libra Navamsa aspected by a malefic; or, Venus in Virgo Rasi and Virgo Navamsa; or Saturn in a Kendra or Lagna unaspected by benefics; or, when the 9th lord is in the 12th, malefics in the 3rd and the 12th lord in the 2nd; or Saturn, Jupiter and Venus in their depression Navamsas; or, the Lagna lord has no strength and is aspected by the 8th lord while Jupiter is combust; the 4th lord is aspected by the 6th lord; or the 8th lord is in the 5th and the Lagna lord is in debility; or, benefics are in the 6th, 8th and the 12th while malefics occupy Kendras and Trikonas with the 11th lord powerless, then one experiences all the wretchedness that is associated with poverty.

One of the best safeguards against poverty of a demeaning nature is to have the Ascendant lord, Jupiter or Mercury aspect the Ascendant. The Ascendant lord in a Kendra invests one with the grit and perseverance needed to achieve success, a large measure of which has to be translated as money, pragmatically speaking. If the Ascendant lord is in a trine, the element of luck is strong. The 9th house is preferable to the 5th. Conversely, shift the Ascendant lord to the 6th, 8th or the 12th and the chart is drained off of much of its energy. Or, substitute the aspect of Jupiter or Mercury with that of Mars or Saturn (as malefics) and you have a chart that attracts strife and failure and therefore, financial inadequacy.

The Ascendant in Chart 1 is occupied by the 8th lord Sun while the Ascendant lord Saturn is in the 8th house, both signs being inimical to both planets. The native belongs to a very poor family that leads a hand-to-mouth existence.

Chart 1: Born 26-1-1979 at 6-40 a.m. at 10 N 46, 79 E 01.

Ketu			Jupt. (R)
Ascdt. Sun Mars Merc.	Chart 1 Rasi		Sat. Rahu
Moon	Venus		

Venus	Ascdt. Sun Mars		Ketu
Merc.	Navamsa		Moon
Rahu		Jupt. (R) Sat.	

Contrast this with Chart 2, where the native who was born in a log-cabin made it to the highest office in the country.

Chart 2: Born 12-2-1809 at 7-30 p.m. (LMT) at 35 N, 89 W.

Jupt. Venus	Ketu		
Sun Ascdt. Merc.	Chart 2 Rasi		
Moon			
	Sat.	Rahu Mars	

Rahu			
Moon Ascdt.	Navamsa		Jupt.
Merc.			
	Venus	Sun Mars	Sat.	Ketu

The Ascendant lord Saturn occupies the most powerful Kendra in the 10th house. Mercury occupies the Ascendant, so does the Sun as 5th (and 8th) and 7th lords respectively.

Chart 1 has exalted Mars in the Ascendant but combust in the 8th lord Sun and joined by 6th and 9th lord Mercury. Unable to afford school, lacking in skills of any kind and an appearance of no consequence, the future holds out no hope in this case. Saturn, the Lagna lord, is afflicted by Rahu in the 8th. Mercury's 9th lordship becomes ineffective as he

Financial Prospects

occupies a Nakshatra ruled by the 8th lord Sun. Jupiter aspects the Ascendant from his exaltation but can be of very little help as he is the 3rd and 12th lord and occupies the Nakshatra of a powerless Lagna lord. Jupiter Dasa begins only when the girl is past 60 years. Until then, it will be of a life of daily struggle. Even in Jupiter Dasa, the situation may improve only slightly which, against the background of the rest of the chart, may mean, may be (?) two square meals a day.

Such charts only help to confirm the premise that the strength of the Ascendant adds to the strength of the Dhana Yogas in a chart; its weakness dilutes them.

Dhana Yogas in the sense of financial luck (not mere stability or absence of poverty) are usually caused by an inter-relationship between the 2nd and 11th houses and their lords. If the 9th house and its lord are also involved, so much the better.

In Chart 2, the Lagna lord is in the 10th house. The 2nd lord Jupiter who is also the 11th lord, occupies the 2nd house in his own sign with exalted 9th lord Venus.

The 2nd lord in the 12th or the 6th, 8th or the 12th, or the 12th lord in the 2nd while the 11th lord is in the 6th, 8th or the 12th makes a chart financially weak.

In Chart 1, the 2nd lord Saturn is in the 8th, the 12th lord Jupiter aspects the Lagna and the 11th lord joins the 8th lord Sun.

Chart 3: Born 3-3-1934 at 10-30 p.m. (IST) at 31 N 35, 74 E 56.

Mars				Ketu	Sun	Merc.	Venus
Merc. Sun Sat.	Chart 3 Rasi		Ketu		Navamsa		Mars
Rahu Venus				Ascdt.			
		Ascdt. Jupt.	Moon			Sat. Jupt.	Rahu

Chart 3 has the Lagna lord Venus in a Kendra but afflicted by Rahu. The 9th lord Mercury and 11th lord Sun combine in the 5th house causing a Dhana Yoga. This is strengthened by 5th lord Yogakaraka Saturn joining them. The native, with a good academic background in physics, went into business in 1977, dealing mainly with semi-conductors and IC chips for computers. Between 1979 and 1985, he made huge gains, this period beginning with the advent of Saturn Dasa. Saturn is with the 9th and 11th lords. In 1986, in the space of 6 months, he suffered heavy losses amounting to about 35 million dollars. How did the losses occur?

The Ascendant lord Venus is afflicted. The 2nd lord Mars is in the 6th in a cuspal degree. The 6th lord Jupiter is in the Ascendant in a cuspal degree. The two planets as 2nd and 6th lords are in a Nakshatra Parivartana or exchange of constellations.

The chart, therefore, holds combinations both for financial success and debacle. Saturn, the Yogakaraka, even though in his Moolatrikona sign occupies a cuspal degree and the constellation of 2nd lord Mars. Therefore, the loss was inbuilt into the Dasa of Saturn. The profits came in Saturn and Mercury Bhuktis as also part of Ketu Bhukti. Saturn and Mercury are part of the Dhana Yoga. Ketu who should give the results of Mars (*Kujavad Ketu*) and of the Moon, ruler of the sign occupied by him, after an initial phase of profit, reversed the trends to collosal losses. The Moon is in the 12th house, Mars is in the 6th house and Ketu brought in losses and liabilities. Venus, the next Bhukti lord, showed no improvement. Normally as Lagna lord he should have helped but there are 3 reasons why he did not. He is afflicted by Rahu, occupies the constellation of the Moon who, in turn, is in the 12th and more importantly because Venus attracts a special rule from **Uttarakalamrita** according to which Saturn and Venus in their mutual periods have the power to reduce even Kubera, the god of wealth, to beggary.

In strong contrast, in Chart 4, the native who was born in humble circumstances through sheer hard work became a highly successful industrialist known for his philanthropic

Financial Prospects

Chart 4: Born 20-9-1948 at 10-00 a.m. at 16 N 55, 74 E 37.

Moon	Rahu		
	Chart 4 Rasi		Venus
			Sat.
Jupt.	Mars Merc. Ascdt. Ketu	Sun	

Mars Jupt.		Ascdt.	Sat.
Sun Moon Ketu	Navamsa		
Venus			Rahu
		Merc.	

disposition. The Ascendant lord Venus occupies the 10th house, the most powerful Kendra, with no afflictions. The Ascendant has 2nd lord Mars and 9th lord Mercury in it with Ketu. The 2nd and 9th lord Vargottama together in the 1st house constitute a powerful Dhana Yoga. With each passing Dasa, the native's financial base has only been growing. Mercury occupies a cuspal degree but the Dasa was over in his childhood when he experienced all that that goes with poverty, hunger, lack of schooling and privation.

A simple Dhana Yoga occurs when the 2nd lord joins the Lagna or the Lagna lord in the Lagna.

Chart 5: Born 8-8-1972 at 5-23 a.m. (EDT) at 42 N 07, 71 W 06.

	Sat.	Venus	
	Chart 5 Rasi		Ketu Moon Sun Ascdt. Merc.
Rahu			Mars
Jupt.			

Sun	Navamsa		Ketu
Merc. Rahu			Sat.
Ascdt. Venus		Moon	

The Ascendant Cancer in Chart 5 is occupied by its ruler Moon, 2nd lord Sun, Vargottama Ketu and 3rd and 12th lord Mercury. The 7th and 8th lord Saturn is in the 11th house. The 11th lord Venus occupies the 12th house.

The birth occurred in Saturn Dasa. Saturn, a malefic, occupies the 11th house and the native was born to parents of no significant means. He became a trash-collector to earn his living. At this point, the Sun-Moon combination in Lagna made itself felt in Ketu Dasa. The previous Dasa of the 3rd and the 12th lord Mercury joining the 2nd lord was nondescript.

Ketu is Vargottama in Cancer ruled by the Moon. The Moon is the Lagna lord. Ketu also reflects the results of Mars and Mars, in this case, is the Yogakaraka placed in the 2nd house. Ketu Dasa, Moon Bhukti in 1996 brought the native a huge windfall. The Sun, ruler of the previous Bhukti, should have given favorable results being the 2nd lord, but did not only because the chart as a whole was still under the influence of transit Saturn in the 8th from natal Moon or *Ashtama Sani*. It is interesting how the Dhana Yoga surfaced. While on his rounds, the trash-collector found a lucky ticket attached to "a discarded soda cup on top of the garbage" piled on his truck which read "Congratulations ! You are the winner of a dollars 200,000 home". The native was told he need not necessarily spend the prize-money on a house; he could do whatever he liked with it.

If the 2nd lord in Lagna favors wealth, the 12th lord there, in combination with other factors, can generate devastating losses.

The Ascendant in Chart 6 is in close conjunction with the 12th lord Mars. The 2nd lord Mercury is in the 4th with the 4th lord Sun and both are afflicted by Rahu. The 11th lord Jupiter joins the 9th lord Saturn (R) which is a Dhana Yoga. The Yoga occurs in the 8th house aspected by 12th lord Mars and carries seeds of loss in it. The Lagna lord Venus is in the 5th aspected by Yogakaraka Saturn but from the 8th. Born in a rich family with ancestral and other properties, the native's industrial unit was progressing well until 1994 when labour problems broke out forcing its closure leading to heavy losses.

Chart 6: Born 31-8-1960 at 11-45 p.m. at 28 N 39, 77 E 13.

		Mars Ascdt.	
Ketu	Chart 6 Rasi		
			Sun Rahu
Sat. (R) Jupt. Moon			Venus

Jupt.	Ketu		
	Navamsa		Moon
			Ascdt. Sun
	Rahu	Sat	Mars Merc.

The 12th lord Mars in the Ascendant exposes the chart to danger of losses. Further, as 12th lord he aspects the Dhana Yoga in the 8th house. Saturn there as Yogakaraka becomes weak, being in the 12th from the 9th. The Moon in the 8th does not help the Yoga. The losses began in Mercury Bhukti of the Moon Dasa. Mercury is the 2nd and 5th lord afflicted by Rahu and aspected by 12th lord Mars. The Dasa lord Moon too is aspected by 12th lord Mars and in the 8th, with 8th lord Jupiter, attracts humiliation with the losses.

Chart 7 of a publishing tycoon with a similarly placed 12th lord is a study in contrast.

Chart 7: Born 18-7-1947 at 1-35 a.m. (EDT) at 40 N 48, 74 W 29.

		Ascdt. Mars Rahu	Venus Merc. (R)
	Chart 7 Rasi		Sun Moon Sat.
	Ketu	Jupt.	

Rahu	Venus	Jupt.	Merc. (R)
	Navamsa		Sun Mars
Ascdt.			Moon
	Sat.		Ketu

The same Lagna Taurus rises with Mars there with exalted Rahu. But while Lagna lord Venus in a trine in Chart 6 is aspected by the 8th house Saturn, in Chart 7 Venus is in the 2nd with Vargottama 2nd lord Mercury making the financial base of the chart formidable. Mars in the Ascendant has not hurt the native because he occupies Rohini ruled by the 3rd lord Moon who is joined by the 4th lord Sun and Yogakaraka Saturn. In Chart 6, the 12th lord Mars occupies his own constellation emphasising losses. Yogakaraka Saturn in the 8th, (as the 9th lord in the 12th from the 9th) in Chart 6 has weakened it while in Chart 7, Yogakaraka Saturn as 9th lord in the 3rd aspects the 9th house.

What has beleaguered the native of Chart 6 with the losses is the fact he is now passing through the Moon Dasa. The Moon is the centre of a Dhana Yoga (Jupiter-Saturn) as well as a Dhana Bhanga Yoga (Saturn-Mars). The aspect of 12th lord Mars on the Dasa lord Moon and Yogakaraka Saturn and 11th lord Jupiter has punctuated his financial success with heavy setbacks causing tremendous stress.

Chart 8: Born 7-11-1867 at 12-00 noon at 52 N 15, 21 E 00.

						Ketu	Moon Sun	
Moon Ketu Jupt.		Chart 8 Rasi						Ascdt.
Ascdt.			Rahu		Ascdt.	Navamsa		Venus Sat.
	Sat. Venus Mars Merc.	Sun			Jupt.	Merc.	Rahu	Mars

One of the best examples of enduring prosperity is of Marie Curie (Chart 8) who discovered radium. The Ascendant lord Saturn who is also the 2nd lord is in the 11th with 11th lord Mars (own sign), Vargottama 9th lord Mercury and Yogakaraka Venus generating a very strong Yoga for wealth. Considered from the Moon, the combination occurring in the 10th house is a Yoga for fame and limelight. Marie was born in an ordinary family where her school-teacher parents could educate her and her four siblings only with great difficulty. She and her husband Pierre Curie worked very hard in their "miserable old shed" which was their laboratory. In December 1903, they won the Nobel Prize for physics with another physicist for the discovery of radium. The Prize not only brought them global fame but also financial benefits. Marie won the Nobel Prize for the second time in December 1911 for chemistry for her work, again, on radium as a metallic element. The first time, the prize came in Ketu Dasa with Ketu in the 2nd house. Ketu should give the results of Mars and Saturn who form a powerful Dhana Yoga in the 11th house from Lagna. The second time, it came in Venus Dasa, Venus being an excellent Yogakaraka both from Lagna and Chandra Lagna and also involved in the Dhana Yoga. The strength of the Lagna lord Saturn supported by the formidable Dhana Yoga shows her rise from humble beginnings to extraordinary heights of success and fame including the monetary benefits accompanying the Nobel Prize.

The Dhana Yogas in a chart of one born in poor or indigent circumstances or of one from a middle-class background promise financial success in life as in Marie Curie's case. If the Dhana Yogas in such a case are marred by strong Daridra Yogas, then one, depending upon the Dasas, may have an initial and heady taste of financial prosperity only to suffer an equally ignoble state of humiliation and loss later. If Dhana Yogas alone occur in the case of those wealthy by birth, then such natives need have no fear of major losses. Dhana Yogas interwined with Daridra Yogas in the charts of those born in affluence show up in the form of heavy losses when Dasas of planets forming the latter Yogas start operating but the Dhana Yogas will continue to sustain the financial foundation of the chart. Charts with only Daridra Yogas of those born in poverty rule out any taste of prosperity in life. Such natives live a life of suffering and penury — unsung, unwept, unhonoured in life as in death. *(09-96)*

Chapter Four

Owning Your Own House

Food, shelter and clothing. Basic needs of man. Of both primitive man and his modern counterpart. Sounds simple enough but today, these basic needs have been transformed into problems of alarming concern and frightening magnitude.

Our cities are dotted with buildings of every shape and size as far as the eye can see, yet finding a decent place to call one's own is an endless pursuit. People have been known to have poured in all their money and resources into acquiring a house and running from pillar to post but finally, ending up with neither a house nor money.

Housing was not such a dreadful problem even three or four decades ago. Both the villager and the urban dweller could easily own a house with spacious rooms and sprawling courtyard. All that was needed was a little money and some hard work. But now even with enormous effort, it is next to impossible to own a house, especially in major cities like Mumbai, Chennai, Delhi and Kolkata. Land is scarce in the cities and costs a fortune. The spiralling prices of building materials, non-availability of reliable building contractors and periodic harassment from petty governmental or quasi-governmental agencies, all conspire to make owning a house as difficult as reaching for the Moon.

This is where astrology is a boon and helps to plan or prune one's aspirations for a house of one's very own. Astrology was basically enunciated by the ancient Rishis to help promote human welfare. Though thousands of years old, the resilient adaptability of astrological lore to changing conditions in the world has invariably left all thinkers amazed at the foresight of the founding fathers of this science. The most ancient of all sciences, the explored potential of astrology is still in its infant stage. But every changing need and weal of society can be brought within its broad framework and solutions worked out to suit the latest need of the hour.

One does not know if housing was ever a problem with the ancients of India. Most times, the skies were the roof and the wide forests their private gardens. But it is incredible that they could envisage possible problems of posterity when they codified and formulated astrological laws. How else can we explain their treatment of the subject of housing. Later writers have only re-written what the ancients had already formulated, and a perusal of the various combinations that indicate acquiring and owning a house must leave one not only a little more humble before this great heritage of ours but also a little more equipped to face the problems of contemporary life.

The chart carrying the planetary positions at the time of birth is a little more than a map of the assets and liabilities each one of us carries over it from the past into the present. Omissions and commissions of previous births are added up and worked out and the results so rationed out can be deciphered according to the disposition of the various Bhavas in the chart.

The fourth house has been assigned house. It is also called Griha Bhava. A strong indication for a house in the chart takes care to endow one with a house of one's own, astronomical costs and paucity of land or sites notwithstanding. This piece of information that a chart provides can help one to plan his resources and go ahead at an appropriate period with one's house-procuring plans. If the 4th house in a chart has no significant worth, it can also help one accept the reality of the situation with pragmatic stoicism and invest his monies in more viable alternatives.

There are some standard combinations common to most classical works that show that a chart holds promise of a house. Only some of them are listed below :

If the lords of the 1st and the 4th exchange houses, the native will acquire a house (*Grihalabhah*).

If the lord of the 4th house possesses strength and be in a Kendra aspected by benefics, the native will get a house.

If the lord of the 4th house has attained a Viseshikamsa and is in its highest exaltation, the native will get a house.

Owning Your Own House

If the owner of the Navamsa occupied by the lord of the 4th house be in a Kendra (quadrant), there will be acquisition of a house.

If the lord of the 9th house occupies a Kendra, the lord of the 4th occupies his exaltation and or a friendly house and if the 4th house be occupied by a planet in exaltation, the native will get a beautiful house (*vichitragrihalabhah*).

If a benefic planet (or Mercury) occupies the 3rd house and if the lord of the 4th as well as the lord of the Navamsa occupied by the owner of the 4th house is strong, the native will own a mansion with an extensive compound.

If the lord of the 4th house has attained a Simhasanamsa, a Gopuramsa or Mridushashtyamsa, the person born will own a mansion with an extensive compound (*prakaradhiyutagriham*).

If the lord of the 4th house has attained a Parvatmsa and the Moon, a Gopuramsa, and be aspected by Jupiter, the native's residence will be a divine one (*daivikam veshma*).

If the lords of the 10th and the 4th houses be conjoined with the Moon and Saturn, the native concerned will possess a lovely house (*vichitram veshma*).

If the lords of the 1st and the 4th houses be posited in the 4th, the native will become the owner of a house all of a sudden.

If the lords of the 11th and 2nd houses occupy the 4th and the lord of the 4th has attained Vaiseshikamsa and is conjoined with or aspected by a benefic, the native will acquire a house of immense value.

The lord of the 4th house occupying it or any other strong planet, there will easily lead to the acquisition of a house.

The condition of the house can be ascertained from the planets in Trikonas and Kendras from the Lagna.

If the 3rd Bhava is occupied by a benefic planet and the lord of the 4th Bhava be strong, the person will possess a strong house (*drudamandiram*).

When the lord of the 4th *Bhava* has attained Gopura and other benefic Vargas, then also it gives a good house.

When the 3rd Bhava is occupied by a benefic planet and when the lords of the 4th and the 1st Bhavas are in strength, the person born will be in possession of a mansion with encircling walls.

There are other combinations also having to do with houses but in a different sense.

If the 4th house and its lord or Karaka be in a moveable sign, the native will reside in many houses (*bahugrihavasah*).

If the 4th house and its lord or Karaka be in a moveable sign, the native will be permanent in one house (*sthiravasah*).

The lord of the 4th house be in a benefic Shashtyamsa, the native will live permanently in one house (*sthiravasah*).

Some classical dicta also help to locate the number of houses one may occupy. For instance, one such dictum says : Find out how many of the lords of the 1st, 4th and 2nd houses are posited in a Kendra or Trikona position. The number of houses occupied by the native will be as many. Of course, it may not be possible to specify the exact number of times one may change house, but it implies, one may have to shift residence quite a few times.

Certain other classical combinations relate to houses but in a slightly adverse vein.

If a malefic planet or Rahu in the 4th Bhava be aspected by an evil planet, the person born will be a sufferer in the matter of domestic comfort (*gehasukhartibhook*).

If Mars or the Sun occupy the 4th Bhava in depression or in an inimical house, the person concerned will be houseless.

If the 4th lord occupies the 12th, the person will lodge in a stranger's house in a foreign land (*anyagehoanyadeshagah*).

If the 4th lord occupies the 8th Bhava, there will be no house owned by him.

If the 4th lord occupies the 6th, he will lodge in the house of a paternal relation (*gnathyadisadgrihah*).

Owning Your Own House

If the 4th lord occupies a Dustana or if the planet in the 4th house has strength for evil, the house falling to the lot of the person will be haunted or dilapidated.

If the lord of the 4th Bhava occupies the 12th from Lagna, the person will have a dilapidated house (*jeernagriha*).

All these various combinations, by and large, emphasise the favorable disposition of the 4th house *vis-à-vis* its lord as the *sine qua non* for owning a house.

The simplest test to determine if a native will own a house is to see if the 4th lord is well-placed and in a Kendra or Trikona. If yes, sooner or later, one will come to own a house.

Venus is the Karaka or natural significator of *griha* or residential house. Venus and the 4th house are important factors in assessing the house-potential of a chart. Other factors help to decide on the quality and size of the house.

The Ascendant in Chart 1 being Taurus, the 4th house is Leo. It is aspected by its own lord Sun, Yogakaraka Saturn, benefic Mercury and Jupiter. The native owned a house with

	Moon	Ascdt.	Sat.
Sun Merc. Jupt.	**Chart 1**		
	Rasi		
Venus		Mars Ketu	

	Ascdt. Jupt.	Rahu	
	Navamsa		
Merc.	Ketu	Sun Sat. Venus Mars	Moon

numerous spacious well-lit and ventilated rooms with a stable for his horses in a sprawling garden with a variety of trees and colourful plants. The house also boasted of a garden room tucked in one corner of the compound surrounded by flowering shrubs and ferns where the native could relax and read quietly with no disturbance. The 4th lord we see is in the 10th with Digbala or directional strength in a Kendra and conjoined with benefics.

The 4th house in Chart 2 is Libra occupied by the Ascendant lord Moon. The 4th lord Venus is in the Ascendant with exalted 9th lord Jupiter. Venus is also Vargottama (since he occupies the same sign in both Rasi and Navamsa). There is an exchange of signs between the 1st and 4th lords and the Moon is extra-powerful being waxing Moon.

Ketu	Sun Merc. Sat.	Sat.	Ascdt. Jupt. Venus
	Chart 2 **Rasi**		
			Mars
	Moon	Rahu	

Ascdt. Ketu			Mars
	Navamsa		Sun Venus Sat.
Merc.			
	Moon Jupt.	Rahu	

The native, a *maharajah*, of a southern state owned some of the most beautiful and breath-taking palaces in the country. Not all charts are as simple as Chart 3 will show us.

			Ascdt. Rahu
	Chart 3 **Rasi**		Sun Mars Merc.
Ketu			
Jupt.	Moon Sat.	Venus	

Sat. Ascdt.	Venus Ketu		Sun
	Navamsa		Merc.
Moon			Mars
	Jupt.	Rahu	

The native has a plot of land but for various reasons has never been able to build a house of her own. She earns well but is forced to stay in a rented apartment.

The 4th house is Libra as in Chart 2 and the Ascendant lord Moon occupies it. It is further occupied by exalted 7th

Owning Your Own House

and 8th lord Saturn. The 4th lord Venus is in the 3rd, the 12th from the 4th, in debility without effective cancellation of debilitation and is hemmed on either side by malefics. Saturn, though exalted in the 4th, is a strong functional malefic. The 4th lord occupies the 12th (not from Lagna though, but from the 4th) and the native lives in another's house (*anyagehanyadeshagah*) in a distant place.

In Chart 1, Venus is the Ascendant lord and a benefic. In Rasi, he is in Sagittarius, a powerful sign, even if not friendly and aspected by Yogakaraka Saturn. In Chart 2, Venus as 4th lord is good for the Bhava in question and powerfully disposed. In Chart 3, Venus enjoys the same lordship as in Chart 2, but he is in debility and in a Dustana with reference to the 4th house. Additionally, he is afflicted by a Papakartari Yoga and occupation of an inimical Navamsa made worse by Ketu being with him.

Chart 4 is a very interesting example of some of the different combinations found in classical works.

Moon Jupt.	Sat. Merc. Ketu Venus	Sun	
	Chart 4 Rasi		Ascdt.
Mars			
		Rahu	

Ascdt.	Venus	Ketu	Merc.
Mars Rahu	Navamsa		
Sun			Ketu
		Moon	Jupt.

The 4th house is Libra occupied by Rahu. The 4th lord Venus is well-placed in the 10th house in Vargottama (since he occupies the same sign in Rasi and Navamsa). The 4th house is afflicted by malefics Saturn and Mercury-Ketu. The Karaka Venus who is also the 4th lord is favorably disposed, being in a Kendra (quadrant). How have these multi-planetary influences affected results pertaining to *griha* or house?

The native built his own house in 1965 but had to leave the city for compulsive reasons two years later. Since then, he has been living in rented houses.

Rahu in the 4th usually denies one the comforts of a home. So while the native has been able to own a house, he has not been able to make a home of it. The 4th lord Venus is, incidentally, in a moveable sign and has given residence in many houses (*baugrihayasah*). This is also due, to some extent, to the afflictions from malefics to the 4th lord and 4th house.

In another case, Chart 5, the native was able to build a beautiful house by the side of a lake. It was an architect's delight and every single detail of colour, decor, design had been planned and executed with painstaking meticulousness. Yet, circumstances did not allow the native to live in it for even a single day.

	Ketu				Ketu	Ascdt.	Merc.
Sat. Jupt.	Chart 5 Rasi		Moon Mars		Navamsa		Jupt.
				Sat.			
	Venus Sun	Merc Ascdt. Rahu			Mars	Rahu	Moon Sun Venus

The 4th house is occupied by its own lord Saturn who is also a Yogakaraka and is Vargottama. He is joined by 3rd and 6th lord Jupiter. Venus, the Karaka, is in close conjunction with the Sun. The combustion of the Karaka Venus did not give the native the benefit of living in his own house. The 4th lord Saturn is in a moveable sign and is partly responsible for the native having to live in different (rented) houses.

The 4th house in Chart 6 being Cancer is occupied by Venus, Saturn and Ketu. While Venus obtains Digbala here,

Owning Your Own House

Saturn and Ketu are not so desirable in this Bhava. The 4th lord Moon is himself, however, powerful in the 11th and full, and also exchanges signs with 11th lord Saturn. While this has given the native a house, Saturn and Ketu in the 4th house have made it musty, ill-lit and dilapidated. But the 11th lord Saturn and the 2nd lord Venus joining the 4th house have made it, inspite of that, a highly priced piece of property because of its vantage location in a big city.

	Ascdt. Jupt.	Sun	
Moon	Chart 6 Rasi		Ketu Sat. Venus
Rahu			Sun
		Mars	

Rahu	Navamsa		Mars
			Sat. Ketu Jupt.
Moon			
Mars	Sun	Ascdt. Venus	

Two factors that keep occurring in charts of those with houses of their own are a well-placed 4th house and Karaka Venus. Where these 2 factors are weakened for one reason or the other, efforts to own a house have rarely fructified. (08-89).

Chapter Five

Progeny

(A) PRINCIPLES OF FAMILY PLANNING

8-15 a.m. August 6, 1945. A whole city was destroyed by a scientific monster and a whole generation of hate and anger took birth as hundreds of men, women and children lay dead or dying with the bombing of Hiroshima.

The greatest tragedy of the nuclear holocaust was directed at infants, born and unborn.

The chart (Chart 1) drawn for this fateful moment is revealing.

Leo rises with Mercury. There is a concentration of affliction on the 5th house. The Nodes, an afflicted Venus and the Moon, Saturn and an adversely aspecting Mars focus their combined baneful influence on the 5th house. Mothers pregnant at the time of the bombing either suffered miscarriages or bore children deformed in various ways.

If this macabre disaster of science is beginning to recede in the minds of men, the tragedy that struck Bhopal a few years ago is still fresh in human memory. Many of the women pregnant at the time the gas leak struck had according to the Relief Commissioner Ishwar Dass, "delivered malformed babies suffering from a *host of mental and physical deformities* (Italics ours). Many of them had an ear missing or a deformed face."

The number of still-births after the tragedy was doubled according to Dr. Dass. A report in early October 1985 said that about 400 pregnancies were aborted and the number of still-births after the tragedy was 52. Out of 2198 children born after the gas leak, many died shortly after birth and many others were deformed. Although these mishaps can be traced to the conception time of the babes themselves, the chart (Chart 2) for the time when the gas leaked out has an afflicted 5th house. "The situation of Mercury in the 5th conjunct

Jupiter and aspected by Saturn is ominous. *Long-term genetic effects are* likely to be considerable. The incidence of miscarriages in women may increase and many children may be born with defects. It is, therefore, necessary that preventive medical steps be taken. Quite a few women may probably become barren. Mars in the 6th house with Venus points to the fact that many, mostly women, may need corrective medical and surgical treatment for a whole bunch of problems."* This assessment made on page 180 in *The Astrological Magazine*, February 1985 has since been proved correct. Again, in the same issue we had warned "Scorpio being the sign of regeneration, the unborn child may have to pay a heavy price for the folly of human ambitions. All over the world deformed foetuses, still-births and congenitically defective babes may reach a new high as a result of this conjunction" and this has now been confirmed. Recent reports have shown an increase in still-births and abortions and also malformed infants among the gas-affected population of Bhopal. Much of this heart-breaking mass infanticide could have been averted and minimised if only the medical fraternity had set aside its inflated ego for a while and paid attention to astrological forebodings. But this is not surprising if we analyse the medical man's priorities. He is not prompted by what is of importance to the patient but by "what is of greatest relevance in the international community of scientists. Sophisticated research, preferably clinic/laboratory based, using the costly apparatus which has been specially obtained, is the order of the day . . . . Moreover, the attitude of modern medical research (including the ICMR) has been to view individuals as collections of organs." Even when certain conscientious workers suggested that the affected people should be enlightened on the uncertainties of pregnant women, it was condemned as alarmist by medical men.

The point, here, is to use these charts bearing afflicted 5th houses for lessons in preparing a Nisheka chart (timing impregnation). A study of the Bhopal gas leak chart (Chart 2) and the Hiroshima bombing chart will teach us just

---

* See page 79.

Chart 1: Hiroshima bombed at 8-15 a.m. (IST) on 6-8-1945 at 132 E 25, 34 N 24.

		Mars	Venus Rahu Moon Sat.
	Chart 1 **Rasi** **Hiroshima** **Bombing**		Sun
			Merc. Lagna
Ketu			Jupt.

	Mars Sat.	Moon	
Jupt. Rahu	**Navamsa**		Merc.
Sun Venus			Ketu

Moon		Rahu	
	Chart 2 **Rasi** **Bhopal** **Gas Leak**		
Mars Venus			Ascdt.
Merc. Jupt.	Sun Ketu	Sat.	

	Ascdt.		Merc. Sat.
Rahu	**Navamsa**		Mars
Venus			Ketu
Sun	Moon	Jupt.	

what to avoid in electing a Muhurtha for Garbhadana. *Mars in the 4th, the Sun in the 12th and the Moon waning* is a combination in clasical works which results in the pregnant woman dying with a child in the womb. Here, the exact result is not important, what is important is the kind of general result that can be ascribed to this Yoga. In Chart 1 of the Hiroshima bombing, Mars is not in the 4th but aspects it. The Sun is in the 12th and the Moon is waning. And we know with what results on expectant mothers !

While modern medicine is still trying to figure out methods to determine the sex of the unborn child, the ancient seers had gone miles ahead in this direction even before the West opened its eyes. They had outlined methods to plan the sex of the child yet to be conceived. Not only that; where the child was already forming in the womb, they had methods to effect a change in its sex. Ayurvedic works carry in detail the various processes that could affect a change in the sex of the child in the womb.

The first time a couple came together was called Nishekam. This was an event of major importance and was timed with great care and precision. No emotional romantic factors determined the epoch as it happens today. The time when the couple came together was deemed to influence not only the quality of their own married life but also of the progeny they would bear in future.

According to the sages, certain Nakshatras such as Rohini, Uttaraphalguni, Hasta, Swati, Anuradha, Moola, Uttarashada, Sravana, Satabhisha, Uttarabhadrapada and Revati are deemed excellent for Nishekam. The week days and Navamas as ruled by the Moon, Mercury, Jupiter and Venus are especially auspicious. So also signs ruled by the natural benefics Mercury, Venus and Jupiter and the luminaries, the Sun and the Moon, are highly propitious.

The first sixteen days from the day the menstrual flow begins are said to be the fertile period. Union on these days results in conception, that on the odd days resulting in female progeny and that on even days causing male births. This way a couple can easily plan their family and also choose the sex of the baby they would like by timing union on appropriate days.

According to classical writers, who have but drawn from what the Maharishis have said, union on different days after the menstrual flow begins is said to cause different kinds of results.

The first 4 nights are not fit for impregnation as they cause adverse results generally.

According to Vaidyanatha Dikshitar, offspring conceived during the rest of the fertile period will be as follows :

1. On the 4th night, it leads to a short-lived son.
2. On the 5th night, a girl will be born.
3. On the 6th, a son who brings glory to the family.
4. On the 7th, a female child who will be barren.

5. On the 8th, a son.
6. On the 9th, the birth of a beautiful daughter occurs.
7. On the 10th, a son born to rule others.
8. On the 11th, a deformed girl will be born.
9. On the 12th, a prosperous boy.
10. On the 13th, a wretched baby girl who will be inclined.
11. On the 14th, a balanced and righteous-minded.
12. On the 15th, a girl who will be the embodiment of good fortune; and
13. On the 16th night, a *sarvagna* or all-knowing or wise son.

Kalaprakasika, the standard work on electional astrology, outlines the dangers of union during the first 4 days of menstruation. The first day can be fatal to the husband, it can render him weak and vulnerable to disease. If it is the second day, the woman is adversely affected in her functional health. On the 3rd day, if it results in conception, birth will be of a mentally retarded boy. The fourth day affects the virility of the father.

The day apart, much importance is given to the Nisheka Lagna or rising sign at union. Yogas or planetary combinations for male, female and eunuch births are also enumerated. By a careful and diligent application of these Yogas, healthy and happy progeny can be obtained. Birth of twins can also be successfully attempted.

Jupiter and the Sun and Moon in odd signs at Nisheka result in male progeny. For a girl, the Moon, Venus and Mars should be in even signs. Jupiter, Venus, Sun, Moon and Mars in dual a Rasi and Navamsa lead to the birth of twins.

The Sun in Nisheka Lagna with Saturn and Mars in the 7th, the Moon, Saturn and Mars in Nisheka Lagna and the Moon in a Martian or Saturnine sign aspected by their respective ruler and not aspected by benefics in the Nisheka chart tends to cause abortions.

As a general rule, benefic influences on Nisheka Lagna and a well-placed Moon result in healthy, intelligent progeny. Malefics influencing the rising sign cause the birth of sickly, crippled, blind, mentally retarded and physically handicapped children.

Charts cast for the conception time can give a picture of the health of the baby to be born. But the problem lies in not being able to record this particular epoch. However, from the birth chart we can easily determine the pre-natal epoch and study it from a purely academic angle. None of the classical works carries any clues to determining the epoch. There are some general principles based upon the relationship of the Moon and the Ascendant which have been verified after elaborate tests as valid. Below is the chart (Chart 3) of a young man who was born by caesarean section. Two days after birth, he was struck by brain fever which caused damage to the left side of his brain. As a result, he lost control over his right limbs. However, mentally he grew up quite normal and intelligent.

Birth and epoch details are withheld for obvious reasons.

	Jupt. (R)		
	Chart 3 Rasi		Lagna Ketu
Rahu Mars Moon			
Venus	Merc. Sun	Jupt.	

	Mars		
Merc. Kettu	Navamsa		
Moon			Rahu Venus
		Lagna Jupt. Sat.	

Pre-natal Epoch: 9-2-1952.

Jupt.			
Rahu	Chart 4 Rasi		
Lagna Sun Merc.			Ketu
Venus		Mars	Sat. (R)

	Merc.		Ketu
	Navamsa		Sat. (R)
Mars			
Lagna			Moon Sun
Jupt. Rahu		Venus	

Malefics Sun and Mercury occupy Lagna at Epoch (Chart 4) and Mars aspects it. The Lagna lord Saturn comes under a Papakartari Yoga. This affliction to the Nisheka Lagna resulted in a partially crippled physical body. Jupiter's aspect on the Lagna lord has modified the affliction.

These directions from the sages were meant to preserve the human race in its best form. Union was not a matter of emotional or physical urge but one of careful planning. If only couples made use of these tips, the world would be free of the horror of mentally retarded and physically deformed children. Prevention is better than cure. But who would today heed the counsel of the Rishis and regulate one's passions when the order of the day is to run after pleasures, come what may. And the result, we see in the deformed bodies and minds of countless infants and children around us. Science with its amazing progress has still not been able to do anything about this vital issue.

Timing progeny on running Dasas and Bhuktis can also prevent many mishaps such as still-births, abortions, spastics, mentally retarded children, mongoloids and physically deformed births.

Afflictions to the 5th house and Karaka Jupiter show up as problems centering round children. A couple may be childless or it may continually lose progeny through still-births, abortions or miscarriages.

Different planets rule over different months of pregnancy. What the ancient seers guaged through their intuitive flashes is confirmed by modern research on the unborn child.

Sloka 16 of Chapter IV of **Brihat Jataka** gives a clear picture of the various stages of development of the embryo. According to it, Venus is the ruler of the first month when the conception takes place. Mars rules the second month when flesh begins to form. The hands, mouth and other limbs form under the rulership of Jupiter in the 3rd month. Bones form in the fourth month when the Sun rules. The Moon ruling the 6th month causes the skin to form. In the 7th month, intelligence or consciousness is infused into the foetus. The ruler of the Lagna at Adhana is the ruler of the

8th month when food is absorbed through the navel. The Moon, again, comes into the picture in the 9th month when the movements are felt. At delivery in the 10th month, the Sun assumes rulership.

Studies made by doctors since 1960 have only rediscovered the truth of what our own sages had revealed to us.

"Henry Truby, former professor of paediatrics, linguistics and anthropology at the University of Miami, U.S.A., points to studies since 1960, showing that the foetus hears clearly from the sixth month in utero and even more startling that it responds to the mother's speech. A six-month foetus is also capable of reacting to music, even in rather discriminating ways. Put on Beethoven — and all forms of rock — and most unborn babies start kicking violently." Mercury ruling the 7th month brings consciousness into the foetus. That is, it can react to external stimuli in positive or negative ways. Mercury rules *dhi* or intellect or the discriminative faculty. At this period, in the growth of the foetus, it recognises sounds such as the mother's or father's voices that can be reassuring. It shies away from strange noises. It can now discriminate between loving sounds and non-loving sounds, which is why, at this stage, Mercury is said to rule over the foetus.

Modern science does not have the answers to all the problems of man. Perhaps, it can help in some ways in a limited manner but not beyond. It is only when orthodox men of science set aside their blinkers and apply their minds, without prejudice, to a study of our ancient science of astrology that many of man's ills find an answer.

(B) YOUR OWN CHILD OR ADOPTION

The joy of parenthood is sought by all, yet it eludes many. Not all do get children, and if they do, the child often proves more a bane than a blessing. No wonder then if Clarence S. Darrow was prompted to say, "the first half of our lives is ruined by our parents and the second half by our children." The first half of the statement may be a topic of controversy, but most of us must concede the truth of the latter half.

Progeny

Inspite of it all, human nature being what it is, every heart is sooner or later seized by the homing instinct.

Where there are no children even after some years of marriage, the craving for a child is satisfied by adopting one. Sadly though, no sooner is this done, then a baby is on the way. Such circumstances can lead to tragic consequences where the adopted child finds itself neglected in preference to the baby born to the couple. If we can know for sure that there can never be a baby of our own, adoption of a child would be blessed two-fold. Not only do the couple find emotional satisfaction, but also a helpless life finds a home. Astrology can enable us to adopt another's child, or wait for our own, however late that may be.

The Rasi chart furnishes the first clue to this aspect of life. The Saptamsa chart and the Beeja-Kshetra determination give a conclusive answer to whether there will be any children or not.

The 5th house, the 5th lord and the aspects on these two are the elements to be analysed. Jupiter, the natural Putrakaraka, must also be studied with reference to position and associations.

Chart 1: Born 9-11-1932 at 1-30 a.m. (ZST) at Kuala Lumpur.

Moon				Sun			Venus Rahu
Rahu	Chart 1 Rasi		Ascdt. Jupt. Mars Ketu		Saptamsa		Ascdt. Merc. Mars Sat.
Sat.				Jupt.			
	Merc.	Sun	Venus	Ketu		Moon	

Chart 1 belongs to a gentleman of about 42 years. He has no children. The Lagna being Leo, the 5th house is Sagittarius whose lord Jupiter is the Karaka for children. He is posited in Lagna, a fiery sign, with Ketu, a withering planet, and an eunuch by nature, and with fiery Mars, Yogakaraka for Leo. The 5th house is subject to a Papakartari Yoga being hemmed between Saturn and Mercury, lord of the 2nd and hence, a Maraka. The 5th lord Jupiter is in Pubba whose lord Venus is a functional malefic. Prospects for progeny seem, therefore, pretty dim.

The Saptamsa chart must be studied with reference to the 5th lord in Rasi and its own Lagna and the 6th houses. The 5th house in this Saptamsa chart happens to have Jupiter, 5th lord in Rasi, as its lord here as well. He is debilitated and ill-placed in the 6th from Lagna, an Upachaya house. The Saptamsa Lagna is occupied by Mercury and Saturn, both impotent planets. Ketu is in the 5th house shrivelling up the 5th house significations. It is further aspected by 2 malefics, Rahu and Venus (3rd lord).

The Beeja determination only confirms the gloomy picture. Adding the longitudes of Venus (165-00), the Sun (203-16) and Jupiter (145-08) and expunging multiples of 360 from the total sum, we get 153-24. This gives Virgo 3-24 as the Rasi and Aquarius in Navamsa. One is even and the other odd, indicating limited virility in the native of the chart.

Let us consider another case of a lady (Chart 2). The 5th house is Capricorn and is occupied by Ketu — one of the worst malefics. It is aspected by an eunuch — Mercury, the malefic

Chart 2: Born 28-7-1943 at 10-30 a.m. (ZST) at Kuala Lumpur

	Mars	Sat Moon	
			Rahu Jupt Sun Merc.
Ketu	Chart 2 Rasi		Venus
			Ascdt.

Jupt. Sun		Sat. Moon	Merc. Ascdt. Rahu
	Saptamsa		Mars
	Merc. Venus		

Sun, incendiary Rahu and exalted Jupiter. However, as lord of quadrants, Jupiter becomes a malefic.

The 5th lord Saturn is in Mrigasira belonging to Mars together with the Moon, also in the same constellation. But Mars is a malefic, being the lord of the 3rd and 8th houses. Both the 5th house and the 5th lord are afflicted.

In the Saptmsa chart, Saturn who is the 5th lord in Rasi is relegated to the 12th (a Trika house) from the Lagna. The Lagna Gemini is itself afflicted by Rahu, Ketu and Mercury. The 5th house in the Saptamsa chart is Libra whose lord Venus is afflicted by the Nodes. Further, he is in the 3rd (an Upachaya) from the 5th. Jupiter, the natural Karaka, is in the 6th from the Saptamsa 5th. Saturn, the 5th lord in Rasi, is in the 8th from the 5th in Saptamsa.

The Kshetra test will let us know for sure if the lady can conceive at all. Adding the longitudes of Jupiter (102-54), the Moon (57-07) and Mars (20-23) we get 180-24 which gives Rasi Libra 0-24, and Navamsa also, Libra. Both are odd signs, and we may safely conclude the lady will not bear children. According to classical texts, if the Amsa and Rasi are both odd in a female chart, the field is barren.

In Chart 3, the 5th house is Aries ruled by Mars exalted in the 2nd house. He is with the hermaphrodite Mercury. The 5th house is occupied by malefic Rahu and aspected by own lord Mars. The Karaka Jupiter is ill-placed in the 6th from Lagna.

Chart 3: Born 25-2-1930 at 4-20 a.m. at Ahmedabad.

	Rahu	Jupt.			Sat.	Sun	Moon Venus
Venus Sun	Chart 3 Rasi			Jupt.	Saptamsa		Rahu
Mars Merc.				Ketu			
Ascdt. Sat. Moon		Ketu		Ascdt. Mars	Merc.		

In the Saptamsa chart, the 5th lord Mars is the same as in Rasi; but the 5th house is occupied by Saturn which is not a good augury for children as Saturn is also classified as eunuch. However, the 5th lord in the Saptamsa chart Mars is in the Lagna aspected by the Moon and Venus. As such, afflicting and redeeming features are equally balanced in the chart.

The Beeja test gives Aquarius 17-33 as Rasi and Pisces as Amsa — one odd and the other even — indicating limited virility. The native was running Rahu Dasa upto February 1970 and Rahu being in the 5th in the Rasi chart did not give him any issues. Jupiter Dasa gave him children, though limited in number, during his period. The next period will be that of Saturn who may not give further progeny.

Afflictions to the 5th house and the 5th lord in Rasi and a poor Saptamsa chart deny the native happiness from children. Depending upon the results of the Beeja-Kshetra test, this unhappiness may be due to lack of progeny or due to wayward or short-lived issues. (01-74)

(C) WHEN JUPITER CEASES TO HELP

Jupiter, the best benefic, is often compared to the friend who turns up in the hour of need. The generator of luck, he bestows upon his favorites success, honour, wealth, happy associations and everything desired. Jovian aspects are like sunshine brightening up the landscape of human lives. But sometimes, sunshine can become unbearable and blinding. So, can Jupiter turn ruthless and whimsical.

Many people with well-placed Putrakaraka Jupiter have lost children notwithstanding his supposedly benign influences.

Two out of three children born to the native of Chart 1 died at very tender ages. Jupiter is in his Moolatrikona sign Sagittarius.

The 5th house is Scorpio subject to a powerful Papakartari Yoga caused by Saturn and Rahu. The 5th lord Mars is in the 2nd from Lagna.

Progeny

Chart 1: Born 20-6-1901 at 7-30 a.m. (LMT) at 25 N 36, 85 E 10 with a balance of 9 years 3 months and 28 days of Mercury Dasa.

	Ketu		Sun Venus
	Chart 1 **Rasi**		Ascdt. Moon Merc.
			Mars Mandi
Jupt. Sat.		Rahu	

	Venus		Rahu Mandi
	Navamsa		Merc.
Moon			
Sun Ketu	Mars	Sat.	Ascdt. Jupt.

The Dustanas — the 6th, 8th and the 12th — from the Putra Bhava are occupied by Ketu, the Sun (and Venus), and Rahu — all malefics.

The 5th house and the Karaka Jupiter are both badly afflicted. However, Jupiter's placement in Sagittarius has softened the affliction by leaving untouched one child at least.

Jupiter though generally well-placed in Cancer, Pisces, Sagittarius and Aquarius is strangely fettered when it comes to 5th house indications. This is borne out by Vaidyanatha Dikshitar in his treatise **Jataka Parijata**, Adh. XIII Slokas 30-31.

मीनस्थोत्यल्पसन्तानsचपस्य: कृछ् सन्तति: ।
असन्तति: कुलीरस्यो जीव: कुम्भेन सन्तति: ।
पुत्रस्याने कुलिरेवा मीने कुम्भे शरासूने ।
स्थितो यदि सुराचार्यस्तत्फलं कुरुते नृणाम् ।

meaning, that

> Jupiter in Pisces gives very few children; in Sagittarius, gives children after much difficulty; in Cancer or Aquarius, no issue at all. When the 5th Bhava falls in Cancer, Pisces, Aquarius or Sagittarius, and Jupiter occupies the same, similar results as in Sloka 30 follow.

Chart 2: Born 6-6-1901 at 1-30 p.m. at 11 N 6, 79 E 44 with a balance of 0 years, 3 months and 12 days of Sun Dasa.

		Sun Ketu	Merc. Venus
	Chart 2 **Rasi**		Mandi
Moon			Mars
Jupt. Sat.	Rahu		Ascdt.

Moon		Ascdt.	
Merc.	**Navamsa**		Rahu
Ketu Mandi			Sun
	Sat. Venus	Jupt.	Mars

The native's wife delivered 5 children of whom 4 died. She also suffered an abortion once.

Jupiter (Chart 2) once again is in his Moolatrikona sign, Sagittarius with Saturn, the 5th lord.

The Dustanas from the 5th are occupied by malefics — afflicted Mercury, Mars and Saturn respectively.

According to Vaidyanatha Dikshitar, Sloka 12 of Adh. XIII from the same text,

पुत्रस्थे मदनाधिपे वितनयो जायाविहीनो थवा।
पुत्रदघृम शत्रृरि: फगृहगा: पापा: कुलध्वंसका:।।
राहौ नन्दनराजिगे तदधिपे दु:स्थानगे पुत्रहा।।
पुत्रस्थे तनुपे तनौ सुतपतौ गृहणाति दत्तात्मजम्।।

meaning, that

> if the lord of the 7th Bhava be in the 5th, the person born will have no children or be bereft of a wife. Malefic planets in the 8th, 6th and 12th places from the 5th Bhava bring the family to extinction. Rahu occupying the 5th Bhava and the lord thereof in a Dustana will cause death of children . . . .

The simultaneous fulfilment of conditions for extinction of family plus Jupiter's position in Sagittarius snatched away several children but left a single child alive. If Jupiter had

Progeny

Chart 3: Born 29-11-1876 at 7-00 a.m. (LMT) with a balance of 13 years, 0 months and 18 days of Venus Dasa.

	Moon				Mars	Rahu	
Sat. Rahu	Chart 3 Rasi				Navamsa		
			Ketu	Jupt. Sat.			
Ascdt. Sun Jupt. Merc.	Venus Mars			Venus Sun Mars	Ascdt. Merc. Ketu		Moon

been in Cancer or Aquarius, there would have been no children left alive.

The native (Chart 3) had no children at all since his wife aborted every time.

The Dustanas from the 5th are occupied by Ketu, Mars and Saturn-Rahu. Reckoned from the Moon also, the 5th is occupied by Ketu and afflicted by Saturn while the 5th lord is in a Dustana (8th from Moon Lagna) indicating extinction of family.

Jupiter though aspecting the 5th has been of no help in continuing the family.

The native (Chart 4) had no children at all since his wife aborted every time.

Jupiter is in Cancer which according to Vaidyanatha Dikshitar indicates no issues.

The 5th is Leo occupied by Jupiter in Bhava and the 5th lord Sun is in the 10th.

The Dustanas from the 5th are all occupied by malefics. The 6th from Putra Bhava is occupied by the Sun, the 8th by Mandi and the 12th by Saturn.

In Navamsa too, Jupiter is in Aquarius stressing the point under discussion.

Chart 4: Born 15-1-1920 at 12 noon (IST) at 31 N 35, 74 E 18 with a balance of 7 years, 2 months and 26 days of Jupiter Dasa.

Mandi	Ascdt.	Ketu	
	Chart 4 Rasi		Jupt. Sat.
Sun			
Merc.	Venus Rahu	Moon Mars	

	Ascdt.		Moon
Jupt.	Navamsa		Rahu
Venus Sun Ketu			
		Mars	Merc Sat.

Chart 5 (Female): Born 30-9-1919 at 8-39 a.m. (IST) at 11 N 6, 79 E 44 with a balance of 12 years, 4 months and 27 days of Mercury Dasa.

		Ketu	
	Chart 5 Rasi		Jupt.
			Mars Venus Sat.
Mandi	Moon Rahu	Ascdt.	Merc. Sun

	Ascdt. Mars	Sun	Merc
Ketu	Navamsa		
Moon Jupt.			
		Venus	Mandi

The native of Chart 5 gave birth to three children, two of whom died.

Jupiter is exalted in Rasi in Cancer.

The 5th is Aquarius whose lord Saturn and Mars and Venus aspect it.

All the Dustanas from the 5th are not occupied. Perhaps this, together with the 5th lord aspecting the 5th, saved the family from total extinction.

Progeny

Chart 6: Born 2-6-1914 at 7-5 a.m. (IST) at 22 N 45, 72 E 41 with a balance of 1 year, 4 months and 24 days of Venus Dasa.

		Sun Sat.	Ascdt. Venus Merc.
Jupt. Rahu	\multicolumn{2}{c}{Chart 6 Rasi}	Mars
			Moon Ketu

Rahu Venus			Sun
Mars	\multicolumn{2}{c}{Navamsa}	
	Merc.	Ascdt. Venus	Jupt.	Sat. Ketu

Chart 6 belongs to a childless gentleman.

Jupiter is in Aquarius while the 6th from the 5th is occupied by Rahu (in Bhava), the 8th by Saturn-Sun and the 12th, by Ketu.

Chart 7: Born 31-7-1910 at 7-06 p.m. (IST) at 8 N 48, 77 E 40 with a balance of 6 years, 3 months and 22 days of Moon Dasa.

Mandi	Sat.	Moon Rahu	Venus
	\multicolumn{2}{c}{Chart 7 Rasi}	Sun Merc.
Ascdt.			Mars
			Jupt.

Merc.		Moon Mars	Jupt.
Venus Rahu	\multicolumn{2}{c}{Navamsa}	
			Ascdt. Sat. Ketu
		Sun	

The 5th house in Chart 7 is occupied by Rahu and the 5th from the Moon by Jupiter. Jupiter's aspect on the 5th Bhava was of little use as the native could not get children.

(Incidentally, our attention is drawn to Venus in the 6th while the 7th is occupied by Mercury. Saturn aspects Venus. This is more a case of impotency than pure "childlessness".)

Chart 8: Born 1-5-1904 at 5-35 a.m. (LMT) at 16 N 57, 82 E 13 with a balance of 0 years, 2 months and 26 days of Saturn Dasa.

Jupt. Ketu	Ascdt. Sun Venus Mars	Merc	
	Chart 8 Rasi		
Sat.			
	Moon		Rahu

		Venus	
Jupt. Rahu Merc.	Navamsa		
			Ketu
Mars	Moon	Sun	

The native (Chart 8) suffered the death of both his children.

Jupiter is in Pisces and Aquarius in Rasi and Navamsa respectively.

The 5th from the Moon is occupied by Jupiter-Ketu in Pisces.

The 5th lord in exaltation gave the native children, but Jupiter-Ketu in Pisces killed them.

Can Jupiter's pleasant smile ever turn into a leer? Perhaps, it can. (10-74)

(D) CHILDREN — BANE OR BLESSING?

Anapatya Yoga is a simple Yoga which is said to deny one children. It is caused by Jupiter and the lords of the Lagna, the 5th and 7th houses being weak. This is the least malefic of the Yogas covering children.

The 2nd, 5th and 7th lords conjoining in one sign and the Navamsa lords of these planets being malefic and also occupying malefic signs denies one children. If the Lagna lord and the 5th lord occupy a Dustana — the 6th, 8th or 12th — Jupiter is in debility while Mercury and Saturn occupy the 5th, one does not get children. If Jupiter in the 5th or 8th is in a Kroora (cruel) Shashtiamsa and the 5th lord is relegated to the 8th, then one is childless.

Rahu aspected by Mars or Rahu in the 5th if in Scorpio or Aries; the 5th lord and Rahu in one sign, the 5th occupied by Saturn and aspected by the Moon; Rahu and Jupiter in one sign, the 5th lord weak and Lagna lord conjoining Mars; the Lagna lord or Jupiter conjoining Rahu while the 5th lord is with Mars; Rahu in the 5th conjoining or aspected by Mercury for Cancer or Sagittarius Ascendants; Rahu in Lagna, Jupiter with Mars and 5th lord in the 6th, 8th or 12th; Rahu and Gulika in Lagna, the 5th lord Mercury in conjunction with Mars and in a Navamsa ruled by Mars are all combinations that deny one children.

A Sagittarius-born with the Moon and Rahu in Lagna, Saturn in the 3rd, Ketu in the 7th, Venus in the 9th, Sun in the 10th, Mercury in the 11th and Mars and Jupiter in the 12th, died childless. The Lagna and 5th lords, Mars and Jupiter, occupy the 12th. The 8th lord is in Lagna and Mercury aspects the 5th.

Whenever Rahu is involved, the childlessness is attributed to Sarpa Sapa or the curse of serpents. In some texts Sarpa Sapa is said to result from destroying life, especially in the formative stages, and includes destroying eggs of any specie and causing abortions.

Childlessness does create a big void in life but it is any day preferable to the more poignant situation of losing one's child to death. In fact, Putrasoka or the grief that results on the loss of one's child is said to surpass all other kinds of suffering.

Afflictions by Mars, Rahu or Saturn or sometimes even Ketu or the Sun to anyone or more of the Sun, Moon, Mars, Mercury and Jupiter in relation to the 5th house result in the loss of children attributed to the curse (*Sapa*) of the father, the mother, the brother, the maternal uncle and the Brahmin (pious and virtuous man) respectively. The Sapa is, at any rate, not necessarily the vocal pronouncement that evil should befall one. It is the reaction attendant on the anguish or suffering (mostly mental), undergone by anyone of this list as a result of the pain (mental, physical, emotional, psychological or even spiritual) inflicted on one by the native at some point of time. This point of time is not limited to this life-time only but could be from some recent or even remote past embodiment. The reaction clings to the native biding its time to manifest as pain again, to enable him to understand at a deeper level his misdeed of inflicting pain on anyone of the individuals in the list above. The pain the native suffers on account of loss of his own children is, therefore, not only punitive but also deterrent and reformative.

The Lagna lord or Jupiter with Rahu while the 5th lord is weak and the Ascendant lord is with Mars; the 5th lord with the Sun, Jupiter in Leo and malefics in the 5th and the Ascendant; or, the Sun in a Saturnine sign hemmed between malefics and in debility in Navamsa; or, the 4th and 5th houses occupied by malefics and the 5th lord Mars debilitated or hemmed between malefics; or exchange of signs between the 8th and 5th lords while the 4th lord and the Moon are in the 6th, 8th or the 12th; or the 9th lord in the 5th, while the 5th lord occupies the 8th with Jupiter, Mars and Rahu; or Rahu in the Ascendant and Saturn in the 5th aspected by or with Mars are some Yogas that show loss of children.

Sometimes, these combinations are present *adverbatim*; sometimes, they occur with some modification. The native of Chart 1 lost two of her sons to violence when they were in their 20's and 40's.

The 5th house in Chart 1 is occupied by the Sun while the 5th lord Jupiter joins the 7th lord Venus in the 6th. Venus

Chart 1: Born 23-3-1929 at 10-51 p.m. (IST) at 18 N 56, 72 E 31.

Sun 11-11	Venus 15-49 Jupt. 19-57	Rahu 2-31	Mars 13-41
Merc. 19-50	Chart 1 Rasi		
			Moon 21-18
Sat. 8-50	Lagna 7-29 Ketu 2-31		

Merc.			Sat.
			Ketu
Mars	Navamsa		
Rahu			Venus
		Sun Moon	Lagna Jupt.

Progeny

who is also the 12th lord being with the 5th lord Jupiter is not a happy feature. The Lagna lord Mars occupies the 8th, another Dustana.

Suputra Yoga is an important Yoga and is said to give one a worthy son. One of the greatest blessings in life is to have a child who cares. In fact, according to **Tirukural**, the best thing a son can do for his parents is "to make others say what penance his parents should have done to beget such a good son." If Jupiter is the 5th lord and the Sun occupies a favorable position, one gets a worthy son. This combination, if taken literally, can hold good only in the case of Leo and Scorpio Lagnas and, therefore, is limited in application. Yet, it gives us a clue to what finally decides one will get a Suputra. It is the Karaka Jupiter who matters more than anything else in conferring on one a worthy child, be it son or daughter or both. Jupiter's occupation of the 5th house or his aspect on the 5th house or the 5th lord, provided there is no malefic influence on the 5th house gives children who care. If malefic influences are *also* present, then at least one child will be affectionate, obedient and concerned with the natives' well-being. Alternately, in the event of both benefic and malefic combinations, it can give children who could generally be described as good but who, at times, may go off at a tangent.

For example, an Aries Ascendant native who has Jupiter in the 1st house, aspecting the 5th house Leo occupied by the 5th lord Sun has a son who is extremely devoted to her. He is ever ready to carry out the most trying and whimsical bidding coming from her, even at the cost of his own personal life. Of course, this is an extreme case, for, one has a duty towards different relationships simultaneously and at different levels; one should not be neglected at the cost of the other. However, in the context of the subject under discussion, the lady should consider herself extremely fortunate in an age where apathy and growing indifference to parents in their old age seem to be the rule. In the same case, with reference to the Moon, the 5th lord Mercury is exalted in the 8th. But the Sun in Leo and Mars in Libra flank the 5th house and 5th lord bringing both under a Papakartari Yoga. One of her children proved to be too demanding and selfish to the core. While this did lead to mental anguish, Jupiter in Lagna worked to diffuse the Dosha in that this child lived far away in her marital home.

Likewise, the aspect of a malefic, particularly, Mars, on the 5th house in the absence of benefic influences can give a child who can become a source of pain, constant annoyance or sometimes even a major problem. Such a native may be exposed to emotional blackmail or even physical violence from one's child. Where the horoscope is otherwise strong, then Mars in such a position gets shorn of its maleficence to some extent and generates only a self-willed, self-centred child.

The consideration of the aspects, occupation or association of Jupiter or Mars is not confined to the 5th house from the Ascendant alone. The Moon-sign is equally important. The Karaka Jupiter is also to be assessed. If malefic and benefic influences are sprinkled evenly, in the event of more than one child, one may be good; the other, difficult. Good and bad Dasas may also influence the behaviour of the child, this way or that.

While the list of Yogas for different causes for childlessness or loss of children is quite long in classical authorities, those for unhappiness on account of children are not many.

The 5th lord's association with the 6th lord is said to make the son शत्रुसमो भवेत् or like an enemy. Likewise, the 6th lord in the 5th is said to make one bereft of happiness from the son. The association of the 5th lord with the 8th or 12th lord is also deemed to come in the way of happiness from children. This combination applies very well in Chart 1 where the 5th lord Jupiter is with the 12th lord Venus in the 6th. The children had monstrous ambitions and, in a mad race for power, developed dangerous animosities for one another. Such a situation can hardly make a patent happy about one's children, no matter, how successful they are.

A Sagittarius Ascendant native with the Sun in Lagna, Jupiter in Aquarius, Saturn in Pisces, Ketu in Aries, Mars, Venus and Rahu in Libra and the Moon and Mercury in

Scorpio, born in a family in indigent circumstances married into affluence. The husband, coming from a highly cultured background, treated her with affection and respect. Two sons were born, both of whom were obedient and brilliant. All these events came about in Venus, Sun, Moon and Mars Dasas.

Both the sons went abroad for studies. In the meanwhile, the husband's health was adversely affected. The first son who had married in accordance with the wishes of his mother came back and prevailed on his parents to go back with him to the United States where he said the father could get the best medical treatment. The lady and her husband wound up their establishment in India and moved overseas to stay with their son. Unfortunately for the lady, the husband succumbed to the illness. She suddenly found herself totally dependent on her sons in a faraway land. Gradually, she began to sense that she was unwanted until one fine day she was asked to pack up and leave.

The 5th house has Ketu. The 5th lord Mars is with Venus and Rahu aspected by Jupiter. Until Rahu Dasa began, everything was fine. Rahu occupies the 11th afflicting the 5th lord Mars and aspected by Jupiter. Rahu should give the results of Venus. Venus, as the 6th lord with the 5th lord is not really desirable. Rahu should also reflect the results of Saturn according to the dictum *Sanivad Rahu*. Saturn, as a malefic, occupies the 5th house from the Moon-sign. Saturn is in exchange of signs with 5th lord Jupiter reckoned from the Lagna but the exchange is not a favorable one. The realisation that the son who had all along been so good had changed and now found her a burden left the native stunned beyond belief.

In combinations showing children, the results are described as सुतसौख्य (happiness from sons) and interpreted as meaning being blessed with children. But the quality of the children is seldom implied. Likewise, when malefic combinations are referred to, the result is automatically thought to imply either absence of children or loss of children, and therefore, no happiness on that score. But life has a funny way of finding new ways of unhappiness and this is never more true than when dealing with children who cause pain and suffering to the parent. The child may become wayward, defiant, disobedient and selfish to the core. Suffering on account of progeny can also include cases where an affectionate and bright child falls prey to a terminal ailment or is hit by some major tragedy. Likewise, in the case of spastics and mentally retarded or physically handicapped children. Especially, in the last named cases, the parent's suffering is infinite and is experienced daily, almost on an hour-to-hour basis.

In Chart 2, the daughter of the native had a nervous breakdown with several relapses. She had difficulty relating to people who began to turn away from her. The native was mad with worry as her daughter exhibited self-destructive tendencies. In this case, the problem was not something confined to a time-frame but a continuing one. The parent was constantly in a state of tension because of the girl's volatile mood swings and with a gnawing fear of the self-injury she could inflict on herself.

Chart 2: Born 22-12-1922 at 11-45 p.m. at 40 N 45, 73 W 57.

Ketu 3-29				Lagna Mars	Jupt.		Sun
Mars 17-12 Moon 5-52	Chart 2 Rasi			Rahu	Navamsa		
							Venus Ketu
Sun 9-15 Merc. 18-30	Venus 4-12	Jupt. 20-22	Rahu 3-29 Lagna 7-29 Sat. 27-51		Moon		Sat. Merc.

The 5th house is vacant but the 5th lord Saturn is in the Ascendant with Rahu; yet, there is a daughter. Such a combination involving the 5th lord generally passes for a Yoga that shows childlessness due to Sarpa Sapa. But Saturn is Vargottama which is good.

The 5th house Capricorn is flanked on either side by malefics Sun-Mercury and Moon-Mars subjecting it to a Papakartari Yoga. The 5th lord Saturn is in Chitta ruled by

Mars, ruler of the 3rd and 8th houses and, therefore, a baneful planet. Mars aspects the 5th lord Saturn adversely.

Chart 3 is of a more pathetic case. The lady has a daughter and is retired with no one else. She subsists on income from Social Security. The daughter is a working woman and well-off.

Chart 3: Born 17-2-1924 at 10-00 a.m. at 47 N 30, 19 E 05.

Venus 13-43		Ascdt. 2-53	Moon 26-24
Ketu 11-09 Sun 6-06	Chart 3 Rasi		
Merc. 12-58			Rahu 11.09
	Jupt. 25-30 Mars 26-57	Sat. (R) 11-21	

Mars	Merc.	Moon	
Jupt.	Navamsa		Rahu
Lagna Mars (R) Ketu			
	Venus Sun		

The daughter constantly pesters the native for money. She even bothers her on telephone and even when the native refuses to see her, comes to her and does not leave until she gets what she wants by forcing the old woman to give her the cheque. The native dreads her daughter and sometimes has to make do with bread and water.

Focus your attention on the 5th house. It is Virgo aspected by Lagna lord Venus from the 11th. The 5th lord Mercury is in the 9th showing the daughter is well-off. But the 5th house is itself caught between malefics Rahu and Saturn (R) on either side. Saturn is exalted and retrograde and occupies a Rahu-ruled Nakshatra. Rahu in Leo is in an inimical sign in a Ketu-ruled Nakshatra and aspected by an afflicted Sun. It is the Papakartari Yoga that is at work making it miserable for the native.

The relationship of the 5th lord with the 6th house or the 8th house factors gives worries of a major magnitude in relation to one's child. If it is the 12th house factors, the problem is reduced in severity.

Chart 4: Born 23-3-1915 at 5-29 a.m. (IST) at 13 N 08, 75 E 51.

Sun 11-03			Moon 11-36 Sat. 4-50
Lagna 22-31 Jupt. 20-12 Merc. 13-36 Mars 20-08	Chart 4 Rasi		
Venus 28-43			Ketu 3-30
			Mandi 22-55

	Mars Lagna Jupt.	Ketu	
Merc.	Navamsa		
Moon			
	Sat. Rahu	Sun	Venus

The 5th house Gemini has Lagna lord Saturn in it with 6th lord Moon. The 5th lord Mercury is with Mars, Rahu and Jupiter occupying a Nakshatra ruled by Rahu. Saturn and Mercury are in Parivartana which is all fine but, because the Moon as 6th lord is also involved, the Yoga is considerably blemished. Mercury is in Satabhisha ruled by Rahu and Saturn in the 5th is in Mrigasira ruled by Mars.

From the Moon-sign, the 5th lord Venus is in the 8th in Dhanishta ruled by malefic 6th and 11th lord Mars. Jupiter, himself afflicted by degree conjunction with Mars, aspects the 5th both from the Lagna and the Moon-sign.

The native's wife died in 1984. He then, at his only daughter's insistence, went to live with her. Venus Dasa had begun and as 5th lord in the 8th could not be expected to give good results. The daughter began to ill-treat the native; the son-in-law was no better until finally, unable to bear the humiliation, the native left them and joined an old-age home.

These examples show clearly what kind of a situation one may expect of one's child in one's old age.

Jupiter and Lagna lord favorably influencing the 5th house from Lagna and the Moon, in the absence of malefic influences on the 6th, give progeny who will be loving and dutiful.

Jupiter and or the Lagna lord favorably influencing the 5th house factors from the Lagna or the Moon and malefic influences also present *vis-á-vis* the 5th houses makes, in cases of more than one child, at least one caring and affectionate. Or, depending upon adverse Dasas, children will inflict suffering on the native during such periods.

If the influence of Jupiter or the Lagna lord is absent and that of Mars or Saturn is predominant, one must suffer selfish, heartless children.

If Rahu or Ketu are also involved, such children get into scrapes and situations embarrassing their parents.

If the 5th house or the 5th lord is caught in a Papakartari Yoga, then the native has no escape from a situation that is perennially painful, difficult, embarrassing and, sometimes, physically also difficult to endure. In such cases, the problems are never-ending and can erupt on an hour-to-hour basis.

The 5th house factors influenced by retrograde planets, such as Mars, Jupiter and Saturn alone or in combination and involving Rahu and Ketu as well as Papakartari Yogas with a special emphasis on the 8th house factor can lead to birth of children with serious handicaps — mental or physical. Jupiter in debility in such cases adds to the severity of the child's handicaps. A Scorpio native with Jupiter in the 3rd in Capricorn in all the Vargas and with no cancellation of debility had a number of children, born healthy. But, except for one, each child as it reached the age of 8 or 9 years, began to develop muscular dystrophy and, in the course of 5 to 6 years, the native had to cope with nearly 4 children with normal intelligence but unable to use their limbs or move about. A Capricorn Ascendant native had a seriously mentally retarded child. The 5th house had Mars (R). Saturn (R) *cum*-8th lord Sun aspect the 5th from Scorpio. The girl used to exhibit violent moods, tearing and scratching her hair, face and clothes.

One of the most malefic factors centering round the 5th house is combustion. It shows serious tragedy in relation to one's progeny.

In the case of a Libra Lagna native, with the Sun and Saturn in exact conjunction in Capricorn, both sons committed suicide in the prime of youth. One fell prey to vices while even in his teens.

Chart 5: Born 16-7-1946 at 2-30 p.m. (CST) at 38 N 19, 88 W 52.

		Rahu 27-25		Ketu			Ascdt.
Moon 0-31	Chart 5 Rasi		Sun 2-01 Sat. 11-36 Merc. 24-13	Merc.	Navamsa		Sun Jupt. Venus
			Venus 11-50 Mars 23-49				Sat.
	Ketu 27-25	Lagna 28-39	Jupt. 27-16		Mars	Moon	Rahu

The 5th lord in Chart 5 is in the 10th combust. The Karaka Jupiter is Vargottama in the 12th house. From the Moon-sign, the 5th lord Mercury is in the 6th with a combust Saturn. The son, indeed, proved to be the native's enemy. In Mercury Bhukti of Saturn Dasa, the son stabbed his father, mother, an elder brother and sister to death and strangulated his kid-brother.

Chart 6: Born 30-10-1946 at 10-55 a.m. (CST) 38 N 19, 88 W 62.

		Rahu 21-48				Jupt. Sun	
	Chart 6 Rasi		Sat. 16-48		Navamsa		Ascdt. Rahu Mars
Lagna 11-13 Moon 17-39	Ketu 21-48 Mars 3-17 Merc. 8-33 Venus 10-42		Sun 15 Jupt. 15-52		Sat.	Venus	Merc. Moon

The planetary positions in the mother's case (Chart 6) are equally interesting. The 5th lord in Chart 6 is Mars placed in the vindictive sign Scorpio with Ketu, Mercury and Venus (R). The 5th house is aspected by Saturn. This is from both the Lagna and the Chandra Lagna both being in Sagittarius. The

Karaka Jupiter is in a Kendra in the 10th but in exact degree conjunction with the Sun aspected by Saturn. The killings occurred in Rahu Dasa, Rahu Bhukti, the Nodal axis afflicting the 5th lord. The 5th lord here also is with the 6th lord Venus and what an enemy it made of the son!

There are a few specific planetary positions relating to inimical and supportive children found in classical works.

A son whose asterism happens to be owned by the lord of the 12th from the Chandra Lagna in the father's horoscope will cause sorrow to his father by his travels and other actions.

If the son's Lagna is the 6th from the Janma Rasi of the father, the son is inimical to him.

If the son's asterism is ruled by the lord of the 6th from the father's Janma Rasi, he becomes inimical to the father.

If the lord of the Janma Rasi in the father's horoscope joins the 12th house or the 12th lord in the son's horoscope, the son will be required to redeem his father's debts.

One born in the 6th or the 8th from father's Lagna will blame and criticise one's father.

If one's Lagna falls in the 2nd, 9th or 11th from the father's Lagna, one will be obedient and dutiful to the father.

One born in the 8th, 9th or 10th constellation from the father's will do the work of his father in a cheerful manner.

One will be equal to his father if one's Lagna is in the 10th from the father's.

In Indian social life, the duties of the parent and child are clearly defined while Indian philosophy discourages infatuation with or excessive attachment to one's kith and kin. This lofty philosophy ensures mental peace while the social definition of duties ensures that parents are not neglected in their old age. However, factually life does not allow such clear definitions to work which is when we have to fall back on astrological help to accept reality and modify our responses in such a manner as to be able to digest unpalatable but unavoidable situations. Advance astrological insights prepare both parent and child to accept the inevitable ebb and tide of life with stoicism (09-97).

(E) ARE TEST-TUBE BABIES SAFE?

Reproduction is a natural process. Babies come naturally. They are conceived naturally, their development is Nature's responsibility and it culminates in their delivery naturally. That is what usually happens. But if we go back in time, there are cases of the unusual unnatural births also. In the days of **Mahabharata**, when Gandhari, the queen of Hastinapura, conceived, something abnormal was waiting to take place. The delivery date came and went like any other date. The distraught queen, unable to bear the suspense any longer, hit herself in frustration on her stomach, hoping the baby would be forced out. Instead, all that happened was the floor was splattered with blood and flesh. Precisely at that moment, the great Vedavyasa arrived. Consoling the queen, he put each of the 100 pieces into a pot with some ghee and other materials (the details of which will be never known) and sealed them. Chanting incantations, he instructed the queen to open them only after a 100 days. At the end of the period, a hundred babies began howling from within these pots waiting to be mothered by Gandhari.

Thus did the first ever set of pot-babies (improvised to test-tube babies now) arrive, conceived naturally but developed outside the mother's womb. This was one step ahead of the test-tube baby of today who is still delivered by the mother after developing in the womb.

The next stage in the evolution of the baby-business was their being conceived naturally but delivered surgically. Although many other babies must have been born earlier this way, it was only Julius Caesar's name that stuck to this kind of delivery perhaps because he was one of the first greats to be born this way.

Thereafter, nothing unusual or exciting took place on this front of baby-business except in some remote cases of science fiction such as Aldous Huxley's. Then, in 1978, Louise Brown was born an *in vitro* baby in England. That is, she was conceived when her mother's egg and father's sperm were joined in a glass dish and then injected into the mother's reproductive system. It made news then; it still does!

It is indeed an achievement, a marvel of science, a breakthrough. On the other side of the coin, it has raised the hopes of millions of childless couples without due justification. This bauble of a test-tube baby leaves the couple chronically depressed and economically shattered in cases when it fails to work. And these are many.

What are the facts of this medical achievement ? And how many can avail of it ? And what are the requisites of availing of this facility ? A leading international journal says more than 3000 IVF (*in vitro* fertilization) babies have been born so far, nearly a third of them in the USA. But two factors come in the way of the common man availing it — economics and the flimsy chances of its success being a mere 10 per cent. That is, if a 100 IVFs are tried, only 10 women stand chances of becoming pregnant. The process is tedious, but this many are willing to go through only if they can get the long coveted gift of parenthood. And, of course, the unscrupulous in the medical fraternity have been quick to cash on this medical achievement.

The process is gruelling, tension-ridden. The woman must take a series of injections which are accompanied by headaches and moods. Daily blood tests and frequent ultrasound examinations necessitate the couple having to stay close to the clinic (and such clinics in our own country are very, very few) away from home. The ripened eggs are then fertilised by the husband's sperm in a dish. If cell-division occurs, they are transferred to the wife's uterus. Then, more injections follow. Blood samples are regularly taken and only then pregnancy is confirmed. The whole procedure costs tremendous amounts in terms of money, resources and hopes. Many times, mistakes occur. In the US, women who have miscarried after IVF have even gone to the courts for damages. In fact, a famous psycho-therapist and physician U.S. couple have already spent 10,000 dollars on two unsuccessful IVF attempts. Another case went through 12 attempts at IVF, spending 100,000 dollars for a son. How many in India have this kind of money when buying essentials itself is a feat of some kind ?

Clinics that offer IVF facilities are choosy and usually take on a case only if the patient is below 40 years. The husband should have normal fertility.

There is no standardisation of the procedure and the potential for abuse is tremendous.

But, after all this trouble and expense, how far does the family stand to gain ? How will such births contribute to society and its welfare ? One cannot be too sure for even in the hands of the great Vedavyasa, the births spelt only ruin and destruction. The Kauravas in their monstrous greed for a kingdom engineered the epic battle of Kurukshetra which nearly killed all the valorous kings of the day. Will results be any better when the doctors are lesser mortals ?

The charts of such births can give a clue to the trends they generate. In India, the first test-tube baby was born on 3rd August 1986. Although the birth brought rejoicing to its poor parents, it faced ostracism from the neighbourhood for its 'bizzare' origins.

	Rahu		
Jupt. (R)	Chart 1 Rasi		Merc. Sun Moon
Ascdt. Marc.	Sat.	Ketu	Venus

	Moon	Rahu Ascdt.		Jupt.
	Navamsa			
	Sun			Merc.
			Ketu Sat.	Venus Mars

The Ascendant in Chart 1, degree-wise, is hemmed between malefics, Mars and Saturn. The Moon who has just emerged from a conjunction with the Sun is in the 8th with Mercury. The 10th lord Mercury in the 8th gives humiliation and, in this case, the neighbours shrank back with fear when the little girl was brought home. Mercury Dasa was on at birth.

The Moon weak in the 8th is afflicted by the aspect of 5th lord Mars. The 5th rules the intellect and the Moon, the mind. The unfavourable disposition of these two factors can result in serious emotional and psychological complexes if the child survives the Balarishta range.

The baby's parents had married in 1991 but the mother could not conceive as the fallopian tubes had been damaged due to infection. The 4th house is aspected by Mars and the 4th lord Jupiter is retrograde in the 12th therefrom.

Considered from the Moon, the 4th lord Venus is again in the 12th from the 4th. And the 9th lords both from Lagna and Chandra Lagna (Moon-sign) are in the respective 12th signs therefrom. These planetary positions are not favorable for normal parental responses and are some kind of a drawback in the chart.

Conceived in the impersonal environs of a non-feeling test tube, one can only hope and pray the little one will grow up into a healthy adult in both body and mind.

A sample astrological survey of some more similar births will show us some common features, not very complimentary though !

On 4, November 1987, three test-tube babies arrived on the same day in the same municipal hospital at Bombay. All the births took place on a Wednesday, between 9 and 12 noon. Incidentally, all the three were delivered by caesarean section.

The first, a boy, was born at 9-25 a.m. (IST). The birth (Chart 2) took place in Uttarabhadrapada, a constellation ruled by Saturn. Saturn is the 4th lord placed in an inimical sign Scorpio. The mother did not conceive for 9 years after marriage due to blocked fallopian tubes. Then after *invitro-fertilization and embryo-transfer,* she became pregnant.

Here the Moon is with Rahu, sharing the same Nakshatra of Saturn. They are aspected by Ketu-afflicted Mars. Mars is the 6th lord. The Mars-Rahu influence speaks of putting the latest technology (surgical, medical) to use in the birth of the baby. While at the technical level it is an achievement, the Moon-Mars-Rahu nexus occurring in the 5th house ruling intellect afflicts the psychological personality of the baby. A split between the mind (emotions coming under the Moon) and the intellect (5th house and lord) seems inevitable as the years pass.

Rahu Moon	Jupt.		
	Chart 2 Rasi		
	Ascdt. Venus Sat.	Merc. Sun	Ketu Mars

Sun Ketu	Jupt.		
Ascdt.			
	Navamsa		Mars
	Moon Merc.		Venus Rahu

The second birth (Chart 3) took place at 10-40 a.m. (IST). The mother had been married for 10 years and was infertile due to an occluded fallopian tube. All the features of Chart 2 repeat here, except that the Lagna is different and the Moon has moved a little ahead.

Moon Rahu	Jupt.		
	Chart 3 Rasi		
Ascdt.	Venus Sat.	Sun Merc.	Ketu Mars

Sun Ketu	Jupt.		
Sat.			Ascdt.
	Navamsa		Mars
	Moon	Merc.	Venus Rahu

The 4th houses the Moon and Rahu. The 5th lord Mars afflicted aspects the Moon. The Moon and the 5th house are, again, inter-related but not in a positive way.

Chart 4 is of the girl born on the same day at 12-05 noon. The mother had the same problem as in the previous case and was issueless for 8 years.

All the planetary positions repeat, save the Ascendant and the Moon's longitude. The Moon, this time in the 3rd house, is strongly afflicted by Rahu and Mars. The 5th house from Lagna is relatively free from affliction. But as in the previous

Progeny

two cases, the Moon is also the 5th lord (with reference to Chandra Lagna) and attracts the affliction from the Nodes and Mars.

In all these charts, the most common affliction is of the Moon. He occupies a watery, fluid sign in all the 4 charts and Mars afflicts him by his aspect. In the first chart, the Moon and Jupiter are in Shashtashtaka. In the latter 3 cases, they are in Dwirdwadasa positions.

Jupiter's position is of paramount importance in evaluating progeny, and, therefore, the creative force behind it. In all these cases, Jupiter occupies a cuspal degree. In Chart 1, he is in the 30th degree of Aquarius. In the remaining 3 charts, he is in the 1st degree of Aries.

Moon Rahu	Jupt.		
	Chart 4 Rasi		
Ascdt.			
	Venus Sat.	Sun Merc.	Ketu Mars

Sun	Jupt.		
Sat.	Navamsa		
Ascdt.			Mars
Moon	Merc.		Venus

Jupiter's weak position could even suggest that the births have been largely manipulated through human ingenuity (in other words, by extraneous forces) rather than through Divine Grace. Such cases in Puranic lore have always led to demonic and Asuric births. The scriptural stories are mere metaphoric allegories that constantly highlight the dangers of man's ego going out of hand and the consequences it can attract. This moral is depicted as puny man's demonical passions and urges interfering beyond a point with the natural order of the Universe and attracting calamitous catastrophes. In all the test-tube births, the heavy afflictions to the Moon would suggest a preponderance of the Asuric Gunas or traits over the Daivika or Divine Gunas. As it is, society is in a dangerous state of chaotic disintegration due to a slackening of values and promiscuous life-styles. If in this kind of weakening social structure, such planetary afflictions as we have identified in test-tube births keep recurring, it can only mean they cannot contribute to the well-being of the social order. These births may make headlines and fetch their engineers approbiums but are a dangerous experiment so far as social mental health is conncerned.

There is the case of an 18-year old who learnt he was the result of artificial insemination. He set out to trace his genetic father against several odds. When finally he succeeded, the genetic father refused to have anything do with him. He had his own family and children and had no intention of blowing up his world with the induction of this experimental dish son. The boy's mother's husband had always distanced himself from him. The poor lad, unable to digest the complexity of his multi-relationship birth, ended up a drug-addict.

Science has this funny but dangerous habit of promising a lot but delivering little. And the little, especially in dish-births, may be fraught with tragic consequences !

Sex-determination tests, for example, are not only unreliable but highly unethical, if you look into that aspect of the issue. A leading fertility expert Dr. Peter Bromwich of the Midland Fertility Services, U.K., believes that the only exact way of ensuring the sex of the unborn babe is through aminocentesis and selective abortion. But this is not only misleading but leaves the couple dazed and psychologically disturbed when the over-exaggerated medical promise of the child of the sex of one's preference fails. A study made in 1982 shows that out of 8000 foetuses aborted in the hospitals of a major city of India after aminocentesis, 7999 were of the female sex. In fact, a North Indian state has banned the sex-selection tests when it found that 30,000 to 50,000 female foetuses were being aborted every year.

Apart from promising babies to childless couples, medical science also claims to induce birth of the child of the sex of one's choice. The procedure involved is long and expensive but is it at least fool-proof in that it keeps up its promise ?

Progeny

A famous film star who already had a girl went ahead with her second pregnancy only after the doctors had assured her it would be a boy. And finally, when the baby came, it was another girl who had all the doctors and medical expertise licking the mud !

All the trouble going to extraordinary lengths burning away one's physical energies and fiscal resources and putting up with tremendous emotional and psychological pressure can easily be dispensed with if recourse is resorted to horoscopic factors.

Moon	Rahu		
	Chart 5 Rasi		Ascdt.
			Sat. Venus
Jupt.	Mars	Merc. Ketu	Sun

	Jupt.		Sat.
	Navamsa		Rahu Moon
		Ketu	Mars Ascdt.
	Merc.		Sun Venus

The 5th house tells one all about progeny. The 5th lord in a male sign aspected by male planets or male planets in the 5th house lead to male issue. A preponderance of female factors and the Moon also joining these factors leads to female issue. Mixed planetary influences cause both male and female progeny. This is, of course, over-simplifying matters.

In Chart 5 of the actress, the 5th house is a female sign Scorpio and its ruler Mars occupies it. It receives no aspects, good or bad. The 5th lord from Chandra Lagna is the Moon himself, Full and in Pisces, a female sign. An astrological appraisal of this chart clearly indicates only female issue and would have prepared the native to accept the fact that no amount of medical skill could give her a son. Acceptance is a great virtue in situations that cannot be altered. False hopes, on the other hand, can be devastating in their impact on the mind.

The classical works are full of tips to understand the progeny potential of a chart. If a case is a hopeless one, there are factors to show that. If the chart admits of the modifying influence of human effort and intervention, then the child of the sex of one's choice can also be planned by using astrological factors.

Some combinations to plan the sex of the unborn baby are given below and relate to the time of impregnation which can be fixed to support one's preference.

1. The Ascendant, the Sun, Jupiter and the Moon — if powerful and in odd signs and odd Navamsas — indicate male issue.
2. The Ascendant, the Sun, Jupiter and the Moon — if powerful and in even signs and even Navamsa female birth occurs.
3. If Jupiter and the Sun are powerful in odd signs, male issue is to be expected.
4. If the Moon, Venus and Mars are powerful and in female signs, female birth occurs.

Not only does astrology offer guidance in planning the sex of the child but also in begetting twins and their sex as well. The combinations do not stop here but cover safeguards to ensure pregnancy is healthy and delivery, smooth. For this, benefic planets should be in the Ascendant or with the Moon or in the 5th, 9th, 2nd, 10th and 4th houses from the Lagna or the Moon. Evil planets should be pushed to the 3rd and 11th houses from the Moon or Lagna. The Lagna or the Moon aspected by the Sun is also desirable.

Timing healthy progeny astrologically covers another area into which medical skill is claiming to make forays. That of ensuring quality births. Sperm banks are mushrooming round the country and offer for sale, healthy sperm screened by experts. You can buy, they claim, looks, health, brains and even success for your future progeny across the counter for a mere Rs. 150 per sample. No one has tested these claims for a long enough period of time to see if the products of such counter-samples will grow up into normal healthy adults or turn out to be monstrous fiends nurtured in test tubes. An error can occur at any stage of this genetic exercise and, as in Puranic times, give rise to demons instead of darlings.

The simple and easy to apply astrological combinations, on the other hand, are a boon to anyone to use with much benefit. Medical science stands to gain colossally from astrology. Compared to the huge expenses involved in genetic engineering, astrology costs next to nothing and gives satisfactory results. To the hopeless cases, it prepares the mind to accept the situation for what it is.

Astrological methods are clear, safe and within the reach of everyone. They do not promise the sky but they can give good progeny with sound body and sane mind.

Chapter Six

Education

(A) DECIDING CHILDREN'S EDUCATION

The ordeals of parents are innumerable. Once upon a time they started when the daughter came of age and the father of the household had to go groom-hunting. But now, son or daughter, the parents' trials and tribulations start even as the toddler crosses into the third year. Schools are the test of parents. There are so many schools everywhere, good, bad, indifferent — and the poor parents have a difficult time getting their little one admission into them. Schools no longer educate the child or bring out the best in him. They teach him to read and write, but most certainly not always the right things which will make him a humane, considerate and responsible citizen when he grows up. They are, simply put, literary centres !

Schools come under two categories in our country — those offering education under the State syllabus (framed by the State in which the school is located) and those that go by the Central syllabus (framed by an all-India body). The latter is said to be a little more demanding on the young one's abilities and is what most parents would like their children to go in for. Come admission time after the summer holidays, harried parents and even worse, harassed children keep shuttling from school to school for admission forms, interviews not only for the youngsters but also for the parents in many cases and trying to mobilise funds for donations which are a rule before admission in many schools. Yet, after years and years of study and hard work, the final result is often far from satisfactory. Why does this happen ?

Many times, parents would like the children to do courses they themselves did not get a chance to do while young. Other parents would like their kids to be one bit better than the neighbours and do all to push them through the Central curricula. Yet others feel that being a doctor or an engineer is a matter of prestige and the child should tread accordingly. Another category looks upon the child's education as a kind of trade. It starts with calculating how much money is invested in its studies. So, by making the child a doctor or architect, it plans not only to get back all the initial capital but sometimes worse, even would prefer compound interest on it in the form of dowry-demands. Naturally, with such attitudes behind parental ambitions — there could be exceptions — for their ward's education, the personality of the youngster often gets battered and bruised shaping up not always very positively.

The aim of education can only be to bring out the best in the youngster, tapping his potential and curbing negative points in him. It must aim at creating a strong moral, spiritual and physical personality with devotion to the pursuit of knowledge. This aim is now lost sight of with other lesser aims taking over. The child's own aptitude is often never taken into account. Its abilities, or rather limitations, are overlooked. Parental ambition, vicarious that is, becomes the decisive factor.

Astrological guidance provides reliable clues to one's line of education consistent with one's flair for a particular branch of study. It also helps one to guage the intelligence quotient of a youngster. Putting the child in a course of study that does not clash with its own aptitude and does not make heavy demands on its intelligence leads to wholesome developement of the child and creates in its mind confidence and other positive attitudes to life and its realities.

Imagine a dull-headed child enrolled in a school that offers the Central syllabus. Failure to understand the lessons, poor performance in tests and fear of ridicule from classmates together with the feeling the parents' expectations are not being met, which can, over a period of time, lead to a severe inferiority complex resulting in a quiet in-drawn nature that withdraws into a shell. Loss of appetite and violent behaviour towards siblings to make up for deficiency in academic performance are but the natural responses of such a child. Let the child move into adolescene and it will soon seek escape routes. Escapism is an unhealthy response to a situation and, therefore, the forms it takes can never be sound. For example, promiscious sex, running away from home, cheating in examination, using drugs are some easy routes such youngsters can take. All these routes need money and that is not always available to a youngster. The solution is crime — petty thefts, shop-lifting to begin with. Maybe as the youngster grows up and gets worldly wise — embezzlement, conning, even crimes of violence may suit his purpose. At this stage, we must ask ourselves this question — was this why we tried to give him education ?

Coming back to astrology, the first factor to look for in examining a chart for its education-potential is to take up its suitability or otherwise for a Central syllabus.

	Jupt. (R)		
	Chart 1 **Rasi**		Ascdt. Ketu Moon Sat.
Rahu			
	Sun Mars	Merc.	Venus

Mars		Jupt.	Merc.
	Navamsa		Sun Ketu
Moon Rahu Ascdt.			Venus
			Sat.

Mercury is the Vidyakaraka and his strength in the chart becomes a primary determinant in the matter. Mercury in the fiery signs, Aries, Leo and Sagittarius and also airy signs — Gemini, Libra and Aquarius — gives a sharp intellect with a flair for figures and numbers (*ganita*). Mercury in earthy signs — Taurus, Virgo and Capricorn — does not give such sharp intelligence but it does not imply dullness either. Such natives usually possess mercantile abilities but these are of little help in academic distinction. Mercury in Virgo is an exception because this sign happens to be its sign of exaltation. Mercury retrograde also gives precocious intelligence and such natives often pursue higher studies and go into research.

Mercury in the Kendras, the 1st, 4th, 7th or 10th is good, especially in the 10th. In the 5th and 9th also, which are powerful Trikonas, he becomes strong.

Mercury when he is Vargottama, that is, when he occupies the same sign in Rasi and Navamsa, makes one highly intelligent.

Children with such a disposition in their charts have a powerful memory, analytical skills and good grasping power. They do well, whether in the State or Central syllabus.

Mercury in earthy signs, generally gives difficulty in mathematic and numbers. Such children do better in courses to do with commerce, humanities and such other fields. If Mercury in an earthy sign is otherwise rendered very powerful, then the intellect gets sharpened and overcomes the results normally attributed to earthy signs. In watery signs again, Scorpio and Cancer, Mercury is not very happy and blunts one's intelligence unless other sources of strength occur in the Navamsa or *via* strong aspects and associations. In Pisces, however, especially if he gets Neechabhanga, he gives a flair for maths and related disciplines.

		Ascdt.	Jupt. (R)
	Chart 2 Rasi		Ketu
Rahu			
	Moon Merc.	Sun Venus Sat.	Mars

	Mars	Sun	
Rahu Ascdt.	**Navamsa**		
	Sat.		Ketu
		Moon Jupt. Venus	Merc.

Mercury, with no particular strength, in the 12th house robs one of strong intellect. Such natives usually have difficulty in understanding their lessons and their performance in school is below the mark. An adverse aspect of Jupiter on Mercury gives wrong judgement, muddled thinking and an "inclination to view things through a false medium". As a result, such natives have difficulty in understanding their lessons and grasping concepts of mathematics and science. A native with Virgo rising and its ruler Mercury in Leo with the Sun could never pass his school examination, inspite of several attempts. Jupiter's aspect from Sagittarius was of no help.

Mercury in favourable aspect with Jupiter makes one liberal, generous, humane, jovial, amiable and endowed with great mental abilities and clarity of thought. Such a disposition contributes to sharpness of intellect. That is, Mercury influenced by functional benefics always tends to confer good results *vis-á-vis* scholastic performance. Additionally in airy signs, the pre-disposition of the native is distinctly intellectual. Such natives are for ever curious and eager to learn more, whatever the subject of their study. Mercury in Libra aspected by Jupiter for a Cancer Ascendant (Chart 1) has made the native an outstanding social scientist with a long string of academic distinctions tagging his name. In Navamsa. Mercury is in Gemini, another airy sign ruled by himself. Note that Mercury is in the 4th in a Kendra aspected by 9th lord Jupiter. Airy signs bring out the best in Mercury.

Mercury with the Sun is sometimes said to blunt one's intellectual abilities and, therefore, not quite comfortable to the pursuit of the higher branches of science. This is a sweeping generalization and not safe to rely upon. Mercury in very close conjunction with the Sun often confers brilliance and a razor-sharp intellect, inventive genius and powerful retentive memory. A Leo-born with Mercury in the 12th Vargottama and with the Sun in exact degree conjunction had a brilliant career in engineering going on to do a doctorate in the subject. The strength of Mercury is of prime importance.

Mercury, if powerful, aspected by Mars or Saturn is not adversely affected. But Mercury weak and so aspected gives dullness of intellect. Mercury's association by aspect or conjunction with Mars confers acuteness and discrimination. It polishes one's logical abilities. It gives skill in mechanical and related subjects, ingeniousness, penetrating brain power, flair for figures, mathematics and higher physics. But with a malefic Mars, intellectual energy goes into wrong channels — violence, fury and domination — and therefore, academic performance is affected. A Gemini native with

Mercury and Mars with Venus in the 12th in Taurus could never pass his college examination.

Mercury, favourably influenced by Saturn, gives an eye for detail, sharp memory and ingeniousness. A Capricornian with Mercury Vargottama in Libra in exact degree conjunction with the Sun aspected by Lagna lord Saturn from the 8th has given exceptional mental abilities, clarity of thought and comprehending powers.

Mercury in good aspect with Venus gives versatile skills and such natives are very knowledgeable in a wide variety of subjects.

Mercury and the Moon in conjunction polishes one's intellectual powers and such natives rise to eminence in science and literature. In Chart 2, Mercury occupies a watery sign Scorpio with the Moon. He is retrograde and as 2nd and 5th lord, a beneficy giving the native proficiency in literature. In Navamsa, Mercury occupies Virgo, his sign of exaltation.

Mercury afflicted with the Moon generates a wayward, volatile personality that fritters away its mental energies and, therefore, becomes incapable of any worthwhile mental pursuit. Such natives usually end up as school drop-outs.

Apart from a strong Mercury, a powerfully disposed 5th house gives high educational attainments and distinction in academics. The 5th lord may be exalted. The planet in the 5th house may be exalted. Or both may be exalted or Vargottama. In fact, if the Dasa of a good 5th lord also runs during the educational years, then one can expect an outstanding and brilliant career in studies. According to **Jataka Tattwa**, T-26 — सुते दशा विद्यार्थदा *the Dasa of the 5th lord gives education*. If well-placed, the performance will be good. If not, educational career will be marked by failure and setbacks.

The Ascendant lord well-placed also promotes academic pursuits, especially, if in exaltation and influencing the 5th house favorably.

There are some specific combinations which lead to *heenadhi* or dullness or deficiency in intellectual strength. Such children are best put in schools with the State syllabus. These combinations have nothing to do with Mercury's disposition in the chart.

Education

The Moon in Lagna, especially if aspected or otherwise associated with malefics, affects educational attainments adversely because of dullnes of intellect.

The 5th house falling in a malefic Shashtyamsa gives the same result. The combined aspect of the Sun, Mars and Saturn on the Moon lead to lack of intelligence. The Moon in the 6th, 8th or 12th aspected by Venus blights one's intelligence. The 5th lord joining a maleficy gives the same result. The 3rd lord with Rahu also robs one of intellectual sharpness. The Lagna aspected by Saturn and the 5th lord with a malefic or Saturn in the 5th give a dull intellect.

Merc. Venus Sat. Rahu	Sun Mars		
	Chart 3 Rasi		
			Jupt.
	Ascdt.	Moon	Ketu

	Sun Moon	Jupt.	
Sat. Rahu	Navamsa		
Merc.			Ascdt. Ketu
	Venus	Mars	

In Chart 3, Saturn Dasa began in the native's thirteenth year. Saturn afflicts the 5th house. Saturn and Rahu afflict Mercury. The native, inspite of repeated attempts, could never succeed in his school examination. Such natives are best trained for some job or craft, or even trade. Scholastic ambitions are not for them.

In Chart 4, too, the 5th house has Saturn but he is a benefic being the Lagna lord. Mercury is with the Sun in the 8th joined by malefic Mars. Endowed with average intelligence, the native barely manged to finish her pre-college course, each time scraping through with the minimum marks required for a pass.

Children with such combinations have difficulty pushing through school. After school too, they are most comfortable in job-oriented diplomas or short term courses.

		Sat.	
	Chart 4		Venus Ketu
Ascdt. Rahu	**Rasi**		Merc. Mars Sun
Jupt.			Moon

			Jupt.
	Navamsa		Ketu
Rahu			Ascdt.
	Sun Mars	Venus	Merc. Moon Sat.

While Mercury and the 5th house govern the intellectual potential of a chart, without the right Dasas operating at the right time, scholastic studies and success can even be ruled out. (08-93)

(B) JUDGING EDUCATIONAL PROGRESS AND PERFORMANCE

Parents face many difficulties to give their children good opportunities in life. Many times, children do not avail of such opportunities. Sometimes, it may be that they don't care; sometimes, it may be that inspite of doing their best, the children cannot come up to parental expectations. Both situations are common occurrences everywhere. Parents are disappointed when this happens and the children themselves suffer from feelings of guilt. There is much unhappiness in the family as a result.

A realistic way of avoiding such situations that create tensions amongst family members, who otherwise deeply care for one another, is to acquaint oneself with the potential for academic pursuit in the child's chart. A proper understanding of the inherent limitations in the chart can put the parent in a better position to cope with the kind of performance the child produces in his academic efforts.

It is possible a child may be highly intelligent but does badly in school. This has happened in the case of many great men and women who have later become celebrities for their intellectual work. But this is more the exception than the rule.

However, there are cases too of children with average performance at school and college who have succeeded in their careers later on in life. Therefore, the mere fact the quality of educational pursuit is not too high in a chart should not dishearten parents. Likewise, just because some have bags of money to give the child excellent opportunities for study should not generate a feeling of achievement because the disillusionment that can follow such euphoria can often be shattering. By properly evaluating the Vidyastana (house of education) in a chart, parents can be poised to grapple with the child for what it is and plan its future accordingly.

Just as certain combinations in classical works provide for *heena-dhi* or dullness of the intellect, there are other combinations that show a high level of intelligence.

If the 5th house is in a benefic sign and aspected or occupied by a benefic, one is a *buddhiman* or intelligent.

If the 5th lord is exalted or between benefics, then also it shows high intelligence. Jupiter in a Kendra or Trikona or if the 5th lord is in a benefic sign and Jupiter occupies the 5th house, again, we have a *buddhiman*. If Mercury is in the 5th or the 5th lord is strong and in a Kendra, the person is intelligent. If the 5th lord is with a benefic and in the 1st, 4th, 7th or 10th, the result is a *Dhaaraanahipatuh* or one endowed with grasping ability. If the 5th lord or its Karaka is in a benefic Shastyamsa and conjoined or aspected by a benefic, a sharp intellect is the result. Likewise, one becomes highly intelligent, if the 5th house or Karaka has obtained Gopura and other higher Amsas. These combinations are listed in Mahadeva's **Jataka Tattwa**.

Chart 5 has an interesting array of planets related to education. The 5th house has no aspects and no planet in it, good or bad. The 5th lord is in a trine but in close conjunction with 6th lord Sun. Mercury is in an airy sign in the 8th in Visakha ruled by Lagna lord Jupiter. The Lagna lord Jupiter is blunted by the aspect of malefic Saturn. He is with Ketu but saved by the association of benefic Mars.

The native is not proficient in mathematics; nevertheless, he is in the engineering course. But he has already lost one year. Now in final year, he has still to finish two papers.

Chart 5: Born 20-11-1968 at 1-20 p.m. (IST) at 22 N 25, 88 E 21 with a balance of 15 years, 3 months and 8 days of Saturn Dasa.

Sat. Rahu Ascdt.			
	\multicolumn{2}{c}{Chart 5 Rasi}	
Venus	Sun Moon	Merc.	Jupt. Mars Ketu

Sat. Jupt.		Merc. Ketu Mars	
	\multicolumn{2}{c}{Navamsa}	Ascdt.
			Moon Sun
	Rahu		

Mercury and the 5th house rule the intellectual potential of a chart but without the right Dasa operating at the right time, scholastic distinction becomes difficult and may even be denied to one.

Mercury, in Chart 5, is in Libra in an airy sign but in a Dustana. The 5th lord Moon is new and lacking in strength (since he is moving to a conjunction with 6th lord Sun). Mercury, even though in a Jupiterean constellation, has not helped the native excel. Jupiter is afflicted by malefics Saturn, Ketu and Mars. Mercury so placed has failed to give good results in his Dasa.

But the native of Chart 6 has done well in mathematics scoring high marks, although Mercury in his case too occupies Libra. But let us see what has made all the difference.

Mercury is in the 3rd, an Upachaya, in Chart 6, unlike in Chart 5, where it is in the 8th house and therefore, a Dastana. Mars, as a Yogakaraka, aspects Mercury favorably. The 5th house has the 12th lord Moon and Rahu, both aspected by Saturn. But benefics Jupiter and Venus flank the 5th house and its occupants. The Moon Dasa is on. Although the 12th lord, the Moon is well-placed in a fiery and powerful sign aspected by Saturn. Saturn's aspect has, to some extent, affected the Moon. The native has obtained high marks in B.Sc. (mathematics).

Education

Chart 6: Born 5-10-1973 at 2-38 a.m. at 22 N 35, 88 E 21 with a balance of 3 years, 8 months and 3 days of Venus Dasa at birth.

	Mars		Ketu Sat.
Jupt.	\multicolumn{2}{c}{Chart 6 Rasi}	Ascdt.
Moon Rahu	Venus	Merc.	Sun

	Jupt.		Ascdt. Sun
	\multicolumn{2}{c}{Navamsa}	Venus Rahu
	Ketu Merc. Sat.		Mars
	Moon		

The major flaw in Chart 5 is attributable to the presence of a strong malefic Saturn in the Ascendant. The Lagna is also afflicted by Rahu.

The right Dasa is of paramount importance. For, even if the capabilities are there, opportunities are not available if unhelpful Dasas operate.

Mercury, in Chart 7, is well-placed in a friendly sign in retrogression.

Rahu Dasa began when the native was about 9 years old and covered most of his educational life. Rahu occupies the

Chart 7: Born 2-6-1963 at 6-59 a.m. (IST) at 13 N 05, 80 E 18 with a balance of 1 year, 11 months and 23 days of Moon Dasa at birth.

Jupt.	Venus	Sun Merc.	Ascdt.
Sat.	\multicolumn{2}{c}{Chart 7 Rasi}	Rahu
Ketu			Mars
			Moon

			Sun Mars
	\multicolumn{2}{c}{Navamsa}	Moon Rahu
	Merc. Jupt. Ketu		
	Venus Ascdt.	Sat.	

2nd house in Cancer in Punarvasu Nakshatra. Rahu is Vargottama and his Nakshatra-ruler is in the 10th house, a powerful Kendra, in his own sign. Rahu is aspected by a well-placed 10th lord Jupiter. The 5th house is well-placed with the 5th lord Venus in the 11th aspecting his own house Libra. Venus occupies his own constellation and is aspected by 9th lord Saturn from the 9th. The native's schooling and college years passed without problems and post-graduate and doctoral studies were overseas, marked by distinction.

Rahu Dasa can give spectacularly good results *vis-à-vis* educational performance and opportunities if the 5th house is well-placed; otherwise, he chokes the educational life of the native.

Chart 8: Born 24-9-1968 at 12-46 p.m. (IST) at 26 N 24, 79 E 30 with a balance of 1 year, 7 months and 6 days of Mars Dasa.

Rahu	Sat.			Sun	Sat. (R)		Mars Ascdt. Ketu
	Chart 8 Rasi				Navamsa		Moon Rahu
			Jupt. Mars				
Ascdt.		Moon Merc. Venus	Sun Ketu	Rahu Jupt.	Moon Merc. Venus		

In Chart 8, the 5th house has Vargottama 2nd and 3rd lord Neechabhanga Saturn aspected by 7th and 10th lord Mercury, 6th and 11th lord Venus, 8th lord Moon and Lagna lord Jupiter. The 5th lord Mars is in a fiery sign with Lagna lord Jupiter and is strongly placed. Rahu Dasa operated during the native's educational life which continued into Jupiter Dasa. Rahu occupies a Nakshatra of Mercury, Revati. Mercury, in turn, is in the 11th aspectiong the 5th. Rahu's sign dispositer Jupiter is with the 5th lord Mars, aspecting the 5th. The native topped his university at both graduate level and also in his master's degree.

Charts 7 and 8 have a well-placed 5th lord and 5th house and Mercury obtaining for them excellent educational opportunities.

Papakartari Yogas afflicting the 5th house and/ or its lord terminate or disrupt educational pursuits.

Chart 9 shifts our focus to the 2nd house as the secondary house of education.

Chart 9: Born 3-4-1965 at 5-25 p.m. (IST) at 14 N 42, 77 E 05 with a balance of 1 year, 8 months and 27 days of Ketu Dasa at birth.

Sun Venus	Merc.(R) Moon	Jupt. Rahu	
Sat.	Chart 9 Rasi		
			Mars (R)
	Ketu		Ascdt.

		Merc. Sat.	
Jupt. Ketu Ascdt.	Navamsa		Moon
		Sun	Rahu
		Venus	Mars

Mercury is Vargottama (Chart 9) in the 8th house aspected by 5th (and 6th lord) Saturn. Being in a fiery sign is a plus point. The 5th lord Saturn is quite well-placed in his Moolatrikona sign but aspected by 3rd and 8th lord Mars.

The native did well in his engineering studies coming under Venus Dasa and part of Sun Dasa. Venus as the 2nd and 9th lord is exalted in the 7th with 12th lord Sun. He is aspected by 8th lord Mars. Mercury is strong, the 5th house is moderately so, but without serious afflictions.

All these charts show that since it is the 5th house and the 2nd house also that are important in judging educational years, Dasas and planets favorably disposed with reference to these houses help education. Planets which aspect these houses, in their Dasas, also help education. That is, a planet placed in the 11th and the 8th, usually does not harm or halt education in its Dasa. The 8th house is a Dustana. Nevertheless, a planet here directly aspects the 2nd and so cannot harm educational continuity. Likewise, if the Dasa is of a planet in the 11th house, here also it influences the 5th house and becomes supportive in the matter.

If the planet concerned is Jupiter, in the absence of afflictions, his position in the 6th, 5th or 11th is helpful. If it is Mars, then his occupation of the 11th or 2nd influences both the 2nd and 5th houses. Mars in the 7th too is good as he aspects the 2nd from here.

Saturn in the 8th aspects both the 2nd and 5th houses and is helpful to studies. In the 12th also, his aspect on the 2nd is good; so also in the 5th when he aspects the 2nd. In the 3rd, he aspects the 5th — good again.

However, in all these cases, Mars, Jupiter and Saturn should otherwise also be qualified to support Vidya; at any rate they must not have, by lordship or association, or otherwise, strength to harm one's studies.

For a Sagittarius Ascendant, Saturn in the 8th gave good grades in school. In college, the Dasa changed to Mercury when the performance improved to distinction. Saturn aspects the 5th house and the 2nd house as 2nd lord.

In another case, Venus in the 11th with 5th lord Jupiter joining him, gave the native good educational opportunities and performance in Venus Dasa.

However, Saturn and the Sun in Aries for a Gemini-born gave schooling in a government school and below average performance in college studies that did not succeed in Rahu Dasa, Rahu being in Aquarius reflecting Saturn's results.

Therefore, in order to assess the intellectual potential as well as the opportunities in a chart, not only should we carefully examine the 5fth house and Mercury, but also the Dasas that run between the ages of 5 and say, about 25 years, which cover the period of school and college education approximately. As always, no single factor can be taken to be decisive in coming to conclusions. (02-94)

Chapter Seven

Health and Diseases

(A) DIAGNOSIS OF DISEASE AND SURGERY

More medical colleges and nursing homes with breath-taking hospital complexes (which would put 5-star hotels to shame, also thrown in for effects, amazing advances in medical research and breakthrough strides in surgery all add up to make the art of healing truly twenty-first centurish and supra-ultra modern. But all this razzle-dazzle in the world of medicine has not contributed one bit to ameliorating disease or giving relief from pain. The agonised whimpers of those who have faced the scalpels bear ample testimony to this sad state of affairs. The medical industry has truly failed in delivering the goods to the suffering, inspite of its phenomenal growth in the last two decades.

Patients are plied with unnecessary drugs. Powerful antibiotics are prescribed for even simple common ailments and fevers, quite unmindful of their dangerous repercussions on the patient.

Studies have shown that the indiscriminate use of antibiotics can damage the body's immune system, the liver and kidney permanently and in children cause ulcers in the food tract and intestines. Even pain-killers can cause death as they lead to intestinal bleeding, blood disorders and even cardio-vascular problems. Obstetric analgesics used frequently to reduce labour pain can cause maternal mortality. And caesarean deliveries are quite unnecessary most of the time. Yet, no one seems to care, so widely is the omniscience of modern medicine and its protagonists accepted.

According to a leading doctor in a Bombay hospital ".....endoscopy is done just because the hospital has the facility". Coronary bypasses are the fashion today but its benefits are only short term, but no doctor will tell you this when he advises you bypass surgery ? Many private nursing homes, it is alleged, keep patients for unnecessarily long periods of time with the sole purpose of billing. All these shocking facts add up only to highlight that the real aim of providing health has been, somehow, lost in the labyrinth of commercialisation of health-care.

Medical help consists of two stages. One, correct diagnosis and two, right prescription. Diagnosis is in the hands of the examining doctor and, if done correctly, can help choose the right kind of treatment. The prescription can be either medication or surgery, both involving drug therapy. Many of the drugs employed before and after surgery can be highly powerful and, therefore, to be administered only after thorough confirmation of necessity and under proper care and supervision. But should diagnosis itself be wrong, as it happens many a time, the patient and his family are not aware of it until the worst has happened. Wrong surgery and wrong medication can often be fatal. Or, it can maim the patient for life and put him at a point of no-return which is perhaps worse than death not only for the patient but his family too.

Many successful and breakthrough surgeries and cures are given wide newspaper and media coverage. But the frightfully large number of cases of wrong diagnosis and, with or without it, of reckless and wrong surgery and drug administration are simply shoved under the carpet. The patient, maimed for life, is asked to leave the hospital or nursing home when the doctors tell him to and the matter is closed there. But that is only as far as the nursing home is concerned. What about the patient ? For him, the ordeal starts now, and with no happy end.

Why do surgeries that are often totally unnecessary or sometimes wrongly advised take place at all ? There are two main reasons and many more sub-reasons. One is the growing trend of commercialization of health-care and two, a dilution in and, even worse, adulteration in the quality of medical skills and personnel. The latter is the logical outcome of indiscriminate licensing of medical colleges by irresponsible politicians. The only factor they consider in granting licences is usually, how much lucre they stand to gain from it. Equally responsible is the reprehensible system of reservations where considerations of caste and community take precedence over merit. One must realise that backward classes cannot be helped by lowering the standard of education to fit them in. All that this can lead to is lowered efficiency and quality of work. Opportunities for education must be provided to all, but the meritorious alone amongst the backward and such other groups must be given seats in courses requiring specialised skills and high levels of intelligence.

Disregard for ethics, callousness, indifference to the Hippocratic oath and the money mania are the ills that plague the world of health cure and caring.

A shocking case is that of a 20-year athletic who was diagnosed as having cancer in a Bombay hospital and put on 4000 rads of radiation. This dosage, by any standards, is said to be in excess of what the human body can take. This led to a hole in his abdomen out of which waste matter kept pouring out.

This is one sample case and, if one carefully investigates the thousands of cases being handled daily all over the country, one would be aghast at the fate suffered by the patients. Yet, hospitals, nursing homes and doctors have a strange mesmerising spell on people who continue to flock to them for the most trifling reasons in the almost superstitious belief that all their ailments will vanish into thin air. So deep-rooted is this feeling that inspite of the ever-increasing tragic results from wrong treatment and callous and even unnecessary surgery, people do not seem to have learnt their lessons.

However, a lucky few have escaped these shocking experiences by recourse to astrology. The chart carries clues to the kind of disease one may suffer from and it also throws light on the need for surgery. If surgery is not astrologically adviseable, the chart can also show you the course of the illness and when it will abate. When a diagnosis has been made, astrology can also help to confirm it. If the chart does not support the diagnosis, it can point to the actual seat of the problem.

The uses of astrology are infinite but it lacks the glamour and sophistication that go with high-tech medicine and surgery and, therefore, is often not taken recourse to before making a major decision regarding health and surgery. But in those cases where astrological help has been sought, results have been very gratifying, not only helping the patient avoid wrong surgery, unnecessary surgery but also in choosing the right line of treatment.

All diseases, according to astrology, can be traced to Karma,

जन्मान्तरकृतं पापं व्याधिरूपेण जायते।
तच्छान्तिरौषधैर्दानैर्जपहोमार्चनादिभिः ।।

meaning,

> Acts (of omission and, or of commission) from previous births are the cause of disease. Shantis, medication, charity, poojas and homas are their pacifiers or alleviators.

When the underlying cause (Karma) or a bodily affliction (in the form of a health problem) gets exhausted by spending itself out, it ceases to trouble one. Where the process of its exhaustion is painful and difficult, the remedial measures suggested in the Sloka are to be taken recourse to. *Oushadhis* cover Ayurvedic remedies prescribed on the basis of the afflictions in the chart. But today, it can also include modern medical and surgical methods. But care must be taken to make sure if surgery is necessary and, if so, the right surgery.

The root of all disease primarily is Karma but that is not something to feel accursed about it. Our governmental agencies go around declaring leprosy is not Karmic (even the use of the word Karma appears to be taboo in our secular state) but only caused by a bacilli. It is true, leprosy is caused by bacilli but what makes some people more vulnerable to this bacilli than others is the Karmic factor. Otherwise, why would leprous couples give birth to healthy offspring though they all share the same squalid living conditions and eat the same food, lacking in nutrition ? Or why would leprosy strike an individual from a well-to-do family, leaving all other members of it out unless it was the Karmic factor that predominated ? And merely because the root cause is Karmic, it does not preclude treatement and cure as made out by our government in its infinite ignorance of Indian knowledge and a deliberate attempt to misinterpret it through the government media. Right medication and highly potent Mantras do work. But the curse of political secularism is on us and revels in ignorance and misinterpretation of all traditional wisdom and this, to our detriment,

The Karmic factor can be clearly discerned from the astrological chart which is a blue-print of the destiny pattern that accompanies every individual at birth.

रोगारिव्यसनक्षतानि वसुधापुत्रारितिश्चिन्तचेदुत्तं ।

— JP XIII-81

Diseases, bad habits and wounds (ulcers, sores, boils, etc.) a person may suffer from are to be understood from the 6th house and Mars.

The 6th house is called Rogastana. Roga or disease is of the body and so automatically includes the Lagna Bhava and its disposition. It is the Thanu Bhava and its strength or weakness has a major say in pointing to good health and, therefore absence of disease of a serious nature or sickness or ill-health.

The Lagna can be said to be strong when it is aspected by its own lord, Venus, Jupiter or Mercury. These planets in Lagna also give good health. In other words, they rule out serious and terminal diseases.

Conversely, when the Lagna suffers serious affliction from Mars, Saturn, Rahu, Ketu, afflicted Mercury and the Sun, the onset of serious health problems at one stage or the other of life cannot be ruled out.

Benefics and strong planets in the Kendras (1, 4, 7, 10) and the Trikonas (1, 5, 9) from the Lagna strengthen it. Strong malefics in the Bhavas cause the Lagna to decay or suffer loss of strength, and therefore, loss of health.

The presence of many favourable Yogas such as Pancha Mahapurusha Yoga, Adhi Yoga, Gajakesari Yoga, Vasumati and other Yogas add to the general strength of the horoscope and therefore, promote good health also.

Chart 1: Born 12-2-1856 at 12-21 p.m. (IST) at 18 N, 84 E with a balance of 12 years, 3 months and 9 days of Venus Dasa.

	Moon Rahu	Ascdt.	Sat.
Sun Merc. Jupt.	Chart 1 Rasi		
Venus		Mars Ketu	

	Ascdt. Jupt.	Rahu	
	Navamsa		
Merc.	Ketu	Sun Sat. Venus Mars	Moon

The native of Chart 1 lived upto 80 years. He led an extremely active life till the end. Mentally also, he was very alert with all his intellectual faculties razor-sharp till the last moment.

The Ascendant lord Venus is in the 8th but three strong benefics Sun, Mercury and Jupiter occupy the 10th house. Mars is in the 6th house with Ketu, but both are aspected by Jupiter. Until the last day, the native used to enjoy two square meals a day, a bowl of fruit and tiffin in the afternoon. He was slim, sturdy and full of energy all the time. He was conscious till the last moment of his life, calling out to his wife he was leaving, seconds before he passed away.

Afflictions to the 6th house, to certain planets and certain signs also show the nature of disease one may suffer from.

Afflictions to the Sun show heart-related ailments and/or of the eyes as the Sun is the natural significator of the heart and the eyes.

Mercury under affliction gives a predisposition to convulsions, epileptic fits and other nervous disorders as he rules the central nervous system.

Mars afflicted causes rashes, boils, skin eruptions, ulcers wounds, all of which can be traced to toxins in the blood. Mars rules the blood and marrow.

When Saturn is influenced by malefics, joint-related diseases, arthritis, bone-dislocations and back-ache can appear. The skeletal system comes under Saturn.

Jupiter afflicted leads to rheumatic pains, diabetes and swellings, obesity.

Urinary problems, eye-infections, sexual problems and skin diseases come under an affliction to Venus.

When the Moon, Rahu and Ketu are involved and adversely placed, serious mental problems and psychological complexes occur.

Planets in the 6th house can point to specific disorders.

The Sun in the 6th causes dyspepsia, burning sensation and gastritis.

The Moon in the 6th gives weak digestion and loose motions.

Mars in the 6th house leads to hyperacidity, biliousness and ulcers.

Mercury in the 6th house does not harm health much unless there are other afflictions; so also Jupiter and Venus.

Saturn in the 6th gives severe constipation and other bowel and anal problems.

Both Rahu and Ketu are generally harmless in the 6th house.

These equations are really over-simplifying matters and the only way we can really understand astrological factors is by a study of cases covering different ailments.

One of the most common ailments today is of the heart. Any pain or discomfort in the heart is followed by ECG and other tests. Most of the time, whatever the medical diagnosis, a strong Sun, and affliction-free Sun rules out any serious heart condition. Even if the pain is severe, one can rest assured it is due to gas, muscular pain and so on, but the heart itself will be quite sound.

Another simple rule one can remember is Mars in the 6th house usually leads to biliousness, acidity and ulcers if one is careless in one's eating habits. In other words, people with this disposition should take care to avoid hot, oily, spicy food and cultivate regular eating habits.

Saturn's aspect on the 6th, that is, if he is in the 4th, 12th or 9th can cause digestive upset and dyspepsia, mostly due to sluggish bowels. Such native if they take steps to avoid constipation, can avoid the condition Saturn can otherwise cause.

Mars or Saturn alone or together in the 7th or 8th can give piles.

In the 8th, Saturn can cause severe arthritis and osteo-related problems, especially during the later years of life. Mars or Saturn afflicting the 3rd house leads to deafness. The degree of deafness must be determined on the degree of affliction.

Saturn in Lagna, especially, if watery signs such as Cancer, Scorpio or Pisces are involved, can show problems related to breathing, such as wheezing, constant cold and sneezing and also asthma.

The Sun in watery signs or with Venus, usually leads to psoriasis and or white patches. Mars and Ketu or Rahu afflicting Lagna or Venus in Scorpio and Pisces as also Cancer give leucodermic patches.

While the planetary positions give a clue to the area of the body which is likely to be affected by ill-health, the onset of the problem can be known by the Dasa or Bhukti or the planet occupying, ruling or aspecting the 6th house. Should such a period coincide strongly with the transits of Saturn in the 1st, 2nd or 12th or the 8th houses from the Moon, the indication becomes stronger. If the indication for a disease is not very strong, then as the Bhukti finishes and as the Moon also frees itself from malefic transits, the disease will automatically reduce or even get eliminated by itself. Recourse to surgery and other forms of drastic treatment becomes redundant.

A thirteen-year old boy (Chart 2) was diagnosed as having very severe ulcers and immediate surgery was advised. In fact, the doctors said it was so serious the boy should be admitted the same day.

Health and Diseases

Chart 2: Born 21-2-1978 at 10-10 p.m. (IST) at 13 N, 77 E 35 with a balance of 6 years, 5 months and 14 days of Mercury Dasa.

Ketu 15-43			Jupt. 3-56
Venus 17-57 Sun 10-36 Merc. 6-09	Chart 2 Rasi		Mars (R) 0-39 Moon 24-56
			Sat. (R) 4-37 Mandi 22-30
		Ascdt. 6-11	Rahu 15-43

Venus		Sat. Rahu	
Moon	Navamsa		Mars
Sun			Lines
		Merc. Jupt. Ketu Ascdt.	

The facts of the case were: The boy had been complaining of stomach pain since about mid-1990. He could take in food only in small quantities. If he took more, he would throw up everything. He occasionally complained of stomach pain also.

The parents of the boy were scared stiff. Surgery, and at such a tender age, was something they could not digest easily. And worse, the cost? How could they mobilize the funds needed, which was a little over twenty thousand rupees? The father of the boy was in some petty trade.

The Ascendant Libra is aspected by 3rd and 6th lord Jupiter and 2nd and 7th lord Mars. The Ascendant lord Venus is in the 5th with benefic Mercury and the Sun, all three planets being aspected by their sign-dispositer Saturn. The Moon is in the 10th in his own sign. All the planets are in trines, quadrants and the 11th house. Rahu and Ketu in the Dustanas are also quite well-placed. So, the Ascendant is reasonably strong.

The 6th house is the Rogastana and Ketu here is quite welcome. The 6th lord Jupiter is in the 9th with no affliction.

These factors rule out severe ulcers as diagnosed by the doctors. So, surgery seemed quite unnecessary astrologically and the parents were accordingly advised.

The Dasa of Venus had begun with Ketu Dasa ending in August 1991. The boy was running Mercury Bhukti of Ketu

Dasa when he first began to get the pain. Ketu is in the 6th and can indicate some defect or deficiency in the body during his Dasa. But Mars who is associated with ulcers has nothing to do with the 6th house, both from the Ascendant and the Moon which is why the medical diagnosis of ulcers could not be accepted.

Saturn, Yogakaraka, aspects the Ascendant as also the Ascendant lord. Saturn rules all growths, lumps, cysts and constrictions.

The boy's parents were asked to seek a second and even a third opinion. This, they did, losing no time. A laproscopy was done and the doctors found a small growth near the deuodenum which was really the cause of all the symptoms the boy was displaying. The doctors now assured the parents medication alone was sufficient to get rid of the growth and there was no need for surgery. The boy's parents were really relieved to hear this. They were also thankful that they had been saved the huge expenses involved in the surgery.

Going back to the chart, the fact Venus Dasa had already begun was more important than anything else in advising against surgery. As a well-placed Lagna lord, Venus becomes a strong benefic and ruling Thanu (body) can set right the defect or fault in the system with only a little effort without any drastic measures.

In another case (Chart 3), the native began to complain of a sore throat about October 1989. It did not respond to the usual remedies prescribed routinely for it and began to get worse. So, the ENT specialists were consulted and they diagnosed it as cancer. They advised removal of the vocal cord and sound box. A hole would be made in the throat to enable the patient to breathe. Otherwise, there was no saying when he woule die which he was sure to, because of the cancerous condition. But if he went through surgery, he would lose his power of speech but live. His family was on the horns of a dilemma unable to make a decision.

An asessment of the Ascendant is important because it is the body which has to take the brunt of the malady. Gemini rises with its ruler Mercury in the 11th house in a fiery sign.

Health and Diseases

Chart 3: Born 1-6-1944 at 7-55 a.m. (IST) at 15 N 54, 74 E 36 with a balance of 8 years and 8 months of Moon Dasa.

		Sun 18-50 Venus 11-44	Sat. 5-50 Ascdt. 15-06
	Chart 3 Rasi		Mars 13-53 Rahu 8-30 Jupt. 28-50
Ketu 8-30			
			Moon 11-46

Jupt. Ketu	Moon Venus		Sun
	Navamsa		
	Mars Merc. Sat.		Rahu

Saturn, a partial benefic, is in the Ascendant. The Lagna is therefore, not unduly weak or afflicted.

The 2nd house rules speech; it also rules the throat. The 2nd house here is Cancer ruled by the Moon who is in the 4th with Digbala and free of afflictions of any kind.

Mars, 6th lord, occupies the 2nd in debility. The 7th and 10th lord Jupiter also in the 2nd is in exaltation. Rahu also joins them. The 2nd house has some afflictions and also some plus points.

Transit-wise, Jupiter was in Cancer. Ketu was also in Cancer. Saturn was in Capricorn aspecting the 2nd house and its occupants. A Rahu-Saturn conjunction was due in January 1991 which would be directly influencing the 2nd house.

The Bhukti at the time the chart was examined was of 6th lord Mars in the Dasa of Jupiter. Both these planets in Cancer were under heavy affliction from transit Saturn, Rahu and Jupiter, the last himself being afflicted as Dasa lord. Since the transit picture was patently malevolent and the natal 2nd house was quite well-placed (ruling out loss of speech), it was concluded that the throat condition would improve after the Saturn-Rahu conjunction in the first phase and in the second phase, with Jupiter's moving out of Cancer, the Dasa lord would be freed of the malefic influence. Therefore, surgery, it was held, was quite unnecessary.

The next Dasa is of Saturn in Lagna who as 8th lord is not good, and as 9th lord, a benefic. The Lagna lord himself is quite well-placed and therefore, death or major disability is ruled out.

This astrological assessment led to the patient opting for therapy other than surgery. At first, the doctors were upset their expert opinion had been questioned but the patient obstinately refused surgery. An understanding between the doctor and the patient was reached that palliative measures would be tried for about 6 months and if the condition got worse, the patient was willing to risk surgery. As Jupiter in transit moved out of Cancer and the distance between Rahu and Saturn increased, the patient began to respond remarkably well to chemo-therapy. The cancerous condition completely disappeared leaving the doctors amazed.

Of course, there is nothing to be amazed if the correlation between planetary factors and human events are understood. The tremendous potential astrology has in safeguarding health and avoiding unnecessary surgeries has never been really explored. And to that extent, we have been the losers. It is but never too late to start and gain the benefits offered by this Vedic science of astrology.

(B) ASTHMA AND CONSUMPTION

अन्तः शशिन्यशुभयोर्मृगगे पतङ्गे
sवासक्षयप्लिहकविद्रधिगुल्मभाजः ।
शोषी परस्परगृहांरेगयो रवीन्दो:
क्षेत्रेऽथवा युगपदेकगयोः कृशो वा ॥ ॥

Brihat Jataka, Chapter 23, Sloka 8 states that,

> When the Sun is in Capricorn, and the Moon is between 2 malefics, the person gets asthma, consumption etc. If the Sun and the Moon mutually exchange their places in Rasi or Amsa, or if the two join together in any one of their houses, the native may be consumptive or a weakling.

Mahadeva also says about the same thing in his **Jataka Tattwa**, H-38, Slokas 44, 45 and 46.

भौमार्क्यदृष्टे लग्नेऽवासक्षयादि: ।

Or, when the Lagna is subject to the aspect of Mars and Saturn, the native will suffer from consumption, asthma etc.

— Sloka 44.

चन्द्रार्कवन्योन्यभांशगौ क्षयो ॥ ४५ ॥

or, if the Moon and the Sun be posited in each other's Rasi or Navamsa, the native will suffer from consumption

— Sloka 45.

सिंहे वा कर्के चन्द्रार्कौ क्षयी ॥

Or, if the Moon conjoined with the Sun occupies Leo or Cancer, the native will be consumptive

—Sloka 46

However, in interpreting these Slokas and applying them to actual cases, we must all along bear in mind that the literal translation is not enough, and the authors in all likelihood intended a liberal interpretation of the axioms. We may therefore extend the meaning of the Slokas figuring the luminaries to include the following in addition to their apparent meaning :

1. The Sun and/or the Moon in the other's debilitation sign, *viz.*, Scorpio and Libra.
2. The Sun and/or the Moon in the other's exaltation sign, *viz.*, Taurus and Aries.
3. The Sun and/or the Moon in the other's Moolatrikona sign, *viz.*, Taurus and Leo.
4. The Sun and/or the Moon in the other's sign, *viz.*, Cancer and Leo.

5. The Sun and/or the Moon in Capricorn and Aquarius respectively aspecting the other's signs *i.e.*, the Sun in Capricorn aspecting Cancer and/or the Moon in Aquarins aspecting Leo.

These combinations may occur either singly or jointly in the Rasi, the Navamsa or the Shashtamsa chart, the last being included as it is an important chart in analysing disease.

Saturn and Mars may afflict Lagna not only by aspect as Mahadeva enunciates, but we may extend the idea to include their occupation of Lagna, for it is well-known that Saturn's aspect is worse than his occupation, while occupation of a sign by Mars is worse than his aspecting it. In most cases, these planets afflict the luminaries also.

The critical part of the analysis of a chart, however, lies when it comes to determining whether the case is one of asthma or of consumption.

Asthma is a condition where the air sacs are plugged by phlegm while in tuberculosis (we are considering only lung cases) the lungs are weakened by the cavities made by the *tubercle* bacillus. So asthma must necessarily involve Jupiter who rules phlegm and also Gemini. For consumption, the focus must be on Gemini alone, the chest portion of the Kalapurusha.

Chart 1: Born 26-8-1922 at 16 Gh. 15 Vgh. after sunrise at 12 N 52, 74 E 04.

Ketu			
	Chart 1 Rasi		Sun Merc. Mandi
	Ascdt. Mars		Rahu Moon Jupt. Venus Sat.

Mars Rahu		Sat.	
	Navamsa		Sun
			Jupt. Venus
	Merc.	Ascdt.	Mandi	Moon Ketu

	Moon Merc. Jupt. Venus		Sun Ketu
	Shashtamsa		Jupt. Venus
Mars			
Sat. Ascdt. Rahu			

In Chart 1, in Rasi, the Lagna is afflicted by Mars and Saturn. Gemini is afflicted by the Mars-Saturn aspect. In the Navamsa, the Sun is in Cancer while Gemini is between 2 malefics, the Sun and Saturn. In the Shashtamsa, too, the Lagna is occupied by Saturn while Gemini is subject to affliction from the Sun, the Nodes and Saturn. The native is a consumptive patient.

Chart 2: Born 3-9-1921 at 3-00 a.m. (IST) at 8 N 45, 77 E 45.

Ketu			
	Chart 2 **Rasi**		Ascdt. Mars Venus
			Sun Moon Merc. Mandi
			Jupt. Sat. Rahu

Mars Ketu			
Jupt. Sat.	**Navamsa**		Ascdt.
Mandi Moon Merc.			Rahu Sun

	Mars		
	Shashtamsa		Sun
	Venus	Ascdt. Jupt. Sat.	Moon Merc. Mandi

Shashtamsa

	Mars	
	Shashtamsa	Sun
Venus		Ascdt. Jupt. Sat.	Moon Merc. Mandi

In Chart 2, in Rasi, the luminaries are afflicted in Leo. The Lagna is occupied by Mars and Gemini is aspected by Saturn. Direct application of the relevant Sloka is sufficient — a case of tuberculosis. The Sun in Cancer in Shashtamsa and Mars aspecting Gemini confirm the result.

Chart 3 : Born 26-7-1914 at 5-24 p.m. at 29 N, 77 E 40.

Chart 3 Rasi

			Merc. Sat.
Rahu			Sun
Jupt.			Moon Ketu Mars Venus
Ascdt. Mandi			

Navamsa

	Sat. Moon Venus	Mars	
Rahu			Jupt. Ketu
			Ascdt. Ketu Mandi
Mars	Moon Sat.	Venus	Jupt.

Shashtamsa

	Sat. Moon Venus	Mars	
			Jupt. Ketu
Sun Rahu	Shashtamsa		
			Ascdt. Merc.

Health and Diseases

In Chart 3, consumption is indicated by the Sun and the Moon exchanging signs with the sign Gemini and the Lagna afflicted by Saturn. The Shashtamsa chart has the Moon in Leo.

Chart 4: Born 28-1-1919 at 3-58 p.m. at Calcutta.

		Mandi Ketu	Ascdt. Jupt.
Mars Venus	Chart 4 Rasi		Sat.
Sun			
Moon Merc.	Rahu		

	Mars	Ascdt. Sun Sat.	Mandi Ketu
	Jupt.	Navamsa	
	Marc. Rahu Merc.		Venus

	Sun Jupt.		Rahu Sat. Merc.	Ascdt.
		Shashtamsa		
				Moon Venus Mars
		Ketu		

Applying the extended interpretation earlier mentioned to Chart 4, the luminaries exchange their exaltation signs in Navamsa. In Rasi, the Sun is in Capricorn aspecting Cancer. In Shashtamsa, the Moon occupies Leo while he is in Aries Navamsa. The Nodes and Mars afflict Gemini in Rasi — tuberculosis.

Chart 5 : Born 16-9-1916 at 10-42 a.m. at 25 N 28, 80 E 23.

	Moon Jupt.		
	Chart 5 Rasi		Ketu Sat. Venus
Rahu			
	Ascdt.	Mars	Sun Merc. Mandi

		Mandi	
Mars Rahu	Navamsa		Ascdt. Jupt. Ketu Sat.
Sun			
Moon	Venus		Merc.

Venus	Rahu		Mars Jupt.
	Shashtamsa		
	Ascdt. Sat.	Ketu Sun	Moon Merc.

In Chart 5, the Moon is in Aries Rasi. In Navamsa, the Sun is in Capricorn and the Lagna is afflicted by Mars, Saturn and the Nodes. In Shashtamsa also, Saturn afflicts lagna, while Mars afflicts Gemini — *tuberculosis* resulting.

Health and Diseases

Chart 6 : Born 13/14-5-1921 at 2-05 a.m. at 28 N 10, 77 E 18.

	Venus Ketu	Mars Sun Merc.	
Ascdt.	\multicolumn{2}{c}{Chart 6 Rasi}	Moon
			Jupt. Sat. Mandi
		Rahu	

	Venus	Mars Ketu	
Ascdt. Merc.	\multicolumn{2}{c}{Navamsa}	
Sun Moon			
Sat.	Rahu		Jupt.

	Rahu Venus		Ascdt.
Moon	\multicolumn{2}{c}{Shashtamsa}	Jupt.
Mars	Merc. Ketu	Sun	Sat.

In Chart 6, the Sun is in Taurus and the Lagna is aspected by Saturn. In Navamsa too, Saturn aspects Lagna, while the luminaries are in Capricorn. In Shashtamsa, the sign Gemini, which is also the Lagna, is afflicted by Mars-Saturn while the Moon is in Aquarius — *tuberculosis*.

Chart 7 : Born 16-11-1914 at 5-00 p.m. at 27 N 55, 68 E 45.

	Ascdt. Rahu Mandi		Sat.
	Chart 7		
Jupt.	**Rasi**		
	Mars Venus Sun	Moon Merc. Ketu	

		Mandi	
Ketu Moon Merc.	**Navamsa**		Sun
			Ascdt. Jupt. Rahu
Sat.			
Venus		Mars	

		Venus	Sat. Ascdt.
	Shashtamsa		Moon Merc. Rahu
Ketu			
Merc. Jupt.		Sun	

In Chart 7, the Sun and the Moon exchange their debilitation signs while Gemini is afflicted by Mars and Saturn. In Navamsa, the Sun occupies Cancer and the Moon, Aquarius. In Shashtamsa too, Mars and Saturn afflict Gemini which is the Lagna as well — *tuberculosis*.

Health and Diseases

Chart 8: Born 18/19-3-1925 at 0-45 a.m. at 33 N 40, 77 E 10.

Sun Merc.		Mars	
Venus	Chart 8 Rasi		Rahu
Ketu			Mandi
Moon Jupt.	Ascdt.	Sat.	

	Sat.		Mandi Venus
Mars	Navamsa		Ketu
Ascdt. Rahu			
Jupt. Merc.		Moon	Sun

Ascdt. Rahu	Shashtamsa		
Merc.			Moon Sat. Ketu
	Sun Mars		Jupt. Venus

In Chart 8, Gemini is caught between Mars and the ascending Node in Rasi. In Navamsa, the Moon is in Libra while the Lagna is aspected by Saturn. In Shashtamsa too, the Moon is in Leo while Mars and Saturn conjointly aspect the Lagna — *tuberculosis.*

Shifting our attention to asthma, we find Jupiter's aspect on or occupation of Gemini and Saturn or Mars afflicting Jupiter as a commonly recurring factor.

The first four interpretations appear either severally or together in consumption cases. However, in asthma cases, we find the following salient features :

(a) The Sun and/or the Moon aspects the other's sign.

(b) Where the Sun and/or the Moon occupy the other's sign (which should indicate tuberculosis), we find this nullified by the Sun and/or the Moon occupying his own

Chart 9: Born 15-4-1922 at 7-30 a.m. at 19 N 58, 79 E 23.

Merc. Ketu	Ascdt. Sun Venus Mandi		
	Chart 9 Rasi		
Mars	Moon		Jupt. Sat. Rahu

	Mars Sat.	Sun	Rahu
	Navamsa		Jupt.
	Merc.		
Ascdt. Ketu	Moon		Venus

	Sun Mars		
Sat. Jupt. Merc.	**Shashtamsa**		Venus
Rahu Moon			
			Ascdt.

sign — exaltation, debilitation or Moolatrikona sign in either one or more of the Rasi, Navamsa and Shashtamsa charts.

The Sun in Chart 9 is in Taurus in Navamsa, but in exaltation in Rasi and Shashtamsa. In Rasi, Jupiter is with Saturn; in Navamsa he is aspected by Mars, while in Shashtamsa, he aspects Gemini — *asthma*.

Chart 10: Born 16-3-1913 at 11-26 p.m. at 10 N 45, 76 E 43.

Sun Merc. Rahu	Venus	Sat. Mandi	Moon
	\multicolumn{2}{c}{**Chart 10 Rasi**}	
Mars			
Jupt.	Ascdt.		Rahu

			Sat.
Moon	\multicolumn{2}{c}{**Navamsa**}	
Merc.			Sun Venus
	Ascdt.	Rahu Jupt.	Mars

Mars			Ketu
Merc.	\multicolumn{2}{c}{**Shashtamsa**}	Moon Venus
Ascdt.			Jupt.
Rahu	Sat.	Sun	

In Chart 10, in Navamsa, the Sun is in Leo. In Shashtamsa, the Sun is in Libra and the Moon in Cancer. Jupiter aspects Gemini in Rasi and Navamsa while in Rasi and Shashtamsa he is aspected by Saturn — *asthma*.

Chart 11 : Born 11-2-1917 at 9-37 p.m. at 15 N 28, 75 E 4.

	Jupt.		Ketu
Sun Mars	Chart 11 Rasi		Sat.
Merc. Venus			
Rahu			Ascdt. Moon

	Venus	Ascdt.	Ketu Jupt.
Merc.	Navamsa		Moon
			Sat.
	Mars	Sun	

	Ketu	Sun Mars	Jupt.	
	Moon	Shashtamsa		
	Ascdt. Venus	Merc.	Sat.	Rahu

Only the Moon is in Aquarius in Shashtamsa in Chart 11. Otherwise, in Navamsa and Shashtamsa, the Sun is in his own sign (as per our definition). Jupiter occupies Gemini in Navamsa afflicted by Mars, while in Rasi, Saturn aspects Jupiter — *asthma*.

Health and Diseases

Chart 12 : Born 28/29-7-1913 at 5-00 a.m. at 32 N 57, 74 E 06.

Rahu		Sat. Moon Mars	Venus
	Chart 12 Rasi		Ascdt. Sun Merc.
Jupt.			Ketu

Mars		Moon	
Ketu Merc.	**Navamsa**		
			Ascdt. Sat. Rahu
	Sun	Venus	Jupt.

	Venus	Ketu	
Merc. Sat.	**Shashtamsa**		Jupt.
	Sun Moon	Mars Rahu	Ascdt.

The Sun in Chart 12 is in Cancer in Rasi and in Scorpio in Navamsa. The Moon is exalted in Rasi and Navamsa. Jupiter aspected by Mars aspects Gemini in Rasi — *asthma*.

We may conclude that in any chart where points (1) to (4) appear and at the same time Jupiter is afflicted and may or may not aspect Gemini, the result would be *consumption*.

Where points (a) and (b) are present, in addition to Jupiter's role (aspect on Gemini is of vital importance), the result would be *asthma*. All the three charts, namely, Rasi, Navamsa and Shashtamsa must be taken into account. (05.74)

(C) DETECTING HEART PROBLEMS

India's number one killer is heart disease. To be more precise, cholera, bronchitis, tuberculosis and other diseases deemed fatal are trailing behind. The heart attack is often a silent killer, sometimes expected but many times like a bolt from the blue.

People suffering heart attacks could be from any group, even in the prime of youth. A decade or so ago, the general feeling was, and fact also corroborated it, people below 60 years were rarely hit by a heart attack. Today, the picture has changed vastly. Age is of no consequence. So also life-styles, stress, overwork, fast life, intemperate habits, smoking and a long list of other minor reasons were often held responsible for an heart attack. However, medical science is discovering, to its chargin, that whether one leads a sedentary life or a fast life, the heart attack strikes. Though smokers are supposed to be more vulnerable, non-smokers are not exempt either from the hit-list of this killer-disease.

What does all this prove ? Very simply that heart attacks are not caused by those superficial reasons although they can hasten one. What really gives rise to this ailment is an affliction in the birth horoscope. That is, years before one picks up any habit that is held responsible for an attack, his pre-disposition to the attack is indicated at birth.

Many families are shattered when the bread-winner succumbs to a heart attack. It is here that one will appreciate the constructive role astrology can play in planning one's life. Doctors, even cardiologists, are themselves caught unawares by a sudden heart attack. Hitech diagnostic tools and wonder-drugs do help. But let us stop for a while to take a look at the economic angle to the help modern cardiac-surgery offers. Bypass surgery costs about Rs. 4 lakhs in India. Much more in the U.S. or the U.K. How many of us can afford this kind of treatment ? In some places, the cost has been considerably reduced to as much as Rs. 20,000 to Rs. 40,000. But even then, how many in our country can shell out this kind of money ? Astrology, in contrast, can provide diagnostic help years in advance to plan and organise one's health, resources and also treatment on economically viable terms. The heart is ruled by the Sun, the 4th house and Leo. Afflictions to these factors at birth indicate the possibility of heart-attacks.

Health and Diseases

In a typical case of heart-disease, the Sun is afflicted by malefics Mars, Rahu, Saturn or Ketu. Affliction by debilitation as well as Papakartari Yoga is also indicative of heart-disease. The Sun related adversely to the 6th, 8th or 12th houses or their lords in any manner always cautions against a pre-disposition to *hridroga* or heart trouble.

This connection between the heart and the Sun is briefly described in the dictum *hridrogam mamasuryaah* and is being increasingly confirmed by research. Scientists have found a distinct nexus between sunspot activity and heart attacks. In a letter to the Academy of Medicine, 2 French scientists wrote in as early as in 1959: "Our first findings point to a really remarkable correlation between increased frequency of myocardial infarctus at certain moments of maximum solar activity, and peaks of geomagnetic disturbance....." Professor N.V. Romenski, Health Director of the Region, Crimea, Sotchi on the Black Sea, also came to a similar conclusion. He established that there was a maximum of ancurisms and fatal attacks during large magnetic storms. As a result, special precautions were taken in hospitals and clinics of the Crimea when these magnetic storms drew near. These precautions led to a considerable reduction in the number of deaths. He also reported a sudden increase to twenty cardiovascular incidents on May 18, 1959 in the hospitals coming under him as compared to two incidents on the previous day, May 17. On May 17, the observatory of USSR Academy of Sciences had noted the occurrence of three powerful solar explosions hurtling towards the earth at speeds of about 10,000 miles per second. The particles of the explosion on May 17 reached the earth on May 18. The connection between solar explosions and cardiac health was simply obvious. Further, during the period from February to August of the same year, when the solar activity was most intense, cardio-vascular incidents had increased three-fold. The French physician working on this hypothesis found that "infarctions do not occur by chance, but follow well-defined solar-coordinates". The period between 1954 and 1958 was one of increasing solar activity. Dr. Gordana at the International Geophysical and Meteorological

Convention of 1960 in Ottawa showed that the period had registered an increased incidence of myocardium infarctions from 200 cases in 1954 to 450 in 1958.

With so much evidence before us, the traditional connection between the Sun and the heart becomes only too apparent.

Chart 1: Born 27-8-1914 at 7-30 p.m. (IST) at 17N, 81E48 with a balance of 17 years, 10 months and 27 days of Saturn Dasa at birth.

Lagna			Sat.
Rahu	Chart 1 Rasi GD VI - 96		
Jupt. (R)		Sun Merc. Ketu	
	Moon		Mars Venus

			Merc. Mars
Rahu	Navamsa		Sun
			Lagna Moon Ketu Jupt. (R)
	Sat.		Venus

The 4th house in Chart 1 is Gemini occupied by Saturn. The 4th lord Mercury is in the 6th in a Nodal constellation. The Sun as the natural ruler of the heart is the 6th lord, in the 6th, afflicted by Ketu and Mercury. Saturn's aspect on him is not redeeming.

Jupiter as Lagna lord is well-placed in the 11th house, so the native always enjoyed good health. Karaka Sun occupies his own sign, so that also gave her no heart ailment. But when she died in November 1982 in the Sun Dasa, Venus Bhukti, it was by a heart attack.

The 6th lord in the 6th gave her good health throughout. It was only in Sun Dasa, the affliction showed up as an attack due to the heavy affliction to the Karaka.

In Chart 2, the 4th house in Pisces. It is occupied by the Moon and hemmed in between malefics Mars and Rahu.

The Sun has no apparent affliction from Mars, Saturn or the Nodes. But he joins Venus, the 6th lord, and Venus Dasa has been on since 1974. Venus is Rogastanadhipati for Sagittarius Ascendants and a functional malefic. According to

Chart 2: Born 2/3-2-1949 at 5-15 a.m. (IST) at 29 N51, 77 E54 with a balance of 1 year, 7 months and 28 days of Saturn Dasa at birth.

Moon	Rahu		
Mars	Chart 2 Rasi GDVI - 244		
Sun Merc. Venus			
Jupt. Lagna			

		Rahu Lagna	
			Sun Sat. Merc.
	Navamsa		
	Ketu Moon Jupt.	Moon	

medical opinion, the native has a heart-ailment and was even advised against marriage. Astrologically, the heart-disease is justified but there is no need to be alarmed. Jupiter, as Lagna lord, occupies Lagna Kendra. The Karaka Venus as well as 7th lord Mercury are well-placed. Marriage cannot be ruled out; nor is it something to panic about as proving detrimental to life. With a little care, the native can be expected to lead a perfectly normal life.

The Sun is the hub around which the solar system revolves. The heart which comes under the Sun generates the life-stream in the human body. Therefore, afflictions to the Sun aptly signify trouble to the heart.

Among the common causes of heart attack are said to be excessive smoking, tension/stress, obesity and, of course, heredity factors. The last is easily explained because family horoscopes show distinctly recurring planetary features and affliction to the Sun in successive generations is nothing unusual.

Smoking also has a strong bearing on heart-health. Arthersclerosis or thickening of the coronary arteries is a common cause of heart attacks. Constant smoking causes the blood vessels to contract forcing the heart to work extra hard to pump blood through them. Usually, Mars influencing the 5th house, directly or indirectly, generarates the smoking habit. Mars rules fire and smoke and very liberally interpreted could tempt one to smoke if the Dasa also warrants it.

Afflictions to the 5th by Mars can generate heart ailments provided the Sun is also sufficiently afflicted. That is one reason why all smokers need not necessarily be heart-patients. In such cases, although Mars influences the 5th, the Sun could be free of affliction or even well-placed.

Chart 3: Born 29-5-1927 at 10 h. (LMT) at 11N, 76 E42 with a balance of 5 years, 11 months and 12 days of Venus

Jupt.	Moon	Sun Merc.	Venus Rahu
	Chart 3 Rasi GD III - 150		Mars Lagna
Ketu	Sat. (R)		

		Sun	Venus Ketu
	Navamsa		
			Mars Merc.
Rahu	Lagna	Sat. Moon	Jupt.

In Chart 3, the 5th has Saturn and the 5th lord is Mars. Both Mars and Saturn are influenced by Jupiter. Mars as 5th lord made the native a heavy smoker in Rahu Dasa. However, there is no trace of heart problem nor any likelihood of heart attacks. The Sun, the Karaka, is Vargottama in the 11th.

Mars influencing the Moon or Lagna usually makes for an extremely ambitious disposition. Where the Dasa and Bhuktis are not favorable, the native may always feel cheated of what is his due. Frustration and stress usually accompany such natives. Their expectations ruled by Mars far outrun the potential of the chart. This is also a reason why apparently successful executives and businessmen suffer from stress and invite heart attacks. Mars again afflicts the Moon or Lagna in addition to an afflicted Sun. Conversely, if the Sun is free of Doshas, the native can stay put he will never suffer any heart problems.

Obesity comes under Jupiter. Too much fat in the body forces the heart to work hard to pump blood to the entire body straining it unduly. Jupiter, therefore, has a role in heart-attacks but always subordinate to the Sun's. Not all obese people suffer heart attacks, so again while excessive body weight seemingly causes heart attacks, the real culprit is the Sun. Common-sign Ascendants or common signs prominent in the chart plus the afflicted Sun make one vulnerable with the medical science attributing it to overweight.

Sometimes, even doctors are confused and misled by symptoms of a heart-attack. But an astrological chart can give a clear clue to the problem as related to the heart, provided the Sun is sufficiently afflicted to warrant it. The nature of the afflicting planet will help explain the why and where of the heart ailment. (05-88)

(D) THE SCOURGE OF AIDS

A new scourge has set in. If WHO reports are to be believed, ten million men and women around the world are affected by AIDS or Acquired Immune Deficiency Syndrome. The United States has the highest incidence of this dreaded visitation from the devil himself, it is alleged.

On October 2, 1985, Hollywood's superstar Rock Hudson died a quiet death while asleep at home. It was about a year before that the fatal AIDS struck him. The death of this noted star sent shock waves all the over the world.

Just as homosexuals were fighting for their so-called rights and their sexual perversions and just about when people had come to almost "accept" their demands as justified, Nature intervened to say *No*. Sexual perversions had to stop, so nature seemed to scream. The killer-virus spreads easily amongst high-risk groups like prostitutes and eunuchs.

What is AIDS and how does it strike ?

Modern medicine knows little about that and less about controlling it. But it is said that once it strikes, it sounds the death-knell for the patient, maybe now or maybe in one, two or even 10 years. For all its advancement, science must accept the scourge as a concomitant of a material civilisation devoid of moral and spiritual values as a challenge which it cannot meet yet.

India's first AIDS death that was noticed was of a Bombay businessman. This highlights the ignorance about AIDS amongst both doctors and the lay public. In 1983, after a blood transfusion in New York, this man developed fever and started losing weight. Inspite of the best treatment, he continued to grow more and more emaciated and finally, when doctors put his symptoms down to AIDS, he was also demented. He died which was the most natural thing to happen in the circumstances lo .ing, just before his death, 30 years older than his age and a mere skeleton.

It is said that there are certain references to this dreaded disease in Siddha literature where it is described as Kuridipandu. It is also said to be a disease of the blood and caused by immoral life and sexual perversions. As most people are aware today, it spreads through sex and sharing of intravenous needles. The AIDS virus is found in heavy concentrations in blood and semen and to a lesser degree in saliva and tears. Women luckily are potently not as good transmitters of the virus as men. While it is true that AIDS is a dreaded striker, the press and the public have over-reacted to its incidence.

AIDS is about as prevalent as any other infection, such as jaundice, for instance. Anyone leading a healthy and regulated life with simple habits can rest assured it can never befall him. Dr. Gerald H. Predland of the Monterfiore Medical Centre in New York has so far treated 300 men and women with AIDS. More than two-thirds are dead. He says conclusively that AIDS is not confined to homosexuals: "Addicts pick it up from unclean needles, taking it home to their women and sometimes implanting it in their unborn young." And he should know !

A lot of feedback on the disease has been thrust on the common man and there is no point in repeating it. Astrological clues to the incidence of AIDS is our interest. We go back to Rock Hudson's chart and also rely on classical works for support.

To start with, blood transfusions and sex against the law of nature lead to AIDS. Blood comes under Mars. And perverse sex under Mars, Venus, Saturn and Rahu, if they are

Health and Diseases

placed in sensitive areas of the chart severally or in relative positions.

The sign Scorpio automatically comes into the picture, ruling as it does the 8th sign of the Zodiac and covering in its ambit base instincts and the brute in man. This sign re-emphasises the role of Mars as he is its ruler. Of the planets in any significant state in this sign is the Moon who debilitates here. The Moon is the Manahkaraka or the ruler of the mind. His fall here bespeaks of a fallen mind, depraved in expression. Let me caution readers here that our purview is confined to bodily urges, particularly of sex and other cravings of the flesh. Therefore, with these 2 planets before us, we can include drug addicts who use intravenous needles. The veins are the channels for the blood to move towards the heart and can be remotely linked to Mars.

					Ketu	Sat.	Ascdt.
			Rahu		Merc.		
	Chart 1 Rasi					Navamsa	
Ketu					Mars		Mars Merc.
Jupt. Venus	Sun Moon Merc.	Mars Sat.	Ascdt.		Jupt.	Venus	Rahu

Chart 1 has Virgo rising involving Hasta ruled by the Moon. The Lagna lord Mercury occupies Jyeshta in Scorpio with the Moon, also in the same constellation. The Moon-Mercury association is a blighting one because it receives no stabilising aspects, good or bad, and Mercury happens to be the Lagna lord, ruler of the psyche. That the Lagna lord and the Moon both happen to be in Scorpio, a highly sensual and sex-oriented sign, ruling the human genitals, is an important pointer to the origins of the wasting disease that eventually struck Rock Hudson who was said to be a homosexual. Homosexuality and lesbianism are perverse urges, immoral and against the laws of Nature. While combinations for such perverse urges are not frequent in our classics there are nevertheless some references to unnatural sexual activity in them. According to **Jataka Tattwa** the native will have intercourse like an animal (*pasugami*) :

1. If the four Kendras be occupied or aspected by malefics.
2. If Gulika associated with a malefic occupies the 7th house.
3. If the Sun be in the 7th house and Mars occupy the 4th.
4. If Rahu be in the 7th house and Mars be in the 4th.
5. If the 7th lord occupies a sign of Mars and be aspected by Venus.
6. If 3 of the Kendras be occupied by malefics.

In chapters on *Stree Jataka* also, there are some combinations listed :

1. If the Moon be in the 7th Bhava, she will lead a depraved life with her husband.
2. When Venus and Saturn occupy each other's Navamsas or aspect mutually, the female born in the 8th rising Navamsa of Kumbha will be afflicted with too much lust.

AIDS results from a sexual life, that is disorderly, whether one's own or of one's spouse. Any one leading a temperate sex life with one's married partner who also has had no experience outside the marital bounds is insured against AIDS. A clean life in sex matters is all that one needs, to be immune to this killer disease, provided he has not had any blood transfusions or used intravenous needles as in the case of those initiated into drugs. Where the combinations given above occur linking the appropriate houses such as 1st, the 7th, the 8th, the 12th as well as the 5th (ruling all urges) and certain signs (particularly Scorpio) and the planets Moon, Mars, Venus, Saturn or Rahu-Ketu, there we have a potential case of AIDS. Should the natives of such charts indulge in homosexual activity or use intravenous needles, they accelerate their chances of being struck by this disease by nearly 75 per cent.

In Rock Hudson's chart, the only affliction is in Scorpio and to the Moon and Mercury, as Lagna lord. The death occurred in Mars Dasa, Mars Bhukti with Mars occupying a constellation ruled by Rahu. Mercury as Lagna lord in Scorpio emphasised the actor's sexual urges, while 8th lord Mars aspecting the 5th from a Nodal constellation gave these urges a perversion. The 12th lord Sun also in Scorpio contributed to the Hollywood star's unnatural relations with men. The luminaries afflicted by Rahu or Ketu cause perversions, their exact nature depending upon the planetary positions in the rest of the chart.

It is a supremely difficult task to identify a potential AIDS chart. But done against the following background, a fair degree of success is possible.

The background of the native in question is of paramount importance. Film stars, those in the show biz, prostitutes, gays, drug addicts stand strong chances of acquiring this killer-disease if in addition to the combinations outlined above, Dasas of malefics, that is of the 6th and 8th lords, run during youth, middle or old age. If such periods are Maraka or just precede Maraka Dasas, little doubt remains as to the nature of ailment. In Hudson's chart, he had just stepped into the Dasa of Mars, who, as 8th lord joins 6th lord Saturn. From Chandra Lagna, he is the 6th lord joining malefic Saturn in the 12th. The constellation of Rahu is to be particularly noted.

In the case of those with a conservative family background and equally conservative food and other personal habits, such combinations may show up to a lesser degree and disturb marital life but not as such a fateful malady.

The tool of astrology is to be employed when one is seized with doubt, confusion and diffidence. The astrologer must be taken into confidence if a correct diagnosis is to be made. Especially, in cases where medical help is of little use, astrological diagnosis will not only help pin the cause but also show the course the affliction can take if left to itself.

A doctor, inspite of all the sophisticated equipment at his command must be given all the details he seeks of the patient.

Or else, he will just shrug his shoulders and shake off the patient. In astrology too, the same holds good. To imagine as many ill-informed and ignorant critics of the science do, that an astrological chart is nothing short of a video tape of a native's life and that an astrologer must read out the man's entire life-story, past, present and future from it, is not only an infantile acceptance of destiny but also the antithesis of sanity and the power of judgement. With a co-operative native, the astrologer can use the planetay positions to string together the past events and relate them to the chart which he will then use to foresee the broad trends indicated in future. What he sees are the trends, and this means, there is always scope for free-will for alleviating what is possible, for mitigating what is difficult and for accepting what is inevitable. Different kinds of Karma, depending upon their gravity and nature, generate different patterns of destiny. The chain of Karmic events drawn is not uniformly made up of the same material. Links generated by lesser kinds of Karma, not so resilient, can be unhooked and substituted by links generated by suitable effort. Karmic causes of a serious nature are links in the life-pattern that are made of stronger stuff and must be accepted for what they are. Links of a malleable and pliable kind can also be appropriately handled.

No one can deny that the world is one of relativities. What is light if there is no darkness ? What is happiness if one does not know what is sorrow ? How can life run if there is no death ? Extend this principle and you have fate and free-will alternate in this world. All things being relative, how can destiny alone be supreme, or even free-will ? The one without the other makes no sense. As we have often stressed in these pages, right effort will play its role in altering the pattern of destiny one carries with one's birth.

Where Jupiter aspects the affliction causing Dasas, and provided he has no Maraka powers, one can hope the patient will turn a new leaf in life and recover. Where the chart shows good longevity with still many years to go and good Dasas, recovery is possible. Medical science may still be struggling with how to grapple with AIDS, but irrespective of that, the solution here, as anywhere else, is prevention. That is why our ancients stressed on Dama or restraint.

Venus well-placed is also a protective influence on a potential AIDS victim. In all cases of a seemingly hopeless nature, we must watch out if the coming periods carry Maraka powers or not.

AIDS, let us all remember, is an affliction not of gays and drug addicts but an affliction of our culture and our times. It is the sad reflection on the lengths to which man can go in the pursuit of sensory pleasure destroying himself eventually in the process. (03 = 88)

(E) WHAT CAUSES MENTAL SICKNESS?

Mental maladies are a great tragedy that laugh at modern advancement. Inspite of spectacular achievement in the outside world of space and technology, man has still to grapple with his mind and ego. The mind is still the breeding ground for some of the most destructive forces in the world — hate, passion, jealousy, depression.

The mind is the most forceful part of the human personality and it is ruled by the Moon. Mercury rules intelligence or the faculty of discrimination.

The 6th house rules ill-health of the body and the mind. Afflictions to these signifcators by Mars, Rahu, Saturn or the sign they occupy cause mental maladies. And what is mental malady ?

According to Hindu Philosophy, kama (desire), krodha (wrath) and lobha (covetousness) are the three gateways leading to hell or misery. An overdose or surplus of any of these or all of these leads to imbalance of the mind and a confused personality. Basically, there is onıy desire — the prime motive for all crime and wrong-doing. The other two, krodha and lobha, are only ramifications of Kama. Kama causes lobha and, kama thwarted results in krodha. And krodha leads to delusion and clouded thinking. This, then, is the anatomy of all mental maladies according to the **Srimad Bhavavad Gita**. Negative Mars rules krodha and negative Saturn, kama.

Saturn and Mars in between them rule *lobha*. These two acting on an afflicted Manahkaraka Moon or an afflicted Buddhikaraka Mercury or an afflicted 4th house (mind) or the 5th house (thinking) cause disturbances in these areas affecting their balance. Rahu or Ketu also included make matters worse. Any miserable or unnatural state of mind is ultimately traceable to either *kama* or *krodha*. No wonder the ancients always advised against these two dark elements in human nature !

We shall study three charts* of mentally imbalanced people. The first belongs to the beautiful Hollywood star Marilyn Monroe, now dead. The second to a woman who killed herself after doing away with her three children between the ages of 9 and 4 years. The third chart is of a man who killed himself after shooting dead his wife.

All three cases are undoubtedly of mentally ill persons. Marilyn was a depressive insomniac while the other two were cases of mental instability and violence.

Saturn is the quiet, brooding planet — gloomy and foreboding. Mars and Rahu on the other hand are violent and explosive.

Chart 1: Born 1-6-1925 at 9-30 p.m. (PST) at 118 W 15, 34 N 03.

	Venus 7-22	Merc. 15-23 Sun 29-04	Rahu 25-54			Rahu Merc.	Venus Mars
Mars 29-22 Jupt. 5-17	Chart 1 Rasi Marilyn		Ascdt. 22-04		Navamsa		Sat. (R)
Moon 27-37				Ascdt.			
Ketu 25-54	Sat. (R) 0-05				Ketu Jupt.		Moon Sun

* All the three charts have been converted to Nirayana from the Sayana charts given in the book *Astro Psychiatry* by Harry F. Darling and Ruth H. Oliver.

The Ascendant (Chart 1) is Cancer aspected by the emotional Moon. Characteristically enough, Marilyn had a deeply emotional personality. The Moon's aspect made it all the more sensitive. Cancer also gave her a fondness for maternal love and an instinct for domestic life. Sadly, she lacked in both, for her mother was always in and out of institutions while the young Marilyn was shunted from foster home to foster home.

The 4th lord Venus although aspecting the 4th is in Aswini whose lord Ketu is in the 6th (Dustana ruling Roga or disease). This situation of Venus not only deprived her of maternal love but also made her mind weak and ill.

The 5th or house of thinking is occupied by a badly afflicted Saturn who is retrograde. The affliction is mostly due to his occupation of a Sandhi position in Visakha ruled by 6th lord (Rogastanadhipati) Jupiter. Saturn in this position made her melancholic and obsessed with death. An insomniac, Marilyn was a victim of moods of intense depression.

Mars, as 5th lord, is no doubt with Jupiter but the latter as the lord of the 6th house has little or no benefic influence to pass on to Mars. This weak position of Mars is heightened by his occupation of Poorvabhadra ruled, again, by the 6th ord.

Mercury aspected by Saturn made for a morbid state of nerves. Mars aspecting Mercury made the actress passionate and unruly in her behaviour.

The Moon in a Saturnine sign should have given some endurance but the sign-dispositor Saturn, himself being full of maleficence, proved totally unhelpful.

Saturn's depressive influence seeped into every core of this beautiful woman's being, dragging her deeper and deeper to a point of no return until an overdose of sleeping pills released her for ever.

Saturn's maleficence was concentrated mostly on the 7th house which he owned and the 5th house which he occupied.

At 18 years, the actress married James Doughtety and divorced him two years later. In 1956, she went through a marriage with Arthur Miller but 4 years later. it was on the rocks. Emotionally snattered by these blows and unable to bear children (she had 2 tubular pregnancies), Saturn's grip on the chart made the woman a spent force. Saturn, malefic and dominating the chart, led to suicide, to self-destruction. Not once did this actress strike out in hysterical violence at anybody. Saturn took care to limit her mental illness and its ramifications to herself.

Chart 2: Born 12-11-1906 at 9-30 p.m. (CST) at 96 W 40, 31 N 11.

Moon 27-47			Jupt. (R) 15-34
Sat. 18-40	Chart 2 Rasi		Ascdt. 29-20 Rahu 15-13
Ketu 15-11			
Sun 10-19	Venus 8-36 Merc. 19-49	Mars 13-05	

Moon Ascdt. Sat.			Ketu
Jupt. (R)	Navamsa		Sun
Mars			
Merc.	Rahu		Venus

This chart (Chart 2) belongs to a suicide-prone homicidal. The man was inhumanly jealous and possessive of his wife who had to flee to her mother's home because he virtually kept her a prisoner. Finally, the poor woman for no fault of hers was shot in the chest and head by the husband who then put a bullet through his own brain.

Cancer, the emotional sign, rises with Rahu therein. Rahu clouds the personality generally. The Ascendant lord Moon occupies another watery sign, Pisces, with no aspects to stabilize the mind.

The 4th is Libra occupied by the passionate and violent Mars in incendiary Swati. The 4th lord Venus is in the 5th house with Mercury. Buddhikaraka Mercury in Buddhistana is not particularly good either for thinking or emotions. However, Jupiter aspects Mars in the 4th but he is in the 12th and Vakra which only aggravates the perverse mode of thinking of the native. The 4th lord Venus and the 5th house

Health and Diseases

are subject to a Papakartari Yoga. The shooting occurred in Moon Dasa, and the Moon in Pisces made the native overly suspicious and vindictive. Perhaps, if the Moon Dasa had not occurred in the lifetime of the man, he might never have been emotionally so out of tune as to kill himself or his wife. (Incidentally, we may note, Mars in the 4th from Lagna and in the 8th from the Moon did kill the homicide's wife before him). But the 8th lord in the 8th aspected by the 9th lord Jupiter, killed the husband also the same day, thus making the couple die almost together neutralising Kuja Dosha to the extent of nearly 99·9 per cent.

Chart 3: Born 9-3-1894 at 3-00 a.m. (CET) 13 E 42, 51 N.

Rahu 20-38 Moon 15-25 Merc. (R) 7-01		Jupt. 4-49					Ascdt. Sun
Sun 27-35	**Chart 3 Rasi**			Jupt.	**Navamsa**		Ketu
Venus 28-58				Rahu			
Ascdt. 8-06 Mars 25-26		Sat. (R) 3-15	Ketu 20-38		Mars Moon	Sat. (R)	Venus Merc. (R)

Chart 3 is of a woman who hanged herself after killing her 3 small children.

The Ascendant Sagittarius is influenced by two malefics, Mars and Saturn exalted but retrograde.

The Ascendant lord Jupiter who also happens to be the 4th lord is in the 6th house, pointing to a sick mind and personality.

The 4th ruling the mind is occupied by the Moon which is bad in itself as Karaka in the relevant house is said to spoil it. Mercury there in association with the Manahkaraka Moon makes matters worse for the former with his Mercurial traits of instability, fickleness, dual and confused thinking, is not only retrograde or Vakra (which means 'perverted' in common parlance) but also debilitated. Rahu throws a cloud over these two planets making for a personality that is afraid of everything and everyone, full of suspicion and saddled with the most unhealthy complexes and phobias. This combination occurs in the watery sign Pisces creating heightened, sensational and intense emotions. Mars aspecting it from a fiery sign makes it in addition explosive.

The 5th lord Mars is in the Ascendant but aspected by a malefic exalted retrograde Saturn. Moreover, he is in Poorvashada ruled by the 6th lord Venus. No wonder, the woman was mentally so unsound as to kill her own children before hanging herself.

The murderous conglomeration of planets in the 4th, each afflicted powerfully, must have robbed the poor woman of all the sane forces of her mind.

Mercury and the Moon associated by conjunction or mutual aspect is generally not favorable. In any chart where such a combination occurs, inevitabley the native turns out to be a complex ridden person with feelings of guilt, insecurity and suspicion. Depending upon other malefics influencing the Moon-Mercury set-up, the mental malady may be mild and hardly noticeable, or dangerously violent. The aspect of Jupiter is a great help in such cases and may even veneer the mind from soaring criminal heights to soaring Divine or intellectual heights.(09-76)

Chapter Eight

Marriage

(A) MARRIAGE TIMING

One of the most commonly encountered problems in astrology is timing marriage. Classical works provide many methods by which marriage can be timed. Applying these different methods to the same charts gives a number of periods when marriage is likely to take place. However, astrological analysis cannot depart from the structure laid by the times and social conditions around one. Therefore, in trying to fix the time of marriage, the important factor is to look for planetary conditions after the 20th year. Even here, marriage may occur soon after one is about 20 years or it may come about when one is past even 40 years. How do we find out then the most likely time for marriage to take place?

As always, the chart is first analysed for factors that delay marriage and then by synthesising appropriate Dasa-Bhukti periods as well as the transits of such planets as Mars, Rahu, Jupiter and Saturn, the event can be identified with a fair degree of precision. Most parents in India tend to get distraught if their daughters do not get married about the time they are 24 or 25 years old.

Rule I

The acquisition of a spouse (whether it is the chart of a male or a female is not relevant) occurs in the Dasa:

(a) of a planet in the 7th house, or
(b) of a planet aspecting the 7th house, or
(c) of a planet owning the 7th house.

When such Dasa runs during the marriageable age of a native, then marriage is indicated during this period.

Chart 1: Born 26-4-1965 at 5-05 a.m. (IST) at 10 N 56, 79 E 46 with a balance of 17 years, 9 months and 8 days of Rahu Dasa.

Ascdt. Merc.	Sun Venus	Jupt. Rahu	
Moon Sat.	**Chart 1 Rasi**		
			Mars
	Ketu		

Jupt. Ascdt.	Sat.		
Ketu	**Navamsa**		
Merc.			Sun Rahu
	Moon		Mars Venus

In Chart 1, marriage took place on 1-11-1987 in Jupiter Dasa. Jupiter Dasa started in the 18th year of the native and runs upto her 34th year. Then, we have Saturn Dasa from 34 to 53 years. Between Jupiter and Saturn, Jupiter is better qualified. Jupiter in 3rd aspects the 7th trinally and favourably showing marriage in his Dasa.

The Dasa balance being of Venus at birth in Chart 2, the Dasa that runs about or after the 20th year is of Mars (20 to 27 years), next of Rahu (27 to 45 years). Between these contenders for marriage, Rahu occupying the 7th house becomes the stronger of the two. Marriage took place in 1968 in Rahu Dasa, Rahu Bhukti.

Chart 2: Born 1-9-1960 at 6-30 p.m. (IST) at 22 N 35, 88 E 21 with a balance of 4 years, 4 months and 10 days of Venus Dasa.

		Mars	
Ascdt. Ketu	**Chart 2 Rasi**		
			Sun Merc. Rahu
Moon Sat. Jupt.			Venus

	Jupt.	Ketu	Ascdt.
Venus	**Navamsa**		
			Sun Rahu
	Moon Rahu	Sat.	Sun Mars Merc.

Marriage

Chart 3: Born 25-9-1945 at 7-23 a.m. (IST) at 13 N 05, 80 E 18, with a balance of 2 years, 4 months and 7 days of Venus Dasa.

	Moon		Mars Rahu
	Chart 3 **Rasi**		Sat.
			Venus
Ketu		Ascdt.	Merc. Sun Jupt.

Sun Mars		Jupt.	Venus
Merc.	**Navamsa**		Sat. Ketu
Rahu			
	Moon	Ascdt.	

The Dasas that run during the marriageable years in Chart 3 are of 7th lord Mars (18 to 25 years) and 9th occupant Rahu (25 to 43 years). As the 7th lord, Mars automatically is the winner; marriage took place in January 1968 in Ketu Bhukti of Mars Dasa.

Rule II

What happens if the Dasa running between 20 and 40 years is of a planet who is neither the 7th lord nor 7th occupant nor aspects the 7th house ?

In such cases, see which of the following pairs is stronger.

A (i) The lord of Rasi occupied by the 7th lord.

(ii) The lord of the Navamsa occupied by the 7th lord.

B (i) Venus

(ii) Moon

The Dasa of such a planet can bring about marriage.

The 7th lord in Chart 4 is Jupiter, the 7th is aspected by Saturn and occupied by Rahu and the Moon. Jupiter Dasa does not occur; Saturn Dasa also until very, very late. Moon Dasa starts only after 46 years. Rule I, therefore, does not apply to Chart 4.

According to Rule II, let us classify planets under the two heads, A and B.

A(i) Lord of Rasi occupied by 7th lord is Jupiter. The 7th lord is in Aquarius ruled by Saturn.

Chart 4: Born 20-11-1950 at 8-00 a.m. at 18 N 50, 72 E 54, with a balance of 13 years, 7 months and 6 days of Mercury Dasa at birth.

Moon Rahu				Sat.		Ascdt.	
Jupt.	Chart 4 Rasi				Navamsa		Rahu
				Ketu			Sun
Mars	Sun Venus Merc.		Ketu Sat. Ascdt.	Merc. Jupt. Moon			Mars Venus

(ii) Lord of Navamsa occupied by 7th lord is Jupiter who as 7th lord occupies his own Navamsa, Sagittarius. The planet in question becomes Jupiter.

B (i) Venus
  (ii) Moon

The Dasas of Saturn and Jupiter are, as we have already seen, out of question. The Dasa of the Moon starts very late. It is only the Dasa of Venus (20 to 40 years) that becomes qualified to give marriage. In this case, the girl got married in September 1972 in Venus Dasa and Venus Bhukti.

Rule III

Apart from these Dasas, the Dasa and Bhukti of the lord of the sign occupied by the 2nd lord can also produce marriage. The Dasa of the planet joining the 7th lord as also of the 9th and 10th lords can also be examined if the Dasas under Rules I and II fail to give results.

The Dasa of Kalatrakaraka Venus is, of course, generally capable of conferring marriage on the native.

Once the Dasa is decided, the time frame of possibility of marriage has to be narrowed down. Which Bhukti becomes marriage-giving ?

The same Rules I and II apply to the Bhukti also but within the time-range defined by the Dasa-period. There is, however, one more Bhukti apart from these that is effective in giving marriage. A planet in the 7th from the Dasa lord is a strong factor in this aspect.

Let us go back to the same charts to work out the Bhukti periods.

If a planet producing marriage in his Dasa is powerful, then it can bring about the event at the beginning of the Dasa.

In Chart 1, marriage took place in November 1987 in Mercury Bhukti, Jupiter Dasa.

Mercury is the 7th lord and aspects the 7th house.

Let us take a look at the transits of all the major planets, plus those of the Dasa and Bhukti lords.

Mars was in the 7th house. Jupiter was on the Kalatrakaraka Venus in the 2nd from Lagna. Rahu was in the Ascendant touching Bhukti lord Mercury. Mercury himself in transit in Libra was influenced by transit Jupiter.

Rahu	Jupt.		
	Chart 1 **Transits**		
	Sat.	Merc.	Mars Ketu

Saturn was influencing Dasa lord Jupiter. The Dasa and Bhukti lords, Jupiter and Mercury, were in mutual aspect in transit.

Jupiter's transit of the 7th lord or Venus is also of importance.

In Chart 2, marriage came about in Rahu Dasa, Rahu Bhukti in 1988. The Bhukti lord Rahu has all the qualifications of the Dasa lord.

In Chart 3, marriage took place on 18-1-1968. The Bhukti was of Ketu in Mars Dasa. Ketu is in the 7th from Dasa lord Mars.

Transit Mars in Aquarius was aspecting Kalatrakaraka Venus in the natal chart. Saturn, in transit, was aspecting

Bhukti lord Ketu. Transit Jupiter was on transit Venus while Rahu and Ketu were influencing the natal 7th house. Transit-wise, Dasa lord Mars was being aspected by Jupiter, while Ketu (who reflects results of Mars) was under the same influence indirectly.

	Sat.	Rahu	
Mars	Chart 3 Transits		
			Jupt.
		Ketu	

In Chart 4, marriage in September 1972 came about in Venus Bhukti. Venus is the Kalatrakaraka. Coming to transits, transit Mars was aspecting natal 7th lord Jupiter. Transit Mars was aspecting Dasa and Bhukti lord Venus.

		Sat.	
	Chart 4 Transits		Venus Ketu
Rahu			Mars
Jupt.			

The Dasas in Chart 5 that cover the period between 20 and 40 years are of Rahu (part) and Jupiter (5 years of Mars + 18 years of Rahu + 16 years of Jupiter). Applying Rule I, Rahu is in the 7th, so also the Moon. The Moon Dasa gets automatically eliminated since Mars Dasa is already on at birth. Rahu becomes a prime factor. Next, as 7th lord Saturn is qualified but his Dasa starts very late, after the 39th year.

Marriage

Chart 5: Born 24-11-1971 at 22 h. 05m. at 28 N 15, 78 E 36 with a balance of 5 years, 0 months and 5 days of Mars Dasa at birth.

		Sat. (R)	
Mars	Chart 5 Rasi		Ascdt. Ketu
Moon Rahu			
Venus Marc.	Sun Jupt.		

Mars	Venus Marc. Sat.	Rahu	
	Navamsa		Rahu
Jupt.			Sun
	Ascdt. Ketu		Moon Sun

Further, since Lagna lord Moon occupies the 7th, such a late marriage is unlikely. No planet aspects the 7th house. Therefore, Rahu becomes the strongest factor in giving marriage in his Dasa.

Applying the same rule to Bhuktis, Rahu, Moon, Saturn become qualified for bringing about marriage. Rahu Bhukti of Rahu Dasa is immediately after Mars Dasa when the girl is only slightly over 5 years. Saturn Bhukti is also too early for marriage. The Moon Bhukti is between May 1992 and November 1993.

Therefore, the Moon Bhukti of Rahu Dasa is ideal for marriage. Marriage took place in this period in July 1993.

Transitwise, both Mars and Saturn were aspecting the Kalatrakaraka Venus. Transit Jupiter was on natal Jupiter and natal 2nd lord Sun. (04-95)

	Sat.	Ketu	
	Chart 6 Transits		
	Jupt.	Rahu	Mars

(B) HAPPY AND UNHAPPY MARRIAGES

Classical works on astrology are full of axiomatic combinations with specific results attributed to them. Sometimes, these combinations can be applied *ad verbatim*. Sometimes, they have to be carefully analysed and interpreted in the light of several factors like planetary lordships, influence of aspects and associations as also the Nakshatra occupied by the planet. There is an interesting combination applicable to marital life.

मन्देऽष्टमे षष्ठे भौमस्ते। राहो भार्या न जीवति।।

If Saturn be in the 8th house, Mars in the 6th house and Rahu in the 7th house, the native will lose his wife.

As with other combinations found in classical works, this too is applicable to both male and female charts.

If you take a hundred charts with this combination (Chart 1) of men and women who have been married for at least 20 to 30 years, you will find the combination working without fail in about 65 cases. In the rest, you will find that it has not failed to work but has been held in abeyance due to either careful matching of charts before marriage or some other exonerating factor in the chart.

The 7th house rules marriage. In this combination, the 6th and 8th houses have also been included. A malefic is placed in the 6th house. Another malefic is also placed in the 8th house. We know malefics in any house generate stress in relation to that house. So, the 7th house here is hemmed between 2 malefics and 2 houses under stress themselves. The 7th house is therefore exposed to great pressure with consequent loss of spouse.

Suppose, we shift the planets a little different from the positions given in the dictum. Put Saturn in the 7th and let Rahu and Mars flank it from the 6th and 8th houses (Chart 2).

There is much stress involved in marital life but because Saturn rules all that is long-drawn and lingering, it may not lead to actual loss of spouse. There may be much unhappiness

Marriage

	Ascdt.		
	Chart 1		
	Rasi		
	Sat.	Rahu	Mars

	Ascdt.		
	Chart 2		
	Rasi		
	Mars	Sat.	Rahu

due to ill-health in the family, or poverty, complicated pregnancies and dissensions and bickerings amongst family members, the result being loss of marital happiness even if the spouse is alive.

Let us now shift the planets a little more differently. Mars comes to the 7th and Rahu and Saturn occupy the houses on either side (Chart 3). What would the result be ? Would it still be loss of spouse ? Mars is an angry, quarrelsome planet. The marriage may survive but happiness will be the casualty with fights, mutual hate, constant friction and acrimony becoming a regular feature of the relationship.

	Ascdt.		
	Chart 3		
	Rasi		
	Rahu	Mars	Sat.

Whatever the afflictions to the 7th house, they have to be interpreted in the light of the inherent characteristics of the planets and their lordships.

Rahu in the 7th is akin to bombing the relationship leaving it burnt out at one stroke. Mars in the 7th can be compared to active combat and artillery fire which can be spread over a long period of time. Saturn in the 7th brings coldness into the relationship leading to indifference. There may be no violent quarrels but the peace is the peace of a graveyard.

The Sun is a haughty, conceited planet and in the 7th, affects the relationship in like manner. Ego conflicts vitiate the marital bond.

Sun		Ketu Mars	Ascdt.
Venus Merc.	\multicolumn{2}{c	}{Chart 4 Rasi}	
			Moon
	Sat. -Rahu		Jupt.

	Venus		Mars
Sun Merc. Ketu	\multicolumn{2}{c	}{Chart 5 Rasi}	Moon
Jupiter			Rahu
		Ascdt.	

Now substitute a benefic like Venus, Jupiter or Mercury in the 7th house. What do we have?

Jupiter in the 7th gives rise to dignity and mutual respect in the relationship. Venus gives warm affectionate ties between husband and wife. Mercury brings in happiness and mirth and the couple are the best of friends with a lot of humour to keep the bond alive and merry.

The position of Venus is a prime determinant of marital happiness. Well-placed, he invariably ensures a modicum of marital happiness even if other afflictions are present.

The 7th lord Jupiter (Chart 4) is aspected by the Sun. The Ascendant and 7th lords are in Shashtashtaka. Mars aspects the 7th house adversely. Yet, the couple is very happy. Venus well-placed in the 9th is with Lagna lord Mercury in a friendly sign.

Jupiter in Chart 5 aspects the 7th house, yet, the girl never was able to experience any marital happiness. The husband was accused of murder within a year of marrige and taken away by the police. He was sentenced to a long term of imprisonment. Out on bail, the case is in appeal.

Marriage

Venus, though Vargottama, is in a cuspal degree and in the 6th from the Lagna which is the 12th from the 7th. The 7th lord in the 6th is not a happy feature, for, it can indicate either litigation or serious health problems affecting marital life. In this particular case, court proceedings did affect the marriage although the case itself had directly nothing to do with the marriage as in cases of divorce or separation.

A clean Venus is the best thing to have for a fairly good quota of marital happiness. Venus aspected by benefic Jupiter gives happiness. Venus influenced by a favorable Saturn is also a desirable factor. Venus in conjunction with malefic Sun or Mars or Rahu or Saturn can ruin marital happiness. With unafflicted Mars, Venus gives happiness and harmony in marriage. Retrograde Venus is a blight on marital happiness.

The Ascendant and 7th lords together or in favorable aspect is good for a happy married life.

The Lagna lord in the 7th is also good. But the same Lagna lord retrograde in the 7th proves to be a bane on marital life.

Kuja Dosha is another factor that needs to be interpreted judiciously. According to definition, Mars in the 2nd, 4th, 7th, 8th or 12th is said to cause this Dosha leading to loss of spouse.

The mere presence of Mars in one of these houses is really not cause enough for concern. It gets neutralised if found in the horoscopes of both husband and wife. Mars with the

Rahu		Moon	Jupt. (R)
	Chart 6 Rasi		Mars (R)
Merc. Sat. Ascdt.	Venus		Ketu

		Sun Merc.	Venus
Ascdt. Sat.	Chart 7 Rasi		Ketu
	Rahu		
		Jupt.	Moon Mars

Moon or aspected by the Moon makes it inffective. Mars in the 8th is usually the most serious form of Kuja Dosha.

However, Jupiter's aspect on Mars is said to contain this Dosha. I have found Mars with or aspected by Saturn also controls the Dosha. There is no textual authority *per se* for this but I have depended on a Sloka from **Jataka Parijata** to support my conclusion.

अर्केण मन्दः शनिना महीसुतः
कुजेन गुरुणा निशाकरः ।
सौमेन शुको सुरमन्त्रिण बुधःबुधने
चन्द्रः खलु वध्यते सदा ।।

In planetary war, Saturn is over-powered by the Sun, Mars is defeated by Saturn, Jupiter is vanquished by Mars, the Moon loses to Jupiter, Venus to the Moon. Mercury is overcome by Venus, Mercury defeats the Moon.

The native of Chart 6 married in 1956. The marriage broke up in 1957-'58. The divorce came in 1966. The second marriage in 1967 was happier but the wife died of an illness in 1987 leaving the native desolate. Mars occupies the 8th in retrogression. There is no aspect on Mars save the Sun's making him retrograde and this only adds to the intensity of the affliction.

In Chart 7, on the other hand, the native married before she was twenty. Thirty-eight years have since passed but Mars in the 8th has been able to cause no mischief. Mars is with the Moon and the Dosha is, therefore, checked.

These cases highlight the fact that no Dosha is absolute in operative strength. The house, sign, planets with it or aspecting it decisively influence the final result. *(07-93)*

(C) BLIGHTING FACTORS IN MARRIAGES

Marriage is a beautiful relationship between man and woman which, starting on the grosser planes, ends in the communion of souls. It is this institution and the sanctity associated with it that has preserved our culture down the ages. Any cracks in it are a warning of grave consequence to society as a whole.

Divorce and separation are as alien to our people as are promiscuous living and free-sex. But we do have exceptions, although they only serve to highlight the richness and stability of the institution of marriage.

Where a chart indicates marital tragedy, it is always best to train oneself into accepting the situation for what it is and, or diverting one's energies into constructive channels of career or profession. When a person realises the stark tragedy of a situation, he cannot overnight accept it philosophically and march on as if nothing has happened. Nor can a young girl who has given up or has been indifferent to education all along in the youthful hope of her rosy dreams coming true, land a job or busy herself otherwise soon enough to drown the sorrow of a shattered life.

Acquiring an attitude of dispassion requires careful cultivation over many years. Training for a job or career is equally long. Hence, when a parent discovers from the chart of his new-born babe that marital happiness will be elusive to it, he can mould the impressionable mind of the child to appreciate the greatness of a dispassionate attitude in life and train him (and her, too) for a career or vocation.

Right attitudes cultivated from childhood form the bedrock of a stable personality which can withstand any mishap in life without reeling under its impact. Would it not be in the larger interests of society that we had mentally strong people than embittered wrecks, frustrated and neurotic who can only spread gloom around ? No one can prevent a tragedy sometimes, but how one reacts to it is within one's conscious control.

Astrologically, Saturn, Mars, Rahu and Ketu in relation to marriage-indicators portend evil.

Barring specific combinations laid down in the classical texts, there are general pointers to marital unhappiness which in its broadest sense can take shape in two ways. Firstly, partners may wage cold war against each other, or one or both of them may be guilty of lapses not easily forgiveable. Secondly, unhappiness may take tangible shape in separation through death or divorce. By divorce, is included the mutually arranged separation which may not be under the seal of a court of law.

Marital unhappiness is indicated not only through the aspects and association of malefics with the relevant significators but also through their being subject to Papakartari Yoga.

The 7th house, the 7th lord and the 8th house are the main indicators in tackling marital problems. The 8th generally governs the longevity or the duration of married life. The 7th house is adjectival in character and denotes the quality of married life. This distinction in the portfolio of these two houses is very narrow and sometimes overlapping too. Venus, as the natural Kalatrakaraka or Bhartrukaraka, has also a say in these delineations, but we shall refrain for the present from dwelling on its role.

Marie Antionette (Chart 1) born with Gemini ascending had a concentration of malefic influences on her 7th house in Sagittarious. Mars aspecting it and the 7th lord Jupiter with Rahu made her marital life a tragedy rendered worse by the hermaphrodite planets—Saturn and Mercury—closing in on it from both sides. The husband, it is said, was so ashamed of his incapacity that he fled from the bridal chamber. In other ways too, he was indifferent to her until his death in Saturn Dasa. Mars aspecting the 8th house from Aridra cut short her married life.

A powerful President and a champion of human rights, Abraham Lincoln (Chart 2) was a helpless husband before

Ketu			Mars Ascdt. 14-0
	Chart 1 Rasi		
Sat.			
	Merc.	Sun Moon Venus	Jupt. Rahu

	Sun Venus		Jupt. Mars
Rahu Sat. Ascdt.	Navamsa		Ketu
			Ketu
	Merc.	Moon	

Chart 2

Rasi

Venus Jupt.	Ketu		
Ascdt. Sun Merc.			
Moon			
	Sat.	Mars Rahu	

Navamsa

Rahu			
Ascdt. Moon			Jupt.
Merc.			
Venus	Sun Mars	Sat.	Ketu

his nagging wife. The 7th Lord Sun in Dhanishta whose lord Mars, himself wicked, made worse by being with Rahu gave Lincoln the realisation married life ``was no bed of roses''. The 7th house comes under the chilling aspect of Saturn and the Sun. The 7th and 8th houses being free of Martian hues took care of the length of his married life. Saturn's influence is always long-drawn and so is nagging !

Chart 3

Rasi

Sun Ascdt.	Ketu	Sat.	Jupt.
Mars Merc.			
Venus			
		Rahu	Moon

Navamsa

Mars	Rahu Merc.	Moon	
Sat.			
		Ascdt. Sun Jupt. Ketu	Venus

A truly tragic instance, the first wife of the native (Chart 3) was an ideal lady but died very young. The second wife proved to be the greatest regret of his life. Either way, the native was deprived of married bliss. The 7th lord Mercury is in the 12th with fiery Mars aspected by Saturn. The 7th itself is afflicted by Mars' aspect from Satabhisha ruled by Rahu. From Chandra Lagna, the 7th is subject to severe Papakartari Yoga caused by Mars and Ketu and with the 12th lord Sun in the 7th. The 7th lord from the Moon, Jupiter, aspects Mars and Mercury but his position in Mrigasira seems to have suppressed his inherent beneficence.

The native lost his first wife at the fag end of Rahu Dasa. Rahu is in the 8th from Lagna and in the 2nd from the 7th with Maraka strength. Jupiter Dasa saw him married again but the Dasa lord being free of Maraka properties and the 7th house afflictions being too powerful to go unnoticed, the 2nd wife emerged a veritable shrew. The native was so disgusted with her mean nature that he lived practically separated from her in later days.

Ascdt.	Mars		Moon Sat.
Ketu	Chart 4 Rasi		Jupt. Sun Merc. Rahu
			Venus

Merc.			
Rahu	Navamsa		Ascdt.
	Mars Sun Moon Jupt. Venus	Sat.	Ketu

Life is a nightmare to the native of Chart 4, a cultured young lady. The 7th lord Mercury is in the 5th house (of emotions) in Cancer (an emotional sign) and in association with the Sun and Rahu. Jupiter has been an helpless onlooker while the husband busies himself with extra-marital adventures. Not only that, his treatment of his wife is cruel and inhuman. Rahu and Mars acting on the spineless Mercury as 7th lord and on Jupiter seem to have sucked the life out of the latter. Jupiter is the 7th lord from the Moon and is with Rahu. Perhaps, this explains his incapacity to save the situation.

Although right now, the native is bearing with her husband's disgraceful conduct, it is highly doubtful if the marriage tie will remain intact for long. The powerful influence of Mars on the 8th house from Lagna and the

Marriage

Sat.	Ketu		
Jupt. Ascdt.	**Chart 5** **Rasi**		
Moon			
Merc.	Sun Venus	Rahu	Mars

	Moon	Merc. Rahu	
Ascdt.	**Navamsa**		
			Venus
Sat.	Ketu	Sun Jupt.	Mars

position of the 7th occupant Saturn (from the Moon) in Mrigasira can destroy the bond.

The 7th house (Chart 5) is relatively free of affliction. In fact, Jupiter aspects it, but sadly from Dhanishta, which is why his marriage broke up so soon. Mars is in the 8th in Chitta, while Saturn aspects it. Within a year of the marriage, his wife began to drift away from him and for no reason. Before the third year was over, she walked away with her divorce decree. This happened at the fag end of Rahu Dasa and Jupiter Dasa beginning, the latter in Dhanishta partaking of the nature of Mars.

Rahu	Moon		
Mars Jupt.	**Chart 6** **Rasi**		
Sun Venus			
Merc.	Ascdt.		Sat. (R) Ketu

	Moon Sat. (R)		Venus
Jupt.	**Navamsa**		Merc. Rahu
Sun Ketu			Ascdt.
		Mars	

Chart 6 belongs to the ex-wife of our previous illustration. The 7th is aspected by only Mars from Dhanishta, his own constellation. The 7th lord Venus is combust. The 8th is aspected only by Jupiter but he is in Swati whose lord Rahu is definitely no well-wisher of married happiness.

Chart 7 Rasi

Mars			Moon Ketu
Sat. Sun Rahu Merc. Venus (R)			
	Ascdt.	Jupt.	

Navamsa

			Sun
			Rahu Ascdt.
Ketu			Merc. Sat.
	Mars	Jupt.	Moon Venus (R)

The native of Chart 7 married in her 17th year and lost her husband some 5 or 6 years later. The 7th lord Venus is in Dhanishta and afflicted by the company of Rahu, Sun, malefic Mercury and Saturn, all of whom except the Sun are in Dhanishta ruled by Mars. Mars aspects the 7th from Dhanishta again, and is in the 8th from the Chandra Lagna. No wonder the marriage tie was severed so early in life.

Chart 8 Rasi

Moon Ascdt.	Sun Merc. Venus		Mars Ketu
			Jupt.
			Sat.
Rahu			

Navamsa

	Jupt.		Ketu
			Sat.
Moon			Ascdt.
	Rahu Sun Venus	Mars	

Rabindranath Tagore (Chart 8) had Mercury, lord of his 7th house, in Aswini ruled by Ketu who imbibes Martian qualities, since he is with Mars, who, in turn, aspects the 7th house. This caused his wife's death in Sun Dasa, Saturn Bhukti — the former in the 8th from the 7th and the latter in the 12th therefrom.

The 7th house in Chart 9 has Saturn and Jupiter combining aspects on it. Jupiter gets tainted by being in Swati belonging

Marriage

Venus		Mars Ketu	
Sun Merc.	**Chart 9**		
	Rasi		
Ascdt.	Moon Rahu	Jupt.	Sat.

	Mars Sat.		Sun
	Navamsa		Ketu
Rahu Venus			
Moon		Merc. Jupt.	Ascdt.

to Rahu. The 7th lord Mercury is in Dhanishta whose ruler Mars is in the 7th from the Moon with Ketu. These Martian influences were instrumental in causing the death of the native's wife.

From what we have seen so far, we may safely conclude Mars in his own or Rahu's constellation gets doubly powerful in causing harm to marriage if afflicting the 7th or the 8th house or the 7th lord. The 7th lord in a Martian star stops at unhappiness without affecting the marriage tie as can be gleaned from Charts 1, 2, 3 and 4. Mars afflicting the 7th or the 8th house snaps the marital bonds through separation by death or divorce as Charts 3, 5, 6, 7, 8 and 9 show.

Other planets related to the 7th house and in stars ruled by Mars emphasize the same results.

Papakartari Yoga in relation to the 7th lord or the 7th house is to be dreaded for it gives a spouse who will be like a thorn in the flesh. Saturn afflicting marriage-indicators gives rise to indifference, bitterness or iciness between partners but rarely separates them as Mars does. Best described as an indicator of cold war between spouses, Saturn may yet never give the outside world any inkling of what is happening within the domestic walls.

Rahu associated with the Kalatrakaraka and Bhava may lead one to break the vow of fidelity on which so much importance is laid in our society. Rahu does not act like Saturn in this lone context. He is in active form turning the hearth into a seething volcano. Instead, Ketu in the relevant sectors is more akin to Saturn. He can shrivel up any warmth between the couple creating bitterness and coldness in their hearts.

These indications from the several planets sprout into real evidence only when allied Dasas and Bhuktis come into operation. Otherwise, they only simmer under the lid. (1-75)

(D) THE TRAGEDY OF DIVORCE

Marriage in our country was always a sacred institution with a religious character imparted to it. Marriage was never a mere contract. It was a *samskara* or sacrament, being the last of the 10 sacraments enjoined on a Hindu. In ancient days, its purpose was for begetting progeny and continuance of the family line.

The sanctity of marriage was highlighted in ancient society. The new bride was immediately given a place of honour in the household. Rights and responsibilities descended on her simultaneously. She was the *dharmapatni* or partner in *dharma* of her husband. She was described as half of her husband. Together they made one unit. The individual ego fused into one self-abnegating whole. The wife, it was emphasised, was a gift from the gods (and which husband who has a happy marriage will dispute this fact) and to be taken care of while she was faithful.

Men and women, as individuals, in those days were more evolved and tolerant of the other's shortcomings. In sharp contrast today a smattering of college education can give either spouse a feeling of omniscient indispensability and a tyrannical urge to exploit the relationship for personal, selfish ends. Both men and women are equally to blame for this sad state of affairs. If more dowry deaths are reported in the dailies, that is only one side of the coin. On the other, we have husbands harassed by shrewish viragos. It is not as if woman alone is being sinned against today. Men too suffer silent torment at the hands of greedy wives who drive them to corruption and crime to satiate their endless desires. In such situations where the aggrieved spouse offers resistance, the marriage is as good as dead even if not legally so pronounced. Sometimes, an exploited spouse has no choice but to opt for divorce. Agreed, divorce does grant some kind of relief or solution to a relationship that is no longer emotionally worthwhile. But why did things go wrong the way they did in the first place? Was it due to greed, avarice, deceit, utter selfishness, infidelity, inhuman cruelty ? May be for one or more of these reasons, apparently. But an honest, impartial and microscopic examination of most divorce cases will show that beneath all these heart-rending reasons is the more tragic one of scant regard for values. That this should happen in a country like ours is, indeed, sad beyond words.

There is a Sanskrit saying *yatha raja thatha prajah*. A corrupt and unrighteous king generates the same qualities in his subjects. People have lost their sense of values. Harmlessness, truth, absence of anger, renunciation, serenity, absence of calumny, compassion, non-covetousness, gentleness, modesty, absence of fickleness and such other qualities of the heart have ceased to function in personal relationships. The family unit is no longer important. The individual alone matters. With such attitudes rampant, children suffer and emerging from homes where both parents center their lives around money and pleasure, they also imbibe the same culture. Educationists are no less guilty for this sad pass. The universities churn out, year after year, youth academically qualified but morally confused. Such young people are unfit to grapple with the problems of life. This is, of course, the natural sequel to an academic life directed and guided by people who are themselves swayed by lucre and are completely impervious to India's ancient cultural values.

In addition, day in and day out, misconceived TV programmes are forever dinning into the ears of young women marriages need not be saved but fought out in law-rooms. That marriage must be approached with hostility and suspicion and qualities like love and understanding must be shown the door.

Most young minds that come out of the university today have lost the ability to discriminate between the real and the fleeting. Instead, they are cloaked in the neo-superstition of legal rights only (forget the responsibilities). When such people enter the institution of marriage, the first petty conflict with the spouse is blown up out of all proportion and taken to the courts. Once this happens, the sanctity of the bond of marriage is forgotten and trampled upon by lies from both sides, prompted and supported by the members of the legal fraternity. This, then, is the diagnosis of divorce in our country.

The charge by those who unconditionally advocate divorce that women are exploited is far from sound. In India, in most cultured homes, the woman is treated with affectionate regard. **Manu Smriti** still regulates the lives of countless Indians, literate or illiterate, and these **Smritis** emphasize a life of regulated discipline, integrity, devotion and respect for elders. At one place, Manu says ``Women must be honoured and adorned by their fathers, brothers, husbands and brothers-in-law who desire their own welfare. Where women are honoured, there the gods are pleased; but where they are not honoured, no sacred rite yields rewards.''

Disputes and differences between the husband and wife could not be taken up by any tribunal or the king's court. With this being the case, no provision was made in astrological texts for divorce. At the most, a wife and husband became estranged or sometimes, separated.

Every classical work has a separate chapter on female horoscopy or **Stri Jataka**. The combinations here cover different aspects of life such as marriage, timing of marriage, nature, appearance and disposition of the female native, personal character and morals of the native, description of the husband and nature of married life. Raja Yogas and combinations for learning, prosperity, lucky progeny etc., and of course, death of husband and widowhood, even combinations for asceticism amongst women are found. With such a comprehensive range of subjects being tackled, if divorce does not find place in this long list, it is simply because divorce just did not exist. A husband died or he deserted his wife, or both husband and wife stayed under the same roof like strangers. Sometimes, a husband might even send away his wife. Combinations like (JPJ, XVI-22) *Balaheenastage pape soumyagrahanireekshite patya visrujyate naari*..... as when a weak malefic planet occupied the 7th and was aspected by a benefic one, the female native would be put away by her husband or as when the Sun was in the 7th, the wife would be cast away (JPJ, XVI-23 *utsrushtaa madanasthite dinakaraha*) or the couple became mutually embittered or the native became a widow if Mars was in the 7th house and many other similar Yogas covered all adverse contingencies in marriage, save divorce. The only instance when something close to a second marriage for a female native was allowed was in the case of *punarbhoo*. This occurred when Lagna or the Moon was owned by Venus and in a Trimsamsa of Saturn (*Lagna bhargavarasige..... punarbhahsieneihi*). This was strictly conditional and occurred also when good and bad planets occupied the 7th house (*Soumya somyayute kalatravane jata punarbhoohu*) but the term *punarbhoo* itself was defined in the texts as when a virgin girl (who had presumably lost her husband) is taken anew as a wife after proper matrimonial rites (JPJ, XVI-20 *Akshatam cha prajaadwaram punarbhoohu samskrutaa punaha*). The condition was too strict to include the case of divorce where the divorced wife today, irrespective of whether the first marriage is consummated or not and whether she has children or not, gets a nearly absolute right to contract a second marriage.

Mars in the 2nd, the 4th, the 7th, the 8th or the 12th from Lagna, the Moon or Venus, was said to cause Kuja Dosha, an affliction which separated spouses or deprived one of a spouse. However, this too did not provide for divorce and covered cases of marital life being disrupted by strife and hostility between spouses.

Divorce was unknown to Hindu law because marriage was regarded indissoluble in this life and extending to after-death. In fact, Manu says "Neither by sale or dissolution can a wife be released from the husband. Let mutual fidelity continue till death." Even otherwise, when divorce was permissible by custom amongst some castes, it did not have the force of law.

It was only in 1955 that the Hindu Marriage Act introduced vital changes in the Hindu Law of Marriage and

Divorce laying down clearly circumstances and grounds in which divorce was permissible. This statutory provision did not bring about any revolutionary changes in social attitudes towards marriage. However, with the passage of time, divorce has now come to be accepted with some reservations, though.

In order to provide for the eventuality of divorce, astrological rules, as found in classical works which do not recognise this contemporary socio-legal solution, need to be interpreted in the light of modern conditions. What amazes one is the far-sighted vision of the Rishis who enunciated the astrological dicta in such a manner as to allow for versatile adaptability to present-day conditions. By a very careful analysis of the different astrological factors related to marriage, factors showing divorce can be identified. It is all a question of careful scrutiny and skilful interpretation.

	Ketu		
Moon	Chart 1 Rasi		
		Sun Merc. Mars	
	Ascdt. Sat.	Venus Rahu	Jupt.

	Rahu	Jupt.	
Moon	Navamsa		
	Ascdt.		
	Mars	Sun Merc. Sat.	Venus Ketu

In Chart 1, the girl got married in February 1981 and the divorce came in August 1983. A typical dowry case, although it did not end in death because the girl acted with pluck and dicided enough was enough when her husband and in-laws started making demands from her father. She left her husband in May 1982 and took a divorce.

In just 14 months of marriage could have driven the girl to divorce, not much can be said for its quality while it lasted. Karaka or the natural significator of marriage is in his own sign Vargottama (being in the same sign in Rasi and Navamsa) but with Rahu. The 7th lord is also Venus, afflicted by the Nodes. The 12th house and 12th lord, Venus again, are afflicted. A malefic Saturn aspects the 7th house.

Marriage

The events occurred in quick succession at the fag end of Jupiter Dasa and the beginning of Saturn Dasa. Jupiter as 2nd lord (Kutumbastanadhipati) is in the 11th hemmed between malefics. The Bhukti lord Rahu is in the 12th with Ketu in the 6th house.

These factors were aided by transit Saturn in Virgo, further adding to the traumatic nature of the incidents of the period. However, because the next Dasa was of a strongly placed Vargottama Saturn (who from the Moon-sign is a benefic), the girl was able to come out of the union easily.

The 7th house from the Moon, Leo, and its lord Sun are afflicted by Mars. The 8th house comes under a Papakartari Yoga caused by the Sun-Mars-Mercury combine on one side and Rahu on the other.

For an indication of divorce in a chart, the first requisite is an unhappy marriage, the exact reason being secondary. An afflicted 7th house or *karaka* Venus shows unhappiness in marriage. Many marriages have, however, survived all kinds of hateful situations and so we cannot stop at this factor alone. The 8th house rules the longevity or duration of a marriage. Afflictions to the 8th house, either from Lagna or the Moon-sign, must also be assessed. Afflictions to the 7th lord or Karaka Venus by Rahu, especially, are a reliable guide to a possible breakdown of marriage.

Mars Ketu	Jupt. Sat.	Merc.			Merc.	Moon	Venus
		Sun		Sat. Rahu			Jupt.
	Chart 2 Rasi				Navamsa		
		Moon Venus		Mars			Ketu
	Ascdt.	Rahu				Sun Ascdt.	

Chart 2 is of an engineer who married in India and was divorced by his wife in the United States after he took her there with him.

The 7th house from the Ascendant has an affliction from Mars-Ketu on one side and Saturn on the other forming a Papakartari Yoga.

The 7th lord Mars is in the 6th, a Dustana (evil house) both with reference to the Ascedant as well as the 7th house. The 8th house from the Moon-sign is afflicted by Mars-Ketu. In Mars Dasa, the wife deserted the husband taking away all his money and jewellery. She took her two children also with her. Unfortunately, for the native, the Dasa lord Mars being also the 2nd lord and in the 6th proved to be terrible. The courts ordered the native to pay his wife and children 75 per cent of his pay as maintenance during the period of litigation. The divorce came in early 1988 after leaving him financially battered and emotionally spent. The period of Saturn's transit through Scorpio was the worst period.

The 8th house which rules *mangalya* is reasonably well-placed and does not indicate death of partner. Jupiter there is helpful in this sense but Mars, the 7th lord, in the 6th and Venus, subject to a Papakartari Yoga caused by the Sun and Rahu, terminated the marriage legally. Jupiter as 6th lord in the 8th and Mars in the 6th as 7th lord show divorce.

Chart 3 is the case of a divorce occurring in the Dasa of an apparently well-placed Kalatrakaraka (significator of marriage) Venus.

The marriage took place in 1976 and the divorce was obtained in 1985. The latter event occurred in Venus Dasa.

Sun	Ascdt. Mars		Ketu Jupt.
Merc.	**Chart 3**		
Venus	**Rasi**		
Rahu	Moon	Sat. (R)	

Sat. (R)			Jupt. Rahu Ascdt.
	Navamsa		Sun Venus
	Ketu	Moon Merc.	Mars

Marriage

The 7th house has an exalted retrograde 11th lord Saturn. The 7th lord Venus has exchanged signs with Saturn. This is not too serious an affliction except that retrograde Saturn as 11th lord in the 7th can indicate more than one marriage which means that under adverse influences the first marriage cannot survive. Coincident with the events was transit Saturn's passage over natal Saturn also marking the beginning of *sadesathe* (or Saturn's seven-and-a-half year transit involving the Moon-sign).

The 8th house from the Lagna has a Papakartari Yoga caused by Rahu and retrograde Saturn. The 8th from the Moon-sign has Jupiter afflicted by the Nodes.

Chart 4 is of a native whose marriage since 1976 was marked by coldness and indifference between both partners until 1987 when it was dissolved legally by mutual consent.

The 7th lord Moon is in close conjunction with Rahu in a constellation ruled by Rahu. The 8th house has Ketu. From the Moon, Ketu afflicts the 7th house and Mars-Saturn, the 8th. Venus, Kalatrakaraka, though in his own sign is under a Papakartari Yoga due to the Sun and Mars-Saturn flanking him on either side. The divorce came about in Saturn Dasa. Saturn in the 8th from the Moon is with Mars.

Whether divorce is destined or brought about by wrong responses to a situation will never find a correct answer. Afflictions to the Karaka and the 7th house do predispose the subject to rather painful reationship. Whether the

Jupt.						Mars	
Moon Rahu	Chart 4 Rasi			Moon	Navamsa		Merc. Sat. Ketu
Ascdt.			Ketu	Sun Rahu			
Merc.	Sun	Venus	Mars Sat.		Venus	Jupt.	Ascdt.

marriage will survive these latent disturbances depends to some extent on the afflictions to the 8th house and to a larger degree, on a combination of adverse Dasas and Gochara (transit influences).

(E) IS MATCHING OF CHARTS NECESSARY?

Any detailed reference to matching charts is conspicuous by its absence in most classical works. An entire chapter, in many of these works, is often devoted to a discussion of the female chart and generally goes by the name *Stri Jataka*. But look for details on how to make a match astrologically and you are more or less stranded.

Jataka Parijata has a lone section *Varavadhujatakasamyoga* under *Adhyaya* XIV which starts with defining Kuja Dosha.

धनावसानरमया१८८ गं
धरासुतो जन्मनि यस्य दारहा।
तथैव कन्याजनन्मलग्नतो
यदि क्षमासूनुनिष्टदः पते: ।।३४।।

meaning,

If Mars occupy the 2nd, the 12th, the 7th, the 4th or the 8th Bhava in the horoscope of a person, he may cause the death of wife. If Mars occupies the same position in the horoscope of the wife to be selected, the planet will prove injurious to the husband.

But, there is no hint of the Dosha's cancellation by any factor. Sloka 37 says —

कलत्रराशित्रितयेथवाऽस्यात्
तदीशसंयुक्तभराशिकोणे।
कलत्रराशिर्यदि पुत्रशीला
तदन्यराशीयदि पुत्रहीन:।।

Marriage

which means,

> If the Janma Rasi (Moon-sign) of the wife be included in the triad designated कलत्रराशि (Kalatra Rasi) or in the triangular signs of the Rasi occupied by the lord of the 7th Bhava in the horoscope of the husband, the latter will have sons. If the Janma Rasi of the wife be other than those that have been enumerated he will have no issue by her. *This part is, of course, open to debate as it again implies the Moon-sign as the ultimate in matching.*

Some light is thrown on matching of charts in Sloka 36 as differentiated from details found in **Kalaprakashika** and other works on Muhurta where the discussion revolves only around *Nakshatra-vichara* or the Moon-signs and constellations of the couple.

Sloka 36 runs as follows:

द्यूनकुटुम्बगतौ यदि पापौ
दारावियोगजदुःखकरौ तौ ।
ताहैशयोगजदारयुतेऽश्चेज्जीवति
पुत्रधनादियुतऽश्च ॥

meaning,

> Malefic planets in the 2nd and the 7th Bhavas are said to bring about bereavement due to loss of wife. If the person be joined in wedlock to a woman born in a Yoga such as this, he is said to live with children, wealth and other blessings.

The results of such a match are पुत्रधनादि युतश्च children, wealth and other signs of good fortune and also, but more important, दारयुतेचज्जीवति — living for long with wife. But as always, results cannot be taken too literally. In the first place, the Yoga talks about bereavement due to death of wife if certain combinations are present in a chart. It then moves on to a clause which also provides the solution. It says the horoscopic deficiency defined can be made good if paired with the chart of a woman which has a similar affliction. Since this is a remedial clause, the remedy should cover the prime affliction in the first place which is bereavement. It is, therefore, an antidote to the problem of loss of partner. Is this antidote potent in the case of all other Doshas too? Does a match between two charts with Dosha ensure perfect happiness?

We may be easily misled into a complacent feeling that since the Doshas are balanced, the couple will live in great harmony and happiness as indicated in the closing part of the Sloka. Far from it, all that the balancing process does is to stall early loss of the mate. It does not improve the quality of the marriage promised in the charts. The following example will show how.

The couple (Charts 1 and 2) married about 8 years ago. They are living together under the same roof but like hostile

	Ketu				Moon Ascdt. Jupt.	Rahu	Mars
	Chart 1 Rasi Wife	Sun			Navamsa		
		Mars Venus Merc.		Sun			Merc.
	Moon Sat. (R)	Rahu	Lagna Jupt.			Ketu	Venus Sat. (R)

		Rahu			Jupt.		Moon Rahu Venus
	Chart 2 Rasi Husband	Sat.			Navamsa		
					Mars		Merc.
	Ketu SunMars. Merc.Ascdt	Moon Venus Jupt.			Ketu	Sat.	Ascdt. Sun

aliens. They do not talk with each other. They cook their food separately.

In the husband's chart, the Nodal axis is spread across the 2nd and 8th houses from Chandra Lagna. In the wife's chart, the axis covers the same houses with reference to the Ascendant. So, there is a similarity in the afflictions in the two charts. This will protect either spouse from dying early which might have been the case if the Doshas had not been balanced. It is only if the results of the malefic Yoga are stalled first that the additional benefits such as children etc., can be enjoyed. That means the basic purpose of this kind of matching is to hold back the danger of *loss of spouse*.

Sloka 34 of Adhyaya XIV covers the 2nd, the 12th, the 7th, the 4th and the 8th houses and has relevance only to Mars occupying these houses and the result is death of wife. Extended to female horoscopes, it invites harm to the husband.

Combining Slokas 34 and 36, the inference is malefics in the 2nd, 4th, 7th, 8th and 12th can lead to the loss of spouse. But if two such charts are paired, the adverse eventuality can be offset.

Dosha means affliction and the results of it are adverse and negative. Does that mean Doshas of any and every kind can be offset by such pairing?

In the wife's chart, the Lagna and the 7th lords are in Dwirdwadasa (mutually adverse positions covering the 2nd and 12th from each other). Further, Mars aspects the 7th house by his 8th house aspect.

In the husband's chart, Mars and Venus as the Lagna and the 7th Lords respectively, are in Dwirdwadasa too. The 7th house is aspected by a combust eclipsed Ascendant lord. These factors have led to absence of harmony between the couple. However, with a change in directional influences, things may improve but always within the broad parameter difined by these afflictions.

When weighing the Dosha content of two charts, the sole purpose would appear to be to ensure a reasonable length of time during which the relationship should endure and not be cut short by the premature loss of one of the parties to the match.

Dosha Samyam becomes relevant only in the context of Mangalya Dosha or coverture. It has nothing to do with the quality of marriage. But it helps, absorbing the tensions some of the afflictions may cause without damaging the infrastructure of the marriage.

Kuta agreement which is so commonly resorted to and relied upon entirely to the exclusion of more important factors by some sections of astrologers seems to do only with mental, psychological and other angles of compatibility that make up the human personality.

If the Moons of the boy and the girl are placed in different constellations, then according to a scale of assessment found in almost all works on Muhurta, the degree of rapport between the pair can be assessed. Where the count is too low, the match may not see much harmony. Viewpoints may differ drastically, attitudes too and, if the rest of the charts so indicate, it can lead to friction while if indicative of harmony, then both parties may be mature enough to respect each others' views and avoid clashing on trifles. The test of Kuta agreement must wait until the other more important aspects of the chart have been thoroughly weighed.

To start with, both charts should have about the same span of life. Where one chart shows Alpayu and the other a very good span of life, in fairness to all concerned, the match cannot be investigated further.

Another important aspect in comparing charts for marriage is to ensure mutual fidelity. No matter what the arguments of the ultra-modern youth or the woman's libber or even the male chauvinist, most of India, why, maybe even 98 per cent of the country, is still anchored in traditional values. Western attitudes and external lifestyles in some major cities emphasizing the pleasure incentive in life are confined only to the novo-rich and thank God, middle class morality has still not slacked its grip on the major chunk of our population. In isolated remote sections of the country, rigid, inhuman mores regulate marriages but they are a negligible fraction. Nevertheless, marriages in India and possibly most parts of the world still seek enduring stability revolving round fidelity.

Marriage

		Ascdt.	Jupt.
Moon	**Chart 3** **Wife** **Rasi**		Mars. Venus Merc Ketu
Rahu			
		Sat.	

	Sun Mars Venus Rahu	Merc.	Moon
Ascdt.	**Chart 4** **Husband** **Rasi**		
Jupt.			Sat.
		Ketu	

This highlights the importance of ensuring in a chart the absence of factors that could influence one to stray away from marital vows and get entangled in extra-marital excursions.

Venus now takes over and a clean Venus is the best thing to have. But this is not always possible and if Venus in both charts is placed in certain ways or influenced by certain factors, then the two charts become capable of catering to each other's appetites and remove the need to seek satiation elsewhere.

Venus influenced by Jupiter is the best bet for a clean conjugal life. Venus with Mars (we are not talking of lordships for the time being) in both charts is a good thing to have.

Jupiter aspectiong the 7th favourably or Saturn influencing it in a constructive sense gives a meagre appetite and when two such people are paired, one can sit back relaxed. Likewise, when Venus is with the Sun or Mars or Rahu or Saturn, subject to the adverse influence of anyone of these planets, one becomes a glutton and has to be paired suitably.

In this pair (Charts 3 and 4) of horoscopes, Venus is heavily afflicted in both charts. The Nodes and Mars afflict Venus and in both, it is the 3rd house from Lagna that is involved. The husband and wife have fighting bouts of such intensity as would put World War II veterans to shame but they make up and continue as before. The husband beats the wife and the wife is no less violent. Once he broke her finger bones and she in turn, broke his back. Anyway, the marriage has literally survived through thick and thin.

Certain simple rules of predictive astrology must also be borne in mind when matching charts. Jupiter's aspect on the 7th house or the 7th lord ensures a reasonably happy and a stable marriage. So also Saturn's and Mars influences, if they are benefics, being either Lagna lord or Yogakaraka and connot be dismissed outright as Doshas.

The 7th lord afflicted by Rahu or the 7th lord in dual signs with serious afflictions indicates more than one marriage. This would automatically imply marriage Number One may not survive for long for any reason, may be due to death of spouse or even divorce (or separation). In such a case, the partner's chart should have a strong 7th and 8th house that can resist the malefic trends indicated in the other chart. And what would make the 7th and 8th houses strong in such a case ? The 7th house (or its lord) should be favorably disposed in trines or Kendras so as to withstand any separation possibilities caused by either legal intervention (influence of the 6th or the 12th lord or houses) or disastrous calamities (influence of the 8th house factors). The longevity of the spouse must be good as to prevent the first marriage terminating through death. So, depending upon the lacunae of one chart, the other chart should be selected so as to be able to overcome the drawbacks of the first chart.

For example, in the chart before us of the boy (Chart 5) the Ascendant lord Venus is exalted in the 11th house, good. The 8th lord Jupiter is in the 12th. No planets are in Kendras. The Moon is full but eclipsed being very close to Ketu. The Sun and Mercury are also eclipsed. Applying other tests too, longevity does not appear to be sound. So, when trying for a match with such a chart, what we will have to do is to look for a girl with a strong Mangalyastana and a sound 7th house that rules out a second marriage and ensures a long marital partnership.

Marriage

Venus Mars	Jupt.	Ascdt.	
			Ketu Moon
Sun Merc. Rahu	\multicolumn{2}{c}{Chart 5 Rasi Husband}	
	Sat.		

	Ascdt.	Merc.	Sun
			Mars Rahu
Ketu Moon	\multicolumn{2}{c}{Navamsa}	Venus
	Sat.	Jupt.	

But unfortunately, the young man of our chart got married to the girl of Chart 6. Not that one chart influenced the other in any sinister manner. Each assessed independently and again, in a mutual sense, did not have the strength to support the weaknesses of the other.

	Mars		
Ketu	\multicolumn{2}{c}{Chart 6 Rasi Wife}	Sun Merc.
Moon			Venus Rahu
Jupt. Sat.		Ascdt.	

	Mars Jupt.	Venus Ketu	
Ascdt. Sun	\multicolumn{2}{c}{Navamsa}	
			Moon Merc.
	Rahu	Sat.	

In the girl's chart, Mars is in the 8th house which is a strong Kuja Dosha factor and he gets no relief here. The 8th from the Moon has Venus afflicted by Rahu. These are Doshas (Mars in the 8th from Lagna and Rahu in the 8th from the Moon) which are said to lead to loss of spouse. And we have seen the boy's chart is weak regarding longevity. So, the girl's chart only seems to confirm what is already apprehended in the boy's chart, without strength to overcome it. And on top of it all, her Jupiter Dasa began just a month after marriage. Jupiter is a malefic no doubt and he is well-placed in Sagittarius, his Moolatrikona sign with Yogakaraka Saturn. Then, how does he become relevant in the context of the afflictions to the 8th house both from Lagna and Chandra Lagna ? Jupiter is with the 4th lord Saturn, and the two are in the 12th from the 4th indicating deprivation of *sukha* or domestic happiness. Especially that the boy's chart does not promise longevity, nothing could be more obvious or plainly logical than loss of husband if the two charts were to be paired. But paired they were in June 1984. The young man who was hale and healthy, collapsed of a massive heart attack in January 1987.

Now, go to the Kuta count and see for yourself how beautifully they match each other. The Moon-signs are in Samasaptaka and applying the usual tests the matching count works out to an excellent 75 per cent or so but to no avail. Kuta agreement then is to be made only after the important factors of longevity and strength of the 7th and 8th houses have been found satisfactory.

Ascdt. Rahu		Mars Jupt.
	Chart 7 Rasi Wife	Moon
		Sun
Sat. (R)	Ketu	Merc. Venus

	Jupt.	Rahu Sun
Merc.	**Navamsa**	Venus
		Sat. Moon
	Ascdt. Ketu Mars	

In the case of the lady (Chart 7), the 7th lord Venus is in the 6th with Mercury aspected by malefics Mars and Saturn. Venus occupies a dual sign and is under Papakartari Yoga. Leaving aside all other factors, this is an indication of more than one marriage. In other words, the first marriage cannot survive, whether for reasons of divorce of death of first partner, the exact reason being of secondary importance. So,

Marriage

the boy's chart should, apart from good longevity, show a stable 7th house if it should be able to stave off the affliction in the lady's chart. Here, the solution of Dosha Samya cannot work. If the girl's chart were to be paired with a boy's chart with similar Dosha (also showing more than one marriage) what purpose would be served by the first marriage except that it would break up to pave the way for the second ?

Venus	Rahu	Moon Jupt.	
Ascdt. Sun Merc. Mars	\multicolumn{2}{c	}{Chart 8 Rasi Husband}	
Sat.		Ketu	

	Moon	Sun Jupt.	
Ketu	\multicolumn{2}{c	}{Navamsa}	Venus
Ascdt.			Rahu
	Merc.	Mars	Sat.

The man (Chart 8) this girl eventually married has the 7th lord Sun with 2 planets, Mercury and Mars and aspected by Saturn from the 11th house. The Karaka Venus is in a dual sign hemmed between malefics Sun-Mars-Mercury on one side and Ketu on the other. This is again a chart indicating more than one marriage. Naturally, after a temptestuous partnership of 16 years or so, the marriage broke-up and the couple divorced. One of the major reasons for the differences between the couple was that neither respected much the marriage-vow of fidelity. What about the Kuta score of nearly 72 per cent ? Did it do nothing to help the couple ? Going by the facts, it obviously did not help much.

In the charts below, both husband and wife show short span of life. The marriage took place in June 1988 and the wife died in 1990.

Another factor, the dreaded Kuja Dosha, which has assumed this status not without valid reasons must be carefully weighed in a compatibility. Most classical works are

	Jupt.	Mars Venus	Rahu
Sat.	\multicolumn{2}{c}{Chart 9 Rasi Wife}	Sun Merc.
Ascdt. Ketu		Moon	

	Ketu	Mars	
Ascdt.	\multicolumn{2}{c}{Chart 10 Husband Rasi}	Sun Merc. Venus Moon
	Sat.	Jupt. Rahu	

agreed on the definition and results of this Dosha. But is it an absolute Dosha or are there factors to cancel it?

Mars in the 2nd, in the 4th and the 12th seems to create high-voltage tension in marriage but in the absence of other disintegrating factors does not generally indicate loss of spouse. On the other hand, Mars in the 7th or the 8th from the Lagna or the Moon or Venus leads to loss of spouse by mostly death, if no other factors obtain to hold such Mars in check. And since the result of the Dosha is death, pairing the chart according to Sloka 36, Adhyaya XIV of **Jataka Parijata** seems to work quite well.

Jupiter's aspect is never without force and holds back Mars Dosha from showing up if he aspects Mars. Jupiter's conjunction with Mars rarely helps. The 5th or the 7th or the 9th house aspect of Jupiter on Mars is a strong protective influence. Saturn's association on the 7th house aspect works equally efficiently. Pairing the two charts that have Mars-Saturn together in one sign or Mars and Saturn in the 7th from each other in both charts removes the evil of Kuja Dosha, even if Mars is in the 7th or 8th house. Mars and Saturn in the 4th and 10th houses from each other also work equally well. There are some exceptions to the rule of Kuja Dosha and these are found in most standard texts and concern the position of Mars in specific signs as cancelling the Dosha.

But one painful truth that has emerged over and over again in the study of horoscope matching is that where the charts of the boy and the girl with similar Dosha (indicating loss of spouse) have been matched, it has resulted in giving about 20 or 25 years or slightly more of marriage and then suddenly erupted. This eruption has always shown up in the female chart more strongly than in the male. Where a female chart has strong combinations for widowhood, such matching has helped to push the tragedy from, say, a few months or one or two years to at least 25 years. Where the astrological indications for widowhood are muted, loss of husband has occurred even say, 50 or 55 years after marriage, but it is always the female chart that has suffered the blow. Why this has happened is not easy to answer and may take us to the theory of Karma and re-birth. Inspite of all the opportunities (leave alone those rare privileged cases) woman may be offered, she has certain distinct disadvantages she must to bear. Perhaps, that is why the subject of loss of spouse is given specific treatment under **Stree Jataka** and a note of caution sounded that great care must be exercised in examining the Mangalya Bhava in the female chart. The woman is always more vulnerable and a prudent father, husband or son will never forget this fact in planning her future. Naturally, the classical wisdom of our seers did not take any chances and emphasised the need to look into this aspect of life more closely and carefully than any other in a woman's chart.

Balancing Dosha is not an absolute remedy and works only where the question of longevity is concerned. It protects one from losing one's partner prematurely by death. It is not a guarantee against unhappiness, infidelity or other problems in marital life although it endows a marriage with the capacity to absorb some of the shocks.

What about the results of children, prosperity and happiness promised by the Sloka ?

Most of us who are acquainted with Puranic literature are aware that, at the end of many chants prescribed by our ancients such as the *Sahasranamas*, *Ashtottari* and other hymns, there is what is known as the *Phalashruti* which promises dazzling benefits should one chant it even once. We know this does not happen in real experience but that does not mean they do not work either. But it is possible the Rishis who discovered or composed these hymns glamourised and exaggerated the results so that devotees stricken with various kinds of physical, mental, spiritual or secular afflictions would take to the chanting with enthusiasm and vigour. Likewise, it appears the other results of prosperity and children may not materialise only by virtue of Dosha Samya unless they are already promised in the chants independently. Otherwise, matching charts would parallel only the sham marriages many people are reported to go through to get a visa abroad. Likewise, charts could be paired only with emphasis on monetary and other material benefits, throwing to the winds the sacred function for which marriage is contracted. There are people who go through marriages only for material considerations but being a Vedic science, astrology and her votaries cannot endorse such mercenary deals.

Matching charts for marriage has its scope and also its limitations. Charts which show loss of spouse within months or a year or two after marriage can benefit from astrological counselling through matching and manage to push the eventuality to a reasonably distant future point of time. Since a chart is bound by Karmic parameters, matching cannot bring about miracles. But it can be an effective tool to fight premature loss of spouse and other problems that occur between spouses. (09-90)

Chapter Nine

Locating Foreign Travel

Travel abroad is no longer an exceptional feat as it used to be in ancient days in India. In fact, at one point of time, why, even as late as about a hundred and fifty years ago, the Sastraic prescription of atonement (*prayaschitta*) for crossing the seas was meticulously undergone by the handful of those who dared to set foot abroad. Orthodoxy frowned on it and those who called themselves ultra-modern were the only ones who dared religious and social ostracism to set foot overseas. Many still long to go abroad but, at least, it is no longer considered a sin to do so. Ask the fresh-from-college youth what he plans to do and, ninety to a hundred, he will tell you, he is looking for opportunities to go abroad and study and work there. It is one of the most natural stages in the academic life of today's ambitious youth. Foreign travel is so common place now that the only barriers which restrict it are economic considerations or lack of opportunities. Socially, it is a prestige issue.

Foreign travel in contemporary life is generally a stroke of good fortune and it is the 9th house or Bhagyastana that can give a clue to it. Sometimes, the 9th ruling *teerthayatras* or pilgrimages is said to be extendable to foreign travel also, since the common feature in both is travel. But this argument does not hold water for, if in the past, crossing the seas was taboo because it was associated with sin, how could then sin be equated with *teerthayatra* or travel to holy spots the very purpose of which was the removal of sin. Moreover, the 9th house is the Dharmastana and travel abroad was generally considered Adharmic since it invited expungatory rites.

Travel abroad can be classified under two distinct heads — occasional or frequent travel overseas and long-term residence abroad. Residence abroad in olden days usually occurred in rather unfortunate circumstances when one was exiled or one fled the country for some reason or the other. *Anyadeshagamana*, as it was called then, was related to the 12th a *dustana* or evil house and carried sinister implications, something in the nature of hopelessness. It was basically associated with adversity or tragic circumstances, since it generally involved separation from kith and kin, financial difficulty and much trial and tribulation and was hence, relegated to the Vyayastana or house of loss.

A few stanzas from **Jataka Parijata** will testify to this definition of foreign residence.

According to Sloka 8, Adhyaya VI, when the lord of the rising sign occupies the 12th Bhava and Mars in conjunction with the Moon is in a malefic sign identical with the 10th Bhava, the person will have to go to a foreign land (*jatasau paradeshagah*) where he may have to live in indigence sacrificing comforts and affluence.

The Ascendant lord in a Dustana (6th, 8th or 12th) is a Dehakasta Yoga and invites for its native bodily suffering, privation, over-exertion and general physical debility. The Kasta Yoga confined to the 12th house is made applicable to residence abroad. It also includes a Moon-Mars Yoga in a malefic sign in the 10th house and this is quite the opposite of an Amala Yoga, which is said to confer good reputation and the results have to be quite contrary implying loss of name, disgrace scandal or loss of social status and therefore, either exile imposed from without or voluntary fleeing.

Another stanza in Adhyaya XI of the same classic says "When the lord of the 12th house from that occupied by the lord of the Lagna is the latter's enemy or is in depression or weak, the person born goes to a foreign country". Here also, the signs involved are not positive and show residence abroad more as an adversity. But this receives some qualification by the nature of the planet influencing the 12th lord from the sign occupied by Lagna lord. If Venus, as a friendly planet, aspects this 12th lord, residence abroad is said to be permanent; if it is the Sun, then residence will be in a small township — if the 12th lord is combust, it could imply a remote place or insignificant town; if, however, the 12th lord is otherwise strong, it could be a metropolis.

Locating Foreign Travel

Travel abroad, if we look at it logically, must involve signs, planets and houses that show movement.

The moveable signs or Chara Rasis Aries, Cancer, Libra and Capricorn, more particularly Cancer since it is a watery sign as well, common signs of Dwiswabhava Rasis Gemini, Virgo, Sagittarius and Pisces, especially the latter two — one being the 9th sign of the Zodiac and the other, the 12th sign as well as watery — and the only other watery but fixed sign Scorpio are important in judging foreign travel and residence.

Of the planets, the Moon, watery and changeable in nature, has an important say in this context.

Of the houses, the 9th and the 12th figure most often in charts showing foreign lands. Sometimes, the 3rd house can also carry some clues because it is related to travel and a planet in it aspects the 9th house linking travel and fortune or more clearly, foreign travel.

Foreign travel always implies coming back home. Foreign residence means making a home outside the country of birth. How do we horoscopically differentiate between these two instances ? Youngsters who go abroad to study also plan career overseas but sometimes, some of them are forced, even if reluctantly, to come back to their countries for lack of suitable opportunities even in the land of opportunity, no matter how hard they try. Some people who go abroad in search of fortune come back frustrated, not alone but with a string of problems trailing them.

A well-placed 9th house (not to overlook a foundationally strong Ascendant) gives travel abroad that brings one success, money and, if the chart warrants it, fame also. In this category, we place successful sportstars, singers, actors and such other celebrities who have an aura of glamour about them.

The Ascendant lord Mars in Chart 1 is in the 3rd house, an Upachaya, and therefore, favorable, with the 3rd lord Mercury and Ketu. The 3rd rules physical prowess, valour, sport. Here, it assumes the tone of an Upachaya or house of elevation and not a Leenastana (house of deterioration) because it is occupied by Lagna lord in a strong constellation with its sign-dispositor also there. The chart also derives

	Ascdt.	Venus Sun	Merc. Ketu Mars
			Jupt.
Moon	Chart 1 Rasi		
Rahu		Sat. (R)	

		Moon Sat. Rahu	
Mars			
Venus	Navamsa		
			Sun
	Merc. Ketu		Ascdt. Jupt.

strength from a powerful 10th house Moon, exalted 9th lord aspecting 10th, exalted 10th and 11th lord aspecting Lagna and Venus, occupying own sign. This replendent array of planetary position has made the native a world class badminton player.

In February 1970, just months after Rahu Dasa began, the native made his mark as junior national champion. Rahu in the 9th is, no doubt, not bad but here because he occupies the powerful sign Sagittarius whose lord Jupiter, in turn, is exalted in the 4th house, he becomes positively favourable. In Setptember 1972, the native participated and won in international tournaments that put him on top of the world in badminton. This period saw him leave the country for the first time and thereafter, countless times. The first time he went abroad was in Jupiter Bhukti. The Dasa lord Rahu is in the 9th aspected by well-placed 3rd lord Mercury. The Bhukti lord Jupiter is the 9th and 12th lord in watery Cancer aspected by the watery Moon, and influencing the 10th house winning for the native international fame, huge prize monies and celebrity status. Rahu Dasa throughout was spotted with foreign trips.

The 4th house, we may note, is aspected by the 4th lord Moon. The 12th lord Jupiter occupies the 4th house. From Chandra Lagna (the Moon-sign), the 4th house is aspected by exalted Chandra Lagna lord. These factors focussing on the 4th house did not allow the native to leave the country for good.

Generalizing but with a wide margin for exceptions, usually a strong connexion between the Lagna, Lagna lord

Locating Foreign Travel

and the 4th house or 4th lord shows, if other factors are present, foreign journeys but residence in the country of birth. The 12th lord in the 4th shifts the emphasis from the 12th to the 4th and therefore, residence in one's own country. On the other hand, the 4th house or 4th lord influenced by 12th house factors with the focus on the 12th make the native spend a large part of his life overseas. The Lagna lord in the 12th or with the 12th lord or 12th lord in Lagna is a strong factor showing residence abroad.

Sun Merc.	Ascdt.	Ketu Mars	
Venus	_ **Chart 2** **Rasi**		
	Rahu Sat.		Jupt. Moon

Mars		Ascdt.	Venus
Jupt.	**Navamsa**		Moon Merc. Rahu
Sat. Ketu			Sun

In Chart 2, the Ascendant is again Aries and it is not influenced by any planet. Mars, its ruler, is in a fixed sign Taurus aspected by Saturn. The native is a research scientist in a European country and his chances of coming back to India for good are practically non-existent. Occasional visits home are not ruled out, though.

The 9th lord and 12th lord Jupiter influences the 4th lord Moon from the 6th. The 4th lord is made full and thereby powerful by the Sun from the 12th. The 3rd lord Mercury is in the 12th. The 4th lord strongly related to the 12th house has given him long term residence abroad.

The native went abroad in the closing years of Rahu Dasa unlike in the previous case. Rahu is in a watery sign Scorpio and in the constellation of 9th and 12th lord Jupiter. Since the sign involved is fixed, the house involved is the 8th, and the aspect is from a fixed sign in the 2nd (both houses having nothing to do with foreign travel), the opportunity to go abroad could come only at the fag end of Rahu Dasa.

The luck factor and the 9th house have a direct bearing on all foreign travel undertaken in happy circumstances. But if adverse houses are involved, one may leave the country in traumatic circumstances. A case in point (Chart 3) is of Albert Einstein. Hounded by the Nazis for his 'un-German' behaviour and exiled from the country with a price on his head, Einstein had an exceedingly powerful chart, nevertheless.

Sun, Merc. Venus Sat.			Ascdt.
Jupt.			Ketu
Rahu Mars	Chart 3 Rasi		
	Moon		

	Rahu Ascdt.		
Moon Mars Venus	Navamsa		Sun
	Jupt.	Sat.	Merc. Ketu

Mars Dasa, Jupiter Bhukti was running when Einstein left Germany, the country of his birth, where he was being persecuted by the Third Riech. Mars is a first-rate malefic for Gemini Ascendant made worse by his occupation of the 8th house afflicted by Rahu. If Rahu had not been in the 8th, the 6th lord Mars (in his own Dasa) in the 8th would have been quite a comfortable disposition. But Rahu has spoilt Mars and the 8th house being involved, humiliating treatment forced Einstein to leave the country of his birth. Jupiter as the 7th lord (Badhaka) is not a benefic but occupying the 9th, does not rule out foreign travel. Transit Saturn in Sagittarius also added to this malefic conflagration by his affliction to natal Moon. With the result, Einstein had to flee to the United States. The rest of the chart being very powerful, this circumstance in his life turned out to be a blessing in disguise. Einstein joined the Princeton University where he made his world-shaking discovery to become one of the most eminent scientists of the century.

Locating Foreign Travel

The Ascendant lord Mercury is in the 10th in a watery sign with exalted 12th lord Venus, 9th lord Saturn and 3rd lord Sun. Einstein did not return to his country of birth even after the war but preferred to stay on in the free atmosphere of the US.

The native of Chart 4 got an opportunity to go abroad in 1985. Since 1978, he had been facing a frustrating period in finding a good job. So, when the offer came, he was sure that meant the end of all his problems.

Venus Rahu			
Sun	Chart 4 Rasi		Sat.
Merc.			Mars Ascdt.
Jupt. Moon	Ketu		

Sun, Ascdt. Moon Mars Venus		Keut Jupt.	
Sat	Navamsa		
	Rahu		Merc.

This was in Saturn Bhukti of Moon Dasa. Saturn, a malefic, is in the 12th house and the Moon is the 12th lord himself. In 1986, however, a fresh set of problems overtook the native and he was forced to return to India in 1987 with no savings whatsoever.

The Lagna lord Sun is in the 7th in a fixed sign aspected by 4th and 9th lord Yogakaraka Mars form a fixed sign.

In this case, the sinister implications of the 12th house have surfaced. The 12th lord is, no doubt, in a powerful sign but in a cuspal degree. The 12th house is occupied by malefic Saturn.

The 9th lord Mars is in the Lagna. The 9th house is occupied by 10th lord Venus and Rahu which is not too bad. But if we have to understand why things did not work well for the native, we have to look at the Dasas. The Dasa is of the Moon who as 12th lord is qualified to give foreign travel. But being weak in a cuspal degree, he does not have enough strength to support the results he generates. In addition, Saturn in transit was in the first stage of his seven-and-a-half year cycle over natal Moon who, in this case, is also the Dasa lord. No wonder then if the Moon was unable to help the native to consolidate his position overseas.

The 9th house suffers from a weak 9th lord and a Nodal affliction which limit its potential for providing good opportunities abroad.

Combinations for travel abroad are not the only determinants. The proper Dasas at the proper time are equally important before one can take off successfully to a foreign country. Adverse Dasas and transit periods, even if indicative of foreign travel, indicate problems and frustrating results overseas. These factors must be kept in mind before finalizing a journey abroad. (09-89)

Chapter Ten

Careers

Chapter Ten

Careers

(A) MARS AND WORKING WOMEN

Every classical work on astrology has an entirely separate section devoted to **Stree Jataka** or female horoscopy. Women were always thought to have distinctly separate roles in life from men. The fields of activity of the two sexes seldom overlapped. This was especially so amongst the more affluent classes as also the upper classes in the sense of Varnas.

Man was the bread winner. He worked at home or outside. Intellectual, commercial or manual labour of the kind that could fetch returns was his prerogative. The women's world was home, spelt in capital letters. She did work but it was confined to the home base. Whether the work involved was physical like cooking, rearing the children, cleaning and other household chores or intellectual or rather mental, like teaching the children their lessons or the three Rs or cultivating literary, aesthetic or other allied interests was not material. Sometimes in the economically poorer sections, the areas of work of the two overlapped but it was mostly on one side. Perhaps, depending upon whether the man was a farmer, potter, blacksmith, the woman also helped in the fields or in the occupation of her husband. But here, her role was only in a secondary capacity. Woman was less ambitious then than her present day sister. She derived great contentment in discharging her part of the family responsibility. *But frankly, it was not a question of exploitation of one sex by the other.* True, there were some cases, but they were rare exceptions and few and far in between. *Woman was primarily the shock-absorber of the family* and, whether it was recognised or not, *her qualities of endurance and tolerance gave a solid and sound foundation to the unit of family.*

Yogas for success and attainment found in *Stree Jataka* were attributed in the majority of cases to the husband. This did not necessarily imply women had a secondary or subordinate status to man in society. All that it did suggest was the existing facts and conditions of those times, where, by and large, roles were compartmentalised.

In Chapter XVI of **Jataka Praijata** Vaidyanatha Dikshita says in *Stree Jatakadhyaya*

अर्थार्जने सहायः पुरुषाणामापदर्णवे।
यात्राकाले मन्त्री जातकमापहाय नास्त्यपरः।।

meaning,

> There is nothing in the world like a horoscope to help men in the acquisition of wealth, to save them like a boat in a sea of troubles and to serve them as a guide in their journeys.

The term horoscope or *jataka* in this context implies the female horoscope. All that this 15th century scholar was saying was *behind every successful man there was a woman or rather, a woman's horoscope.*

Two Slokas later, he comes up with a seemingly contradictory statement:

स्त्रीणां जन्मफले नृत्योग्यमुदितं यत्ततपौ

meaning,

> Whatever affects may accrue from the horoscopes of females that is applicable only to men, should be ascribed to the husband

which can startle many of us. Was he hinting that women could not achieve anything ? Was he saying women could have no careers ? Far from it. He was talking only about the majority of women. For a couple of Slokas later, he talks of Yogas that make women learned and great and wield power.

Says he:

चन्द्रास्तगृहोपगः शुगकरो राज्यास्पदं यच्छति

meaning,

> if the planet in the 7th Bhava from the Moon be auspicious, the Yoga will secure to her sovereign authority (a royal domain) and later,

चन्द्रे कर्कटकोदये च बलिभिः शुक्राज्ञजीवेन्दुभिः ।
नानाशास्त्र कलारसज्ञाचतुरा विख्यातते जस्विनी ।।

that is,

> when the Moon occupies Cancer identical with the Aacendant and when all the benefics, Venus, Jupiter, Mercury and the Moon are powerful, the female born will be highly learned in many sciences and arts, and will be famous for her spiritual powers.

Again,

कामस्थैरथवा विलग्नभवनार्द्धमास्थितैः खेचरै
प्रव्रज्यामुपयाति ।।

meaning,

> when a male planet is in the 7th Bhava, the female concerned will devote herself to asceticism corresponding to the planets, if any, in the 9th Bhava.

These lines clearly underscore the fact that *women ruled and also shone as intellectuals in ancient India*. The difference, may be, lies in that their number was less compared to the number of women with careers today. But an honest appraisal of figures will show the percentage of working women, then and now, is about the same. It may seem like we have more women with vocations now, but actually, it is because improved communications and media have been responsible for publicizing the fact of working women. Most of rural India has only housewives and many of them too are working women, even if unofficially. It is only in the big cities that women work and their number is infinitesimally dismal compared to the total population of the country. If working women seem to have multiplied, so also has the population shot up leaving the percentage of such women quite low.

The justification of setting apart a separate chapter to female horoscopes was only to cover the exceptions amongst women. To most women today, as also then, final fulfilment lies in running a household than in pursuing a career. Psychologically it is a pursuit that gives them emotional satisfaction.

In Stree Jataka, we are told that combinations applicable to women are to be scrutinized at the time of marriage. Contemporary requirements of horoscopic analysis for marriage now carry the additional burden of determining if the horoscope shows a working woman. Today, many eligible men seem to prefer working girls for partners. With the cost of living spiralling up at an astronomical rate, this is perfectly understandable.

What features indicate a career woman in a chart ? What makes a woman continue her vocational life even after marriage ?

Chart 1: Born 19-3-1942 at 15h. 15m. (IST) at 13° N, 77° E 35' with a balance of 4 years, 5 months and 16 days of Ketu Dasa at birth.

Sun	Moon	Jupt. Mars Sat.	
Merc. Ketu	Chart 1 Rasi		Lagna
Venus			Rahu

	Sat. (R)	Ketu	Jup.
Merc.	Navamsa		Moon
	Mars Ven. Sun Lagna	Rahu	

Careers

A powerful 10th house indicates a career. A working woman has to face more challenges than a man. This would necessitate a powerful Lagna or at least, a powerful Moon.

A study of a few charts of women whose careers have been remarkable can throw up some enlightening clues.

The native of Chart 1 is a medical doctor. The Ascendant is Cancer with its ruler Moon in the 10th house in a powerful Kendra. The Lagna lord is exalted in Navamsa and Dasamsa. The native is also working for her doctoral degree. The Moon-sign is also strong with its dispositer being in Vargottama (occupying the same sign in Rasi and Navamsa). The 10th house has the Lagna lord in it while the 10th lord Mars is in the 11th (Upachaya) with 9th lord Jupiter.

In Chart 2, of a medical officer, Aries rises with its ruler Mars in the 5th, a trine. The Moon occupies a Kendra in his own sign in Vargottama.

Chart 2: Born 3/4-8-1929 at 0-30 (IST) at 10 N 10, E 10 with a balance of 3 years, 7 months and 20 days of Jupiter Dasa at birth.

	Rahu	Jupt.	Ven.
			Moon Sun Merc.
	Chart 2		
			Mars
Sat. (R)		Ketu	

	Sat. (R)	Ketu	Jupt.
Mars			Moon
	Navamsa		
	Mars Venus Sun	Rahu	

The 10th lord is in the 9th in a strong sign, Sagittarius, and the 10th house is aspected by as many as 3 planets.

Chart 3 is of an Italian actress with a fan following all over the world. Born in the slums of a small town Naples in Italy, she had an impoverished childhood and often went without food for many days.

Chart 3: Born 20-9-1934 at 2-10 p.m. (CET) at Naples, with a balance of 3 years, 9 months and 2 days of Mars Dasa at birth.

							Rahu	
	Chart 3 Rasi		Ketu Mars		Sun	Navamsa		
Moon Rahu Sat.			Venus		Sat. Mars			Merc. Lagna
Lagna		Jupt.	Merc. Sun		Ketu Jup.			Moon Venus

The Lagna is a powerful sign Sagittarius with the ruler Jupiter in the 11th in an Upachaya (house of elevation).

The Moon-sign or Chandra Lagna is Capricorn with the Moon there joining Saturn in Vargottama and as his sign dispositor. The Moon is also aspected by Mars who gets Neechabhanga (cancellation of debility) strength by reason of Jupiter (who exalts in Cancer) occupying a Kendra from the Moon.

A typical case of the rags-to-riches story, the native is said to be an extremely hard-working actress with a strong sense of perfection. Notable is the fact that the husband is an internationally reputed film director. Going by classical texts, the Yogas (none of them has been identified here) in the chart should apply to the husband. What draws the native also into the orb of influence of these Yogas is a strong Ascendant *cum* Moon-sign.

We may note here, in passing, that Mars aspects the Lagna lord Jupiter and the Moon. The Lagna lord is himself in Chitta, a constellation ruled by Mars. Perhaps, the Martian connection is essential for the individuality of a native to fight through and find an independent niche for itself in this world.

Going back to Charts 1 and 2, the Martian influence is not to be missed. Chart 1 has the Moon in a Martian sign and the 10th lord is Mars. The 10th lord from the Moon, namely Saturn, joins Mars.

In Chart 2, the rising sign is Aries. The 10th house from the Moon-sign is also Aries. Can we, therefore, conclude that Mars influencing the Ascendant, the Moon or the 10th house or their respective lords in any manner, whatsoever, indicates a career woman ?

Let us take the case (Chart 4) of a South Indian singer, internationally famous. She is known for her docility. Her own daughter says of her 'Mother was never cut out to be independent'. The native's music is so spell-binding that once even Mahatma Gandhi was moved to tears by her rendering of *bhajans*. Her concerts have fetched fabulous amounts all of which have been given away in charity.

Chart 4: Born 16-9-1916 at 9-30 a.m. at 13 N 05, 80 E 18 with a balance of 5 years, 10 months and 9 days of Sun Dasa at birth.

	Jupt. (R) Moon		
			Sat. Ketu Venus
	Chart 4 Rasi		
Rahu			
		Mars Lagna	Sun Merc.

		Lagna	
Rahu Mars		Navamsa	
	Sun		Jupt. (R) Ketu Sat.
	Moon	Venus	Merc.

Libra, the Ascendant, is occupied by Mars and aspected by 10th lord Moon and Jupiter. The Lagna lord Venus is in the 10th. The Moon-sign lord or Chandra Lagna lord Mars aspects it, so also Saturn. The 10th house has Lagna lord Venus, Yogakaraka Saturn and Ketu.

Mars influences the Lagna, the Moon as well as the 10th lord.

She is the perfect anti-thesis of today's liberated woman. Yet, she has been more successful in her career than any of her more liberated, assertive contemporaries.

We would be surely doing injustice to the wonderful womanfolk our country has produced if we do not take a look into the chart (Chart 5) of our late prime minister Mrs. Indira Gandhi who eclipsed all the men around her with her political skills.

Chart 5: Born 19-11-1917 at 11-30 p.m. (IST) at 25 N 27, 81 E 51 with a balance of 1 year, 3 months and 25 days of Sun Dasa at birth.

		Jupt. (R)	Ketu		Moon Lagna		Jupt.	
	Chart 5 Rasi		Sat. Lagna			Navamsa		Rahu
Moon			Mars		Sat. Ketu			Sun
Venus Rahu	Merc. Sun					Merc.		Mars

The Lagna is aspected by Lagna lord Moon and the Moon-sign is aspected by its sign-disposiṭer Saturn. The 10th lord Mars is in the 2nd in exchange of signs with 2nd lord Sun. The 10th house is Aries, a Martian sign. There are a host of strong points in this chart to explain the great heights of political success the native achieved in her career but that is not our concern. We are concentrating only on those factors that give enduring careers, irrespective of the quality and nature of success accompanying them.

Yet another example of an outstanding career women with an impeccable record for excellent discharge of duty is of Queen Elizabeth, the II (Chart 6).

The Lagna in Chart 6 is Capricorn. It is occupied by an exalted Mars in Parivartana (exchange of sign) with Lagna lord Saturn in the 11th. The Moon aspects Lagna from his

Chart 6: Born 21-4-1926 at 1-40 p.m. (GMT) at 0 W 06, 51 N 31.

Venus Merc.	Sun		Rahu
Jupt.	Chart 6 Rasi		Moon
Lagna Mars			
Ketu	Sat.		

			Rahu Sun
	Navamsa		Sat.
Lagna Venus Moon			
Ketu		Venus Jupt.	

own sign rendering himself strong by a reciprocal aspect from exalted Yogakaraka Mars. The 10th lord Venus is exalted with 9th lord Mercury. Looking at the picture from Chandra Lagna, the 10th house Aries has an exalted Sun with its ruler Mars aspecting it in exaltation.

In all these cases, we notice **Stree Jataka** rules relating to marriage, children, husband and widowhood apply. But rules beyond the ken of *Stree Jataka* also work on these charts. Astrological rules, even if some of them were earmarked for women only, apply equally well to both sexes. No matter what the changes wrought by the times in social life and conditions, astrological dicta apply with an amazing universality. Although the oldest of applied sciences, astrology is also the most modern in application. It is a holistic science aimed to help one (man or woman) make one's life happier and find fulfilment. Women and men both stand to benefit immensely from a careful pursuit of astrology. (04-87)

(B) MEDICAL PROFESSION

The purpose of a doctor is to heal. In Sanskrit, the terms *bhishaj* (भिषज), *vaidyaha* (वैद्य:), *chikitsakaha* (चिकित्सक:), *angadakarakaha* (अंगदकार:), *sastragna* (शास्त्रज्ञ), *jeevadah* (जीवद:), and *rogaharin* (रोगहरिन्), all mean a doctor generally.

Etymologically, they are derived from different roots but in essence imply one who heals. Just as Varahamihira prescribed certain qualifications for an astrologer, so did Charaka draw a list of qualities that make one a doctor.

The **Charaka Samhita** is a work of great antiquity. It is a voluminous treatise on Ayurveda or the science of life. It is believed to have come down to us from Maharishi Atreya. The text is said to have been compiled by the Sage Agnivesa. The volume as available to us today is the revised version edited by Charaka and Dridhabala.

The introductory chapter tells us that disease is to be avoided because it is considered an impediment to the goal of human life. Birth as human is a rare gift and is to be utilised only for the realization of the Ultimate Truth. "When diseases arose like so many impediments to the austerity, fasting, study, continence and vows of embodied souls, the great sages — the doers of good — feeling compassion for creatures foremost, met together on the sacred slopes of the Himalayas .... " is how the origins of Ayurveda took shape. The sages meditated in their search for a means to ameliorate human suffering. They saw Indra, the king of the Devas (goas), in their minds' eye. They resolved to learn the science of life from Indra who had acquired it from the Aswinikumaras or the Divine twin-physicians.

Sage Bharadwaja approached Indra on behalf of the other Rishis and learnt it from him. Thereafter he taught it to all the other sages of his day "without either adding or withholding any part". And so, from master to disciple, the science changed hands generation after generation until it came to us in its present form as the **Charaka Samhita.**

This science is described as "the most meritorious of all the sciences because it teaches mankind what constitutes their good in both the worlds". This was how the science of medicine was understood by the Hindus. Herein was laid what was wholesome for life and what was not. It was compassion for fellow humans that gave birth to this science.

Modern medicine is a far cry from this definition. And about doctors today, perhaps, with some exceptions, the less said the better. A doctor, according to the Samhita, must possess "a clear grasp of theoretical knowledge, wide practical experience, skill and purity of body and mind". Contrast this with what makes one a successful doctor today — a degree, financial backing and political clout. Compassion is something unheard of with this tribe.

The qualifications of a patient are also enumerated as "recollection, obedience to instructions, courage and ability to describe his ailments". Whether he could pay fat bills during and after the treatment, unlike today, was of no consequence. Of the physician's conduct, it was said "Friendship towards all, compassion for the ailing, devotion to curable patients and a sense of resignation towards the dying constitute the four-fold nature of the physician's profession". Unfortunately today, save for a handful of dedicated medical students and doctors, universities churn out medicos in hundreds every year who are more qualified to run nursing homes by their business acumen than by their humaneness and medical skills. This brings us to the point. When looking for a medical career in a chart today, it is futile to look for combinations that show mercy, compassion and devotion to the ailing. We must look for other combinations.

Clues to which planets have a significant bearing on the medical profession are found scattered in some of our Puranic stories.

It is believed Ayurveda was first obtained by Daksha-prajapati from the Creator Brahma. The Aswinikumaras received it from Daksha and later taught it to Indra.

The constellation Aswini is ruled by the Aswini twins. We also know Ketu rules Aswini and that he exalts in Scorpio. He is comfortable in this sign ruled by Mars. Mars also rules Aries. Mars, in turn, is associated with fevers, cuts, wounds, knives, metallic appliances etc. Therefore, Ketu, Scorpio, Aswini and Mars become relevant to our study. Because of Ketu, we include Rahu also who rules all kinds of potions, poisons and chemicals.

A few examples will help us get a better perspective of the whole point.

Chart 1: Born 11-6-1956 at 9-57 p.m. (IST) at 18 N 31, 73 E 55 with a balance of 12 years, 4 months and 17 days of Saturn Dasa.

		Sun Merc. (R) Rahu	Venus (R)
Mars	Chart 1 Rasi RP 90/83		Moon
Lagna			Jupt.
	Sat. (R) (Ketu)		

Lagna Merc.		Jupt. Rahu	
Venus	Navamsa		
			Sat.
	Ketu		Sun Moon

Three Vargas are important to us — Rasi, Navamsa and the Dasamsa, the last being the relevant Varga for looking into all matters related to career and vocation. Navamsa is important because it is rated *on par* with the Rasi by all classical writers.

In Chart 1, the Moon aspects Lagna from Cancer, which has an unquestionable link with healing. As the 4th sign of the zodiac, it rules the roost, the place where one finds ultimate security and protection from an hostile world. It shows the home, where one retreats for solace and recovery against external afflictions. In this sense, Cancer also sweeps within its ambit, places or people that aid in recovering one's health, mental or physical, and this would include doctors, nurses, nursing homes and hospitals. The Moon governs all life and under him come herbs and *aushadhis* or medicine. The Moon is also, therefore, important to us, especially in relation to the sign Cancer.

What do doctors have to contend against ? Disease and death. Naturally, that brings Karaka Saturn into the picture. For this, not only do they need weapons (instruments) and grit but also skill to deal with cuts, wounds and fevers — all these coming under Mars. Therefore, a Mars-Saturn nexus emerges. It may be onesided or mutual, preferably mutual, but nevertheless imperative.

Going back to Chart 1, Scorpio is powerful with Lagna lord there and also Ketu. The sign Cancer is prominently placed. The 10th lord is Venus and he occupies Gemini in Aridra ruled by Rahu.

From Chandra Lagna (the Moon-sign), the 10th is Aries, a Martian sign and its ruler occupies Satabhisha ruled by Rahu again. Mars and Saturn are in mutual Kendras (quadrants).

In the Navamsa, the 10th lord Jupiter joins Rahu. Mars aspects Saturn. In Dasamsa[1], the Ascendant has Ketu in it and Mars aspects both Lagna, Lagna lord Jupiter and also the 10th. Mars-Saturn are in mutual aspect.

Chart 2: Born 28-10-1952 at 4.30 a.m. (IST) at 15 N 20, 75 E 12.

	Jupt. (R)		
Moon	Chart 2 Rasi G VIII/92		Ketu
Rahu			
Mars	Merc. Venus	Sun	Lagna Sat.

		Lagna	
Ketu	Navamsa		Merc.
			Rahu
Sun			
	Venus Moon Jupt. (R)		Sat. Mars

In Chart 2, the 10th lord Mercury is in the 3rd in Scorpio. He joins Venus. Mars aspects the 10th house. Mars and Saturn are in mutual Kendras.

From the Moon-sign, the 10th is Scorpio occupied by Mercury and Venus. The 10th lord Mars is in Poorvashada

---

[1]D-10 of Chart 1: Sagittarius — Ascendant and Ketu; Aries — Mercury (R); Taurus — the Moon; Gemini — Rahu and Mars; Virgo — Saturn and Jupiter; and Libra — the Sun and Venus (R).

ruled by Venus. In Navamsa, Mercury (the 10th lord in Rasi) is in Cancer. The sign Scorpio is strengthened by three planets there which includes Venus. Mars-Saturn joins the 5th.

Ketu-Rahu influence Scorpio in the Dasamsa[2] and Mars is in the 10th aspecting Lagna. Lagna lord and 10th lord Mercury join Cancer.

Chart 3: Born 19-3-1942 at 3-45 p.m. at 13 N, 77 E 35 with a balance of 4 years, 5 months and 16 days of Ketu Dasa.

Sun	Moon	Moon Sat. Jupt.	
Ketu Merc.	Chart 3 Rasi G VIII 184		Lagna
Venus			Rahu

Lagna	Ketu	Moon Mars	
	Navamsa		Jupt.
Sat. Merc.			Venus Sun
		Rahu	

In Chart 3, Lagna is Cancer and the 10th, Aries, with the Lagna lord Moon there in Aswini. There is a Mars-Saturn combination in the Rasi. The 10th house from the Moon is occupied by Venus and the 10th lord Saturn joins Mars. The 10th lord Mars joins the Moon in Navamsa. In the Dasamsa[3] Lagna has Venus, Ketu-Rahu influence the 10th house and Lagna lord Jupiter is in Cancer.

Chart 4 has Cancer as the 10th sign with the Moon and Ketu there. From Chandra Lagna, the 10th is Aries whose lord Mars joins Venus in Pisces. Cancer and Scorpio being

---

[2] **D-10 of Chart 2**: Virgo — Ascendant; Scorpio — Jupiter (R) and Ketu; Sagittarius — Venus; Aquarius — the Sun and Saturn; Aries — Moon; Tarus — Rahu; Gemini — Mars; and Cancer — Mercury.

[3] **D-10 of Chart 3**: Sagittarius — Ascendant and Venus; Capricorn — Saturn; Pisces — Rahu; Taurus - the Moon, Mars and Mercury; Cancer — Jupiter; Virgo - Ketu; and Scorpio — the Sun.

Chart 4: Born 31-1-1953 at 0-30 a.m. (IST) at 13 N, 77 E 35, with a balance of 3 years, 0 month and 22 days of Mercury Dasa.

Venus Mars	Jupt.			Lagna Moon		Merc.	Sun
Sun Merc. Rahu	Chart 4 Rasi G. VII L		Moon Ketu		Navamsa		Rahu Mars
				Ketu			Venus
		Lagna Sat.			Sat.	Jupt.	

closely related to medicine, their trinal sign Pisces can also be taken into account. What is more, Pisces by itself, also rules hospitals and nursing homes amongst other things. Mars aspects Saturn.

In Navamsa, the Moon (lord of the 10th in Rasi) is in Pisces. Cancer is emphasised by the Nodes and Mars there. Dasamsa[4] Lagna is aspected by a Scorpio-influenced Mars-Saturn combine. The 10th lord in Dasamsa joins the Moon.

We have seen in this sample study Venus has a dominant role in the charts of medical men. Classical works do not carry many combinations for doctors. Of the few found in them, Venus is included in most. This can be traced to Venus being Sukra or Bhrigu who, according to the **Puranas**, was the preceptor of the *Asuras*. It is said, in those times, the *devas* and the *asuras* were involved in endless wars, each claiming supremacy over the other. Countless numbers died in these wars but the *asuras* always rose up with renewed vigour. Their preceptor, Sukracharya, knew the science of life, the art of reviving the dead. Every time there was a war,

---

[4]**D-10 of Chart 4**: Virgo — Ascendant; Scorpio — Ketu and Jupiter; Sagittarius — Venus; Aquarius — Sun and Saturn; Aries — Moon; Taurus — Rahu; Gemini — Mars; and Cancer — Mercury.

Sukracharya would work on the dead and the maimed *asuras*, and with his secret knowledge bring them back to life. As a result, the *devas* continually dwindled in numbers. They were now panicky. Not only were the *asuras* invincible but also in colossal numbers. So, they devised a strategy. They prevailed on Kacha, the son of their own mentor Brihaspati, to learn the secret art from Sukracharya. Kacha, disguised as a student, went to the *asura*-master and expressed a desire to learn at his feet. He soon won over Sukracharya with his exemplary conduct and succeeded in ferreting out the secrets of life and death. This is how Sukracharya of the **Puranas** and Sukra (Venus) of Jyotisha became associated with doctoring.

There are a few more charts here that will emphasize the role of Venus in a medical career.

Chart 5: Born 8-3-1956 at 3-23 p.m. (IST) at 28 N 51, 78 E 49 with a balance of 0 year, 8 months and 3 days of the Sun Dasa.

	Venus	Ketu			Lagna Moon		Merc.	Sun
Sun Merc.	Chart 5 Rasi G VII 66		Lagna			Navamsa		Rahu Mars
Moon			Jupt. (R)		Ketu			Venus
Mars	Sat. Rahu					Sat.	Jupt.	

The Lagna Cancer is aspected by its lord Moon in Chart 5. The 10th is occupied by Venus who is in Aswini. The 10th lord Mars is in the 6th in a constellation ruled by Venus. Scorpio has a Neechabhanga Rahu in it. In Dasamsa[5],

---

[5]D-10 of Chart 5: Virgo — Ascendant; Libra — Sun and Saturn; Scorpio — Moon; Capricorn — Rahu; Pisces — Mercury; Aries — Mars; Gemini — Venus; Cancer — Ketu; and Leo — Jupiter.

Mars-Saturn are in mutual aspect while Lagna lord Mercury is in Pisces. Venus is in the 10th.

Combinations found in classical works can also be explored with success.

For instance, in **Jataka Tatwa**, it is said Rahu and the Sun conjoined with a benefic and also with a malefic when occupying a Navamsa of the Atmakaraka planet, make the native a doctor dealing in (the art of) cure of poison. Another Sutra says if the Navamsa occupied by the Atmakaraka planet be aspected by Mercury, the Moon and Venus, or if the 2nd lord occupy the 7th, the person concerned will be a physician. According to the next one, if the Navamsa mentioned above be aspected by Venus and the Moon, the native will be an alchemist. An alchemist is not a doctor really, but we could include anaesthetists and pathologists also under it but with suitable modifications of these planetary equations. According to Jaimini, Rahu in Karakamsa makes one eke out his livelihood by Dhanurvaidya or as druggist and alchemy is indicated by the Moon occupying the Karakamsa aspected by Venus. When an Amsa of Mars is occupied by the 10th lord from Lagna, the Moon or the Sun, (*Dhatwagniprahara nasahasih*) one earns his livelihood from metals, cooking and all sorts of action in connection with fire, from bravery and using weapons. Surgery is skill in handling implements and instruments on the human body. That is, one may be a surgeon in such a case provided other combinations indicate the medical profession. According to Varahamihira, the Sun, being the ruler of the Navamsa occupied by the 10th lord, makes one's avocation relate to drugs and practice of medicine (*Bhaishaja*).

Apart from the planetary inter-relationships that we have discussed above, we may also make a note of the Sun-Rahu combination for doctors. A Mars-Rahu and the Moon-Rahu association also produces medical men.

In this case of a doctor who had also a world-wide reputation, Mars, the Sun and Rahu combine in the 10th in Chart 6. The 10th being Cancer and its ruler, the Moon, joining Saturn (masses), the native was moved to take up a medical

Chart 6: Born 6-8-1906 at 12-38 p.m. (LMT) at 17 N 46, 83 E 17 with a balance of 6 years, 11 months and 8 days of Rahu Dasa.

			Jupt.		Merc. Sat.		Lagna
Moon Sat.		**Chart 6**	Rahu Mars Sun	Moon Venus			Ketu
Ketu		**Rasi** **RP 23/6**	Merc.	Jupt. Sun Rahu		**Navamsa**	
		Lagna	Venus		Mars		

career for humanitarian reasons. He treated thousands free and with great dedication. Other factors pointing to a medical career include the 10th from Chandra Lagna (Moon-sign) being Scorpio and its ruler joining Rahu-Ketu.

The Sun and Rahu joining an exalted Mercury in a powerful quadrant (Chart 7) have made the native a very skilful cardiologist. The Moon is also with the Nodal axis and in Pisces. The 10th lord Jupiter joins Aries, a Martian sign in the Rasi, and Scorpio, a Martian Navamsa.

Chart 7: Born 18-9-1940 at 7-23 p.m. (IST) at 8 N 48, 78 E 11 with a balance of 6 years, 0 month and 28 days of Mercury Dasa.

Lagna Moon Ketu	Jupt. Sat.					Merc.	
		Chart 7	Venus	Lagna Moon Venus			Rahu
		Rasi	Mars	Ketu		**Navamsa**	
			Sun Merc. Rahu	Venus Mars	Jupt.	Sat.	

Careers

Chart 8 has a prominent Mars-Rahu association with Jupiter in the 10th also aspected by Mars. In Navamsa, the 10th lord Mercury is influenced by the Nodes and Mars and Saturn are in mutual aspect.

Chart 8: Born 13-9-1945 at 1-00 p.m. (IST) at 16 S 30, 68 W 09, with a balance of 16 years, 0 month and 16 days of Mercury Dasa.

			Rahu Mars		Jupt.		
	Chart 8 Rasi GIV 240		Venus Sat.	Rahu Venus	Navamsa		Sat.
			Sun Merc.	Mars			Ketu Merc. Lagna
Lagna Ketu	Moon		Jupt.	Sun Moon			

No planetary combination can be exclusively and independently used to identify a medical career. Only by a skilful use of several combinations on the lines discussed here is it possible to find out if the chart is of medical men. In this discussion, we have confined ourselves to charts of medical men who are academically qualified for it and are legally registered as doctors. Combinations analysed here are irrespective of the degree of success in healing or of the specific field of specialisation of the native concerned. Many of them have an outstanding reputation for their services to the public but we have not touched on the astrological reasons for this.

(C) LAWYERS AND JUDGES

The term *law* is used in more than one sense. You can use it to mean a rule prescribed by authority for human action. It can also be used to imply, as in science and philosophy, a uniform sequential order. But when you talk of justice, jurisprudence, judges, courts and lawyers, it is the first meaning we refer to. Jurisprudence is the study of what law is. Law primarily means and deals with the solution of social conflicts. It is simply meting out justice between man and man. "When I think of the law" wrote a famous judge, "as we know her in court-house and the market, she seems to me a woman sitting by the way-side, beneath whose overshadowing hood every man shall see the countenance of his desires or needs. The timid and the over-borne gain heart from her protecting smile. Fair combatants manfully standing to their rights, see her keeping the lists with the stern and discriminating eye of even justice. The wretch who has defied her most sacred commands and has thought to creep through ways where she was not, finds that his path ends with her and beholds beneath her hood the inexorable face of death."

Law and justice are two different things but the aim of all law is to ensure justice. However, many a time, the two run parallel and hardly meet. Justice is the quality of being or doing what is just, that is, just in law and equity. And a judge in the widest sense of the term is an officer appointed to administer law. The duties of a judge are difficult and often likened to walking on the tight rope. Striking a medium between the law and equity is a task that requires unusual intelligence and a great restraint on emotions and fairness of heart.

Lawyers, on the other hand, are those whose main occupation is to help in the administering of law. They differ from administrative officers in that the State confers important privileges on them in connection with the administration of justice. They are an indeterminate official class and their official relationship continues, unlike those appointed like the judges and other judicial officers, as long as they like, and their compensation comes not from the State (there are exceptions and we are speaking only of the rule) but from their clients.

Judges and lawyers are linked to law closely but their functions differ widely. Justices deal out justice, lawyers fight for their clients. The judge must be an impartial assessor but the lawyer compulsorily has to take up sides. This means a judge's sense of fairplay, equity and natural justice must be

Careers

highly evolved calling for a strong clean Mercury (faculty of discrimination) and Saturn (the great leveller) as well as Jupiter (speech and equity). For a lawyer, Mercury ruling intelligence must, indeed, be powerful but not necessarily blemish-free. Jupiter (speech) must also figure prominently. Saturn rules restrictions and limitations which is what law is all about in inter-relations of various kinds in society and he too must come into the picture. However, for a lawyer, the role of impartial judge is fatal and which is why Saturn, though involved, need not be very strong or unafflicted.

Classical works do not give many combinations for lawyers or judges but the characteristics of planets they furnish can be developed as we have done above to draw broad astrological parameters to fit in both lawyers and judges.

Jaimini attributes to Mars in the Karakamsa or the 5th from it a legal education. While a lawyer or a judge must necessarily pass a prescribed course in law before he can be admitted to the bar, not every one with a law degree is a lawyer or a judge. Many politicians after a brief stint in the courts have bid good-bye to the legal profession.

	Mars	Moon	Rahu
	Chart 1 **Rasi**		Venus Merc.
Jupt.			Sun
Ketu	Ascdt.	Sat.	

		Rahu	Sat. Kara- kamsa
	Navamsa	Merc.	
	Moon Venus		Sun
	Ketu	Mars	Ascdt. Jupt.

Chart 1 is that of a chief minister of a southern state whose dalliance with law was exceedingly brief and that too, if newspaper reports are to be believed, not because he cared to be a lawyer but only at the instance of his father.

Saturn is the Atmakaraka and occupies Gemini in Navamsa. Mars occupies the 5th from Karakamsa, the sign occupied by the Atmakaraka. The native did his law course, practised for a while and then pushed off in other directions.

Mars in the 5th may give a legal education but the rest of the chart and the strength of the Yogas will ultimately decide if one will continue in the courts of law. The Sun in the 10th in his own sign Leo Vargottama had other plans for the native and led him to a highly successful but challenging political career.

The native of Chart 2 was a lawyer for about 7 years after which he contested the assembly elections and progressively rose in eminence until he was prime minister of the country.

	Ketu				Ketu Mars			Ascdt. Sun
Jupt. Sat.	Chart 2 Rasi					Navamsa		Moon Merc. Sat. Ascdt
Merc. Venus Sat. Ascdt		Rahu	Moon Mars				Rahu	

Jupiter is strong having obtained cancellation of debility. Saturn obtains his own Varga in both Rasi and Navamsa. Mercury is powerful in Sagittarius in Lagna Kendra with 9th lord Sun. These factors combined to give a career in law. We may note that the Yoga arising from a combination of the 9th and 10th lords is responsible for a career (10th house) related to law and Dharma (9th house) but basically, because of the disposition of Jupiter and Saturn. But the influence of the Moon and Mars on the 10th house diverted the native's ambitions into political channels where he became an outstanding personality.

Saturn is the great judge who keeps watch over the wheels of destiny and sees to it they grind slowly but surely. Jupiter is the advisor, the counsellor. This would mean Jupiter and Saturn have a big say in the legal profession.

The importance of a Jupiter-Saturn link cannot be underestimated in the charts of those whose careers are related to law. We can even say this could be a basic requirement of a chart for a lawyer. And in order to be a judge, one must have the minimum qualification of having been a lawyer except in a very small percentage of cases where judicial officers are selected through the Public Services Commission channel. Therefore, the lowest common factor for both lawyer and judge is a Jupiter-Saturn nexus. This may be of any kind — association, mutual aspect, one-way aspect, an exchange of signs between the two, or of Nakshatras, sometimes even of Navamsa positions, or even an indirect connection through the aspect and or association of a third planet. Once this is found, we have a chart with the potential career in the law courts. Now, we try to find out what transmutes it into the chart of a judge. Saturn is important, for, it is he alone who can confer on one the capability of impartial judgement. Even Jupiter, described as the best of benefics in most circumstances, must concede to Saturn here. The former can get swayed by feelings of compassion which a judge must keep in rein if he is to deliver a proper verdict. Saturn must occupy a powerful place in the chart. Afflictions to Saturn can rob one of the opportunity of becoming a judge.

Another distinguishing feature of a judge is a relatively unafflicted Mercury. A strong Mercury with afflictions can

Ketu				Moon	Ven	Sat Merc	Sun
	Chart 3 Rasi				Navamsa		Rahu
			Ascdt.	Ketu			Jup
Merc. Sun	Venus	Mars	Moon Jupt. Sat. Rahu		Mars		Ascdt.

create a legal genius but is of little help in making one a good judge.

Jupiter and Saturn combine in the 2nd in Chart 3. Mercury is powerful in the 5th with Lagna lord Sun in a powerful sign, Sagittarius. Mercury is additionally strong by virtue of an exchange of signs with 5th lord Jupiter. Further, as sign-dispositor, Jupiter is in a Kendra from Mercury. This is a very striking illustration of a career in the courts.

The 9th and 10th lords are in Parivartana (exchange of signs) but in the 3rd and 4th houses. The 10th lord Venus aspects the 10th. Venus, as 10th lord, is aspected by Saturn in Rasi.

Jupiter aspects the 10th. The native began his career as a lawyer and then became a judge to occupy the highest judicial office in the country at the time of his retirement.

Mars Sat.			Rahu		Moon		Venus Rahu	Merc.
	Chart 4 Rasi		Jupt.			Navamsa		Mars Sat.
Venus			Ascdt.		Jupt.			Ascdt.
Merc. Sun Ketu		Moon				Ketu		Sun

Chart 4 is that of a High Court Chief Justice who later practised as a Supreme Court advocate. The native who had a very lucrative legal practice was not only known for his razor-sharp intelligence and legal acumen but also for a very witty disposition. The Lagna lord Sun is powerfully placed in the 5th with its ruler exalted. Mercury and Ketu join the Sun. Saturn is aspected by Jupiter while 10th lord Venus is in the 6th. Saturn joins Yogakaraka Mars in a Jupiterean constellation. Saturn aspects the 10th house and is further strengthened by his exact conjunction with Yogakaraka Mars. The chart derives its strength from two sources : (1) The disposition of Lagna lord Sun in the 5th in a powerful sign with 2nd and 11th lord Mercury and (2) the Vipareeta Raja Yoga involving all the three Dustanas — the 8th lord Jupiter is in the 12th, 12th lord Moon is in the 3rd, 3rd lord Venus is in the 6th and the 6th lord Saturn is in the 8th.

His judgements were noted for their incisiveness and for upholding justice. Jupiter in the 12th also gave him a deep insight into Vedanta and scholarship in Sanskrit. Many times, to the consternation of the entire court, he would ask the witnesses questions in Sanskrit where the parties involved belonged to the priestly class and felt more at home in the language of the gods. But the rest of the court would watch the proceedings dumbly. This judge had the distinction of having all his pronouncements upheld by the Supreme Court. The individual strength of the relevant planets play a big role in the calibre of the performance of the judge.

Ketu		Moon	
	Chart 5 Rasi		
			Ascdt.
Mars	Venus	Jupt. Merc (R)	Sun Sat. Rahu

Rahu			Moon
	Navamsa		Sat.
			Sun
	Merc. Jupt.		Venus Ascdt. Ketu

Chart 5 is that of a highly successful Supreme Court advocate. This example is a good illustration of what differentiates a lawyer from a judge. Jupiter and Saturn are linked in Navamsa. Mercury is well-placed in close association with Jupiter. Being retrograde, he is extra-powerful and bestows on the native brilliant intellectual abilities. But Saturn, though with Lagna lord Sun, is combust in him and afflicted by Rahu. In Chart 3 too, Saturn is in the same sign Virgo, closer to Rahu, but saved by being away from the Sun and by his nearness to Jupiter.

Jupiter and Saturn are connected in Navamsa in Chart 6. Jupiter aspects the 10th. Saturn is exalted. Mercury occupies a favorable position in the 11th with 10th lord Venus and Lagna lord Sun. The chart is that of a High Court Judge.

Chart 7, in contrast, is that of a successful lawyer.

Leo Lagna rises here too with its lord Vargottama in Lagna with Mercury and the Moon. Jupiter and Saturn have no direct link. Mars, however, is with Saturn and aspects Jupiter establishing a relationship between the two. Mercury is powerful in Lagna but blemished by his closeness to his enemy Moon who gets worse being New Moon.

		Moon	Merc. Sun Venus
Ketu Mars	\multicolumn{2}{c	}{Chart 6 Rasi}	Ascdt. Rahu
	Jupt.	Sat.	

	Venus	Moon	Rahu
Sun	\multicolumn{2}{c	}{Navamsa}	
Jupt. Mars			
Ascdt. Merc.	Ketu		

Rahu		Mars Sat.	
	\multicolumn{2}{c	}{Chart 7 Rasi}	Venus
			Ascdt. Sun Merc. Moon
Jupt.			Ketu

			Ascdt. Moon
	\multicolumn{2}{c	}{Navamsa}	
	Ketu		Sun Sat. Rahu
			Mars Venus Jupt.

Chart 8 has a similar connection between Jupiter and Saturn as in Chart 7. But this is the chart of a High Court judge. Mercury is Vargottama and unsullied being powerfully aspected by Jupiter. Saturn is very strongly placed being both exalted and Vargottama.

Moon Rahu		Jupt.	
	\multicolumn{2}{c}{**Chart 8**}	
Venus	\multicolumn{2}{c}{**Rasi**}	
Ascdt. Sun	Merc.	Mars Sat.	Ketu

		Sun	Mars
	Rahu		Venus
	Jupt.	**Navamsa**	Ketu
Ascdt.	Merc.	Sat. Moon	

Some of the points that emerge from this study are a Jupiter-Saturn nexus is nearly a must in careers of law and judgeship. Mercury, unsullied, and Saturn also clean and strong lead one from the bar to the bench. A study, such as this, can give broad identifying clues to a career in the courts but no hard and fast rules can apply in astrology. No single combination can be confirmatory. Each chart must be assessed on its own strength, the power of the general factors that could give a legal career applied judiciously and only then counclusions drawn. (09-88)

(D) ART AND ARTISTS

The concept of art and with it of the term *artist* has, over the centuries, taken forms and hues that were never recognised at one point of time as aesthetic or creative.

Art can be defined as the creation of beauty. Art and beauty are inseparable. The one can rarely exist without the other. Yet, if we look at Nature, there is neither beauty nor ugliness in Her. These characteristics are not attributes of Nature. They are only the artist's emotional reaction to matter. Beauty, therefore, becomes subjective aesthetic emotion. The artist has the rare power of giving form to emotion. He can make it audible as in music, or visible as in painting, dance, sculpture, and share his experience of the emotion with others.

If we look at the exquisite temple carvings in Belur in Karnataka, beauty spews through stone — trees, monkeys, fruits, mountains, sculpted men and women beckon you with their captivating and eye-catching figures and forms. The Greek mind, in contrast, evolved and confined art to ideal conditions of the human form. To the Greek artist, the goal was perfection of symmetry and rhythm in the human form beyond the pale of Nature. Until the Renaissance in Italy, Nature in the form of a tree, mountain, landscape, river was taboo to Greek art. There was no emotional response in Europe to Nature and Her varied creations from the artist. Giotto introduced mountains in his pictures and suddenly, they attained beauty in Europe. Beauty, therefore, is not in the subject, but in the artist's mind. That is why the concepts of beauty keep changing with generations and also with races, regions and individuals.

Art concepts change as people begin to look at art in different ways. Some forms are for all time such as the frescos at Ellora or the Ajanta paintings. A *Ravi Varma* or Leonardo da Vinci's *Last Supper* retain their enchanting appeal forever. Pablo Picasso, perhaps, would have been treated with utter contempt by the classical age artists. But a *Picasso* today commands a fabulous price and art lovers fall on top of one another to be able to grab one at art auctions. Is the artistic content and quality of a piece to be judged by the money it fetches ? Or is it the impact it creates on the mind of the art-lover? Whatever it be, true art is an expression of the innermost perceptions of the artist. The medium may vary but the content is the outpouring of the creative mind. It is the beauty that the artist sees in life around him which he pours out through his mind. Art is simply the expression of beauty as each artist sees in in his own way. Art applies only to those activities that tend towards aestheticism.

Aesthetics, astrologically, is associated with Venus. Varahamihira (B-II 10) describes Venus as

भृगुः सुखी कान्तवपुः सुलोचनः कफानिलात्मा सितवक्रमूद्धजः

Bhrigu or Venus is said to be easeloving, कान्तवपुः with a beautiful body, सुलोचनः with beautiful eyes, bilious and wind and with curly (wavy) hair.

The Greek name for Venus is *Aphrodite*, meaning to bring forth, to bear or to produce, and covers the creativity in man. Venus is in exaltation in Pisces, the last sign of the Zodiac ruled by Jupiter. Venus is at home in Taurus. This sign happens to be the exaltation sign of the Moon, Manahkaraka or the ruler of the mind and emotions. Art is subjective and beauty is said to lie in the eye of the beholder, in his mind, in his Moon. In fact, emotional impulse, said Tolstoy, is indispensable to all artistic creation. Art in that sense in not representative, rather it is interpretative. Art, especially in India, aims at depicting the spirit than the semblance of a thing. The artist seeks to interpret the inner meaning of his subject, to convey his mood through the medium. The outpouring of this mood, of this stream of emotion is art ruled by Venus. The Moon and Venus, between them, bring out the best forms of art.

A well-placed Venus in the relevant areas of the chart gives a predisposition to an appreciation of beauty around one and inclines one to express it through music, poetry, painting, drawing, dance, sculpture and other forms. Venus, according to **Uttarakalamirta** V-43 governs विचित्रकविता (*vichitrakavita*)) variegated colours, poetry, नृत्तं (*nrttam*) dance, वीणा (*Veena*) Veena, वेणु (*venu*) flute, विनोद (*vinoda*) amusement, कलानिपुणता (*kalanipunata*) proficiency in art, नाटकालंकृत (*natakalankritih*), decorating the stage, वाद्य (*vadya*) instrument, भरत शास्त्र (*Bharatasastra*) the art of dancing as propounded by sage Bharata and काव्यादौ रचना (*Kavyadau rachana*) or literary composition and poetry-writing.

Venus is comfortable in Libra and is in fall in Virgo.

Venus in Taurus gives creative ability of a kind that is pleasing to the eye, soothing to the mind and refined to the senses. In Virgo, where Venus is at his worst, the effect is often short of being eerie and wierd. Art lovers may object to this classification but where an art form confuses rather than soothe, that is the mildest way the difference can be brought out. Pablo Picasso had Venus in Virgo in contrast to Leonardo da Vinci's Venus in Taurus.

The degree of expressional power acquired by the artist, the emotional urge in him and the skill in adjusting the rhythmic relations of lines, colours, forms, sounds or words distinguish an artistic production as good or bad. It is here, we realise the significance of the 5th house which rules *dhi* or intellect in this context. The 5th house rules the discriminative faculty under which comes one's power of expression. The 5th house also rules the creative energy in man at all levels of existence — physical, mental, moral, spiritual, intellectual and also aesthetic. This energy inspired

	Sat. (R)	Jupt. Ketu	Mars			Mars	Venus
	Chart 1 Rasi		Ascdt.		**Navamsa**		Ketu
					Sun Jupt. (R) Rahu		Merc.
	Merc. Moon Rahu	Sun	Venus		Moon	Ascdt.		Sat. (R)

by the way man perceives the world around him results in some creative form of work — a piece of art — painting, sculpture, poetry, music, dance and other forms. The Moon ruling the mind and therefore, the subjective perceptions of an individual must in some way or the other be connected with the 5th house or its lord. Venus is the Karaka of art, of creativity and connected with the 5th house provides the inspiration to bring out the creative energy in man, to externalise it in some form that we call art. The 5th house, the Moon and Venus, connected directly or indirectly, seem to be the astrogical significators of the artist.

Scorpio rises in Leonardo da Vinci's chart (Chart 2) aspected by the 7th lord and Karaka Venus from his own sign, Taurus. The Ascendant lord Mars is in Aquarius, a spiritual sign with the 5th lord Jupiter and the 9th lord Moon. The

Careers

Merc.	Sun	Venus	Ketu
Moon Mars Jupt.	**Chart 2 Rasi**		
Rahu	Ascdt.		Sat. (R)

Moon Venus Jupt.	Ketu		
Ascdt. Merc.	**Navamsa**		
		Mars Rahu	Sun Sat. (R)

9th lord Moon, in turn, is with the 5th lord Jupiter channelising the energies of this man into art — painting — that has so far been unrivalled in Europe for its sheer intensity and depiction of emotion and passion. Venus, in his very own sign, is in Krittika ruled by the exalted 10th lord Sun. This painter was one of the earliest to recognise the changes light can bring in a subject. He found that as the subject receded from the eye, delicate changes in illumination and hue demanded re-production.

Contrast Leonardo da Vinci's work with Pablo Picasso's (Chart 1) and his creations and at once, the difference between the two stands out. This difference also highlights the totally different kind of results Venus can produce in Taurus and in Virgo.

In Picasso's case, the Ascendant lord is in Scorpio, its sign of fall afflicted by Rahu and Mercury. The Moon in the 5th has given creative abilities but the state of the Moon describes the subjects and quality of his paintings. Jupiter as 9th lord influences the Moon but Jupiter himself is retrograde and afflicted by the Node Ketu and shows the totally unconventional style developed by this artist. Venus, the Karaka for art, is in debility in Hasta ruled by the debilitated Moon. In Navamsa, Venus is better placed being in Taurus and many *Picassos* are indeed masterpieces by any standards.

Under the head art, a whole lot of creative activity can be brought in. We can have dance and music, classical. We can also include pop-singing and film acting though these categories would somehow tend to lower art to a crassy, coarse level. Saturn rules all that is coarse, all that appeals to the masses and dispenses with the refinement and austere discipline required to master the classical arts. According to **Uttarakalamrita** (V-50), Saturn rules रतिरतोवस्त्रादिशृङ्गरता (*ratirato vastradi srungarata*) or dressing up for armorous interviews. No offence meant but this expression comes very close to describing pursuits such as film-acting, modelling and modern dancing (brake dance etc. which involve a whole variety of wierd and wild gyrations of the human anatomy). The purpose in these forms of art (?) is more often than not to draw the attention of the viewer to the physical endowments of the model, actor or actress.

Mercury, according to **Uttarakalamrita** rules लिपिलेख्य (*lipilekhya*) or writing, शिल्पि (*silpi*) sculpturing and नर्तनम् (*nartanam*) dancing. Mercury favorably associated with Venus gives skill in music, poetry, drawing. When Mars influences these two planets, painting and sculpture are shown. Mercury joining the Atmakaraka shows शिल्पि (*silpi*) or skill in art.

	Moon Jupt.		Ketu
	Chart 3 Rasi		Venus Sat. Ketu
Rahu			
		Ascdt. Mars	Sun Merc.

Ascdt.			
Mars	**Navamsa**		
Sun			Sat. Jupt.
Moon	Venus		Merc.

Chart 3 has the Ascendant lord Venus in the 10th house with Yogakaraka Saturn and Ketu. Venus, the Karaka, is with 5th lord Saturn. The Moon is also aspected by the 5th lord. The native M.S. Subbulakshmi is a vocalist, a prominent singer of classical music unrivalled for the fervour and devotion she puts into her singing. Venus is in Cancer, a deeply inspirational sign, in the most powerful Kendra. The 2nd lord

Careers

Mars influences the 10th lord Moon. The emphasis in career is on the Vakstana (2nd house showing speech) coming under the 2nd lord Mars making her a singer of rare virtuosity. The Jupiterean influence on the 10th lord and the Lagna has led her to devotional traditional sublime music.

When art takes the form of dance, the emphasis shifts from Vakstana to *deha* or *thanu*. In other words, when the Lagna lord is strongly placed, particularly in the 9th, then one attains proficiency in dance. If the 9th house is well-placed, since it rules *dharma* and *sampradaya*, one may excel in classical dance forms. In the horoscope of Rukmini Arundale (Chart 4), the Ascendant lord Venus occupies the 9th house with sign-dispositer and Yogakaraka Saturn and benefic Mercury.

Mars Jupt. Ketu	Ascdt.		
Sun	**Chart 4 Rasi**		Moon
Merc. Venus Sat.	**Rukmini Arundale**		
		Rahu	

Rahu			Ascdt. Venus
	Navamsa		
		Moon	Sat.
		Mars	Merc. Jupt. Ketu

Rukmini Arundale became a world-famous exponent of Bharata Natyam and founded the internationally renowned Kalakshetra at Madras on the lines of the ancient Gurukula system. She brought new dignity and respect to this form of dance rescuing it from a state of disrepute to which it had fallen some 50 or 60 years ago. Venus, the Karaka, is powerfully placed with 5th lord Mercury and is in mutual aspect with a powerful Moon in Cancer.

In the chart of a top Bombay film actress of yester years who is equally renowned as a Bharata Natyam dancer, the Ascendant lord Moon is in the 9th house. The Moon is Full and forms the center of an Adhi Yoga involving Venus and

Mercury. Venus occupies its own constellaton Purvaphalguni but is joined by Saturn (malefic, being the 7th and 8th lord) and the native is better known as a popular film actress. Malefic Saturn has tended to make Venus (in an inimical sign Leo) coarse to that extent.

In the case of yet another actress turned politician, Venus is exalted in the 10th. The Ascendant lord Mercury is in the 9th with the aspect of a Full Moon. A one-time popular actress, she was a good Bharata Natyam dancer also before stepping into politics.

When the Ascendant lord occupies a Kendra in strength, art takes on the form of cinema or stage acting skills. A film-maker *cum* actor known for his colourful stories and spectacular sets, Raj Kapoor (Chart 5) had the Moon in the Ascendant in his own sign. Venus is in a Kendra in the Moolatrikona sign Libra aspected by 5th lord Mars from the 9th. Venus is with a powerful malefic lord Saturn, drawing the native to the cinema world. Additionally, Mercury and Jupiter combine giving the man a flair for comedy.

Mars			
	Chart 5 Rasi		Ascdt. Moon Rahu
Ketu			
Sun Merc. Jupt.	Venus Sat.		

Ascdt. Sat.			Venus Jupt.
Rahu	Navamsa		
			Mars Ketu
		Merc.	Moon

Woody Allen (Chart 6), famous comedy star of Hollywood, who made news in the early 90s, though of an unpalatable kind, has Venus well-placed as Karaka in the 3rd house in Chitta ruled by Yogakaraka (primarily 5th lord) Mars. The Moon is also in a Martian constellation Dhanishta. The Lagna lord Sun is in the 4th, a Kendra. Mercury and Jupiter are together. A highly successful star, Woody Allen was very popular with the audiences.

Careers

			Ketu
Moon Sat.	**Chart 6 Rasi**		Ascdt. Moon Rahu
Mars			Ascdt.
Rahu	Sun Merc. Jupt.	Venus	

	Ketu		
Mars	**Navamsa**		Ascdt.
Sat.			Mars Ketu
Sun	Jupt.	Venus Moon Rahu Merc.	

Mia Farrow (Chart 7) who was Woody Allen's wife was as successful as her ex-husband in films. The Ascendant lord Mars is exalted in the 10th. Venus is exalted in the 12th aspected by Saturn, a malefic. Jupiter-Mercury are related to give a mobile face and versatile acting skills.

Venus	Ascdt.		Sat. (R) Rahu
Sun Mars Merc.	**Chart 7 Rasi**		
Moon Ketu			Jupt. (R)

		Merc. Rahu	
Mars Jupt.	**Navamsa**		
Sat.			
	Venus Ketu	Moon	Sun Ascdt.

No discussion on art can really be complete without homage to that peerless saint-singer Thyagaraja and what better way to do it in these pages than to understand the horoscopic features of this great devotee's chart.

The Ascendant is Cancer (Chart 8), the sign of spiritual sublimity and inspiration, occupied by the Moon himself, the Lagna lord. Venus, the Karaka, is in the 11th house in Taurus where he is at his steady best. He is joined by Saturn, the 7th and 8th lord from Lagna. Venus occupies Rohini, ruled by the Lagna lord Moon who, in turn, is in Cancer. The music that flowed from Thyagaraja came from the depths of his soul. Venus aspects the 5th house. The Ascendant lord Moon is with Ketu, the Kaivalyakaraka, and indicates the fervor and devotion in the songs he composed so effortlessly as he dwelt on his Ishta, Lord Rama. The charts of such personalities who have overcome the dualities of life cannot always be assessed the same way as of those caught in the quamire of *samsara*. But a few general clues are always to be found so long as they take on a human body on this earth.

If Venus or the 10th house is free of the influence of Rahu or malefic Saturn, the artist belongs to a form of art that has innate dignity in it. It is the kind of art that leads to moods of elevation and peace and appeals to the higher sentiments in the human mind. Rahu strongly related to the Ascendant, Venus or the 10th draws one to art forms that aim at stimulating or titillating the senses — films, pop-music, dance, modelling. Saturn's influence as a malefic draws the attention to the body as is the case in cinema, nautch, brake-dance and other similar kinds.

	Merc. Sun	Venus Sat	Mars
	Chart 8 Rasi		Ascdt Moon Ketu
Rahu			Jupt.

	Merc.	Rahu	
Ascdt.	Navamsa		Venus
	Mars Ketu	Sun Jupt.	Moon Sat

Summing up, Venus strongly placed in his exaltation, Moolatrikona or own sign or even in his Neecha Rasi in a Kendra or Trikona influenced by the 5th lord gives creative abilities. This is further heightened when the Moon is also involved with Venus or the 5th house or lord.

Venus, dignified and with benefics (functional), leads to interest in classical forms of art. Afflicted Venus gives a flair for cinema acting and such other forms.

Mercury and Jupiter together produce mimics and actors, the latter with a distinct flair for comedy. Emoting comes easily to such natives.

The Ascendant lord in addition if related to the 9th house again emphasises classical, traditional forms of art, particularly dance. The Ascendant lord in Kendras shows films. Apart from these factors, if Yogas for fame and financial success also obtain, such natives reach the top in their chosen line. Where the Dhana Yogas are lacking, talented though they be, good opportunities may never come their way. They live and die unknown. (09-93)